CROSSING CULTURES
IN THERAPY
pluralistic counseling for the
HISPANIC

CROSSING CULTURES
IN THERAPY
pluralistic counseling for the
HISPANIC

ELAINE S. LEVINE
New Mexico State University

AMADO M. PADILLA
University of California, Los Angeles

Brooks/Cole Publishing Company
Monterey, California
A Division of Wadsworth, Inc.

To our parents,
Harry and Evelyn LeVine
and
Manuel and Esperanza Padilla,
with appreciation for
their cultures, transmitted,
and values, upheld

Printed in the United States of America

10 9 8 7 6 5 4 3 2 1

Library of Congress Cataloging in Publication Data

Levine, Elaine Sue.
  Crossing cultures in therapy.

  Bibliography: p. 274
  Includes index.
  1. Hispanic Americans—Mental health services.
2. Minorities—Mental health services.
3. Psychiatry, Transcultural. 4. Counseling.
I. Padilla, Amado M., joint author. II. Title:
Pluralistic counseling for the Hispanic.
RC451.5.H57L47   362.8′4   79-9504
  ISBN 0-8185-0337-8

Acquisition Editor: *Claire Verduin*
Production Editor: *Sally Schuman*
Interior and Cover Design: *Ruth Scott*
Typesetting: *David R. Sullivan Company, Dallas, Texas*

Preface

In recent years there has been a growing need for effective therapeutic and counseling techniques for use with people other than majority-group members. The use of traditional therapeutic approaches with ethnic or racial minority-group members has increasingly been challenged, and the term *pluralistic counseling* has emerged to describe counseling techniques that are geared to the culture, language, and socioeconomic position of minority individuals. Our interest in this evolving discipline led us to examine the pluralistic-counseling literature, and, in the process, we made two observations. First, what literature exists is scattered throughout a large number of diverse professional journals and varies greatly in quality. Second, the literature is neither systematic nor complete: it does not present the comprehensive coverage that is essential to the therapist who works with "culturally different" clients.

Our purpose in writing this book is to present systematically the basic concepts of pluralistic counseling and to show how they may be applied in therapy with the Hispanic client. Many of the principles of pluralistic counseling are therefore explained here in terms of the Hispanic client, who brings a particular set of linguistic, cultural, and economic circumstances to the therapeutic encounter. The principles themselves, however, can be applied with appropriate modifications to therapy with people from any minority group.

We begin the book with a discussion of the relationship between culture and personality, and then we proceed to an examination of the elements of pluralistic counseling. We go on to present an analysis of historical differences, life-style differences, and dilemmas that confront Hispanics in the United States. We explore the sources of psychological stress and maladjustment, and we suggest modes of intervention from a pluralistic perspective. The numerous case histories we use throughout the book serve as concrete, real-life illustrations of the principles we discuss. We have also included a glossary of Spanish words and phrases that are used in the text.

This book is intended for the diverse group of individuals who have occasion to work with Hispanics and other minority-group people. Specifically, it is written for professionals and students in the human-

V

services fields—psychology, psychiatry, social work, and counseling —and we believe it will also be useful to educators, medical and nursing personnel, and students of culture. Furthermore, this book is designed for both minority-group and majority-group readers.

As is true with any project of this nature, this book could not have been written without the support and encouragement of many people. First of all, we would like to acknowledge the financial support we received from New Mexico State University's Mini-Grant 3106–244 and from Avila College to E.S.L. and from the National Institute of Mental Health Research Grant MH 24854 to the Spanish Speaking Mental Health Research Center at the University of California at Los Angeles, A.M.P. Principal Investigator.

We also thank John N. Herrera, University of Washington, George Iglesias, Pima Community College, Manuel Miranda, University of Minnesota, Jose Szapocznik, University of Miami School of Medicine, Jimmy R. Walker, The University of Texas at El Paso, and John M. Whiteley, University of California, Irvine, who reviewed the manuscript and offered insightful comments and criticisms.

We are grateful, too, to the many typists and other assistants who brought their efforts to this project, especially Dolores Campos, Jan Fields, Wayne Theye, and Anne Treviño. A special word of thanks goes to Frank X. Acosta, who took time from his busy schedule to read and comment on the entire manuscript. Much of what is most useful in this book is due to his skill, judgment, and advice in early stages of the writing. And, finally, we thank the many unnamed clients whose cases are reported here and the authors who have written about them.

Elaine S. LeVine
Amado M. Padilla

Contents

PLURALISTIC CONSIDERATIONS IN THERAPY   257

CROSSING CULTURES
IN THERAPY
pluralistic counseling for the
HISPANIC

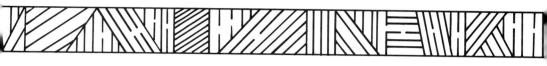

Chapter 1 Culture, Personality, and Therapy

In the time it takes to turn on a television set, images of humanity are transmitted to us from all niches of the world. As technology enables us to view the diversity of life, from the desert of Australia to the ghettos of the United States, it also forces us to become increasingly involved with one another. Our society is disquieted by our diminishing sources of fuel and food and by the ominous threat of nuclear war. The comfort of the middle and upper classes in North America is disrupted not only by the press for effective international relations but also by the upheaval of disenchanted groups within the United States. The media have taught ethnic minority groups in the United States about the pleasures afforded by money and technology. Members of these groups expect the opportunity to live satisfying and productive lives within their chosen environments, and they have learned to struggle for their rights through economic and political action.

Mental-health specialists of every persuasion are becoming increasingly aware of the desires and rights of ethnic minority groups. Beginning with the community-mental-health movement of the 1960s, a belief that mental-health care is a right and privilege of all citizens, not just of the wealthy or the middle class, has emerged. With this change in philosophy the need for culturally relevant therapy has developed, and skill at *pluralistic counseling* is becoming a must for the therapist who intends to provide service in our technological age. Ours is an era in which the "culturally encapsulated counselor" (Wrenn, 1962) no longer has a place.

In our presentation of the essentials of pluralistic counseling (we will define the term in detail later), with its appreciation of ethnic and class differences, we have chosen to concentrate on counseling with the Hispanic population in the United States, for several reasons. The term

1

Hispanic, as we use it here, is a generic label for a diverse group of Spanish-speaking and/or Spanish-surnamed people in the United States who reflect varied histories and a wide range of values. (The very diversity of the group makes selection of a name difficult, and this term is not universally accepted.) Hispanics constitute the second-largest minority group in the United States, and the problems of providing adequate mental-health care to this population have been well documented (Padilla, Ruiz, & Alvarez, 1975). In addition, this population is one marked by historical, cultural, and ethnic diversity. Because of this rich diversity, the Hispanic population is a good model for demonstrating how a pluralistic-counseling orientation is nurtured and carried out. Although we have tried to present as much detail as possible about the pluralistic society in which Hispanics live and to make this book a thorough guide for counseling Hispanics, we will also show how the principles discussed can be applied to other ethnic groups.

DEFINITIONS OF CULTURE

The term *culture* came into anthropological use from the German word *Kultur*. The educated classes of Europe were presumed to be less ignorant than lowly peasants and to have a greater understanding of the truth and a greater appreciation of the finer things of life. In essence, the educated were "more civilized." The degree to which other people differed in their customs, beliefs, and arts from sophisticated Europeans was a measure of how ignorant and uncivilized they were. Society was conceptualized as existing on a continuum ranging from primitive ignorance to progressively greater enlightenment, as reflected in increasing advances in technology, material standards of living, medicine, political management, the arts, and the governing moral code. Accordingly, the more a society possessed and manifested "enlightenment," the more *Kultur* it had and the more civilized or cultured its members were. It was on this foundation that Edward Tylor (1903) came to define culture as "that complex whole which includes knowledge, belief, art, morals, law, custom, and any other capabilities and habits acquired by man as a member of society" (p. 1). In this view discrete cultures were not recognized; societies differed only in their degree of general culture or enlightenment.

The celebrated anthropologist Franz Boas, however, conceptualized culture differently. According to Boas, culture is the distinctive body of customs, beliefs, and social institutions characterizing each separate society (Stocking, 1966). In this view societies are differentiated by their culture. Culture is composed of the same elements found in Tylor's definition, but those elements—knowledge, beliefs, arts, and the like —are considered unique in every society. New members learn their culture from significant others, such as parents, siblings, teachers, and friends. Cultural variety, therefore, results from differences in history and in environmental limitations among societies rather than from differences in degree of enlightenment.

Today social scientists attempt to make their definitions more operational by viewing culture as a product of human learning. Goodenough (1963), for example, states that culture "consists of standards for deciding what is, standards for deciding what can be, standards for deciding how one feels about it, standards for deciding what to do about it, and standards for deciding how to go about doing it" (p. 259). This definition focuses on behavior rather than on customs or institutions. This more operational definition of culture will be implicit in this book as we delve into the standards that members of different cultural groups possess and examine points of agreement and conflict in those standards.

DEFINITION OF PLURALISTIC COUNSELING

With these broad definitions of culture as background, we can define pluralistic counseling as therapy that recognizes the client's culturally based beliefs, values, and behaviors and that is concerned with the client's adaptation to his or her particular cultural milieu. The pluralistic therapist considers all facets of the client's personal history, family history, and social and cultural orientation.

The therapist obtains relevant data about the client's culture in a variety of ways: through observation of speech, posture, and gesture, a technique borrowed from the anthropologist; through the interview, for life history; through the study of folklore, art, and religious beliefs; and through the use of projective and standardized tests (Barnouw, 1963). As is true in all therapy, the individual client is the prime concern in pluralistic counseling, but the pluralistic therapist is, in addition, vigilant to all the ways culture affects the individual. To help clients clarify their personal and cultural standards, the pluralistic therapist needs to be aware of both the minority and the majority cultures, the points of contact between those cultures, and the process by which cultural standards influence the individual.

IMPACT OF CULTURE ON THE INDIVIDUAL

How culture influences the individual has been a prime concern of behavioral scientists, particularly those specializing in the study of culture and personality, and requires special consideration. Honigmann (1967, p. 62), in his discussion of the relationship between culture and personality, asks "Which is more useful: To conceive of personality as sundered from culture—connected with culture by the conjunction 'and' or to image personality as largely contained in culture?" A number of theoretical alternatives have been offered about the relationship between culture and personality. LeVine (1973) has organized these theories into five categories.

1. Anticulture and Personality ($C \rightarrow P$). A number of theorists have followed Goffman's (1961) lead in stating that *culture determines personality* and that the individual changes the culture's systems very little. Theorists adopting this anticulture-and-personality position believe that culture provides broad guidelines for behavior. Through culture individuals learn language, and from language develop values, attitudes, and behavior. According to this approach, culture determines thought and behavior, and an individual's personality is the sum total of how others view him or her. Personal differences are basically irrelevant, and survival of the individual depends on group functioning not on individual ideas. These theorists predict that behavioral science will advance to the point where interpersonal rather than personal dynamics will become the subject of investigation.

2. Psychological Reductionism ($P \rightarrow C$). The psychological reductionists, such as Roheim (1943) and McClelland (1961), postulate that all human activity can be explained by studying individuals. All societal institutions (for example, political, educational, and religious institutions) reflect the individual personalities that make up society. According to this view, *society is an abstraction created by individuals*, and the culture is merely the subjective macrocosm of the individual personality. By studying the individual, therefore, one can build a construct of culture.

3. Personality Is Culture ($P = C$). Theorists such as Gorer and Rickman (1950) and Benedict (1946) have *equated* dynamics of personality and culture. These theorists postulate that individual personalities have composite parallels, called "national character" or "modal traits." Benedict (1946) stated that in childhood, people develop a "world view"—an underlying set of attitudes—and the composite of these attitudes makes up the national character. Gorer and Rickman (1950) applied the concept of national character to specific cultures; for example, they suggested that the swaddling of Russian youngsters creates anger and manic/depressive mood swings and results in the Russian modal trait of moodiness, due to repressed anger. In similar fashion, Gorer and Rickman (1950) stated that the early toilet training of Japanese children led to the development of compulsiveness as a modal personality trait.

According to this position, infants and children grow up with predispositions and characters in common with the adults in their culture. This intergenerational effect accrues over time, because the older generation has undergone the same transformation (or socialization) that they are imposing on their children. National character, therefore, in Gorer's sense, is analogous to genetic structure in the geneticist's sense. That is, it is assumed that the "character" of each individual in society is constant and that this "character" determines the response that the individual will make to his or her environment (Wallace, 1970).

4. Personality Mediation $(C_1 \rightarrow P \rightarrow C_2)$. The personality-mediation approach advanced by Kardiner (1939), Linton (1945), and Whiting and Child (1953) posits a *chain reaction* in which culture creates individual personality and the individual in turn embellishes and changes the culture. These theorists believe that the economics and the child-rearing practices of a culture are primary determinants of individual personality. Individuals are primary determinants of folklore, religion, magic, and art. Theorists adopting a personality-mediation approach see individuals and cultures as two distinct processes that interact and impact on each other in a generally systematized fashion. Individuals stand between the culture of the past and the culture of the future—the culture they have been socialized to accept and the culture they can create.

5. Two Systems $(P \leftrightarrow C)$. Spiro (1951), Hallowell (1955), and others are unwilling to make assumptions about whether culture or personality is the more basic human process. To these theorists culture is neither formative nor reflective of individual personality. Rather, individuals and their culture are in *continuous interaction* and *continuous compromise*. The individual operates for his or her own benefit and for that of the group. The culture's institutions attempt to maintain group productivity and individual happiness. The two-systems theorists believe that the fate of an individual is to compromise continuously between personal desires and needs and pressure to conform from the larger reference group.

SELECTING AN APPROACH

In all five systems culture and individual personality overlap conceptually but differ as to whether the individual or the culture is viewed as the prime determinant of behavior. This issue leads to an important question in pluralistic therapy: how much must therapists know about a cultural group to be effective with clients from that group? Some theorists would answer this question by saying that, the more we know about a culture, the more effective we will be as therapists. They might add that, if we help clients know and appreciate their cultural background, we will be assisting them in their search for identity in a time of rampant change and social alienation (Giordano, 1973). In contrast, other theorists suggest that information about culture is of secondary importance since the therapist's function is to help people find personal direction in their lives.

Assumptions about the interaction of culture and the individual will affect goal setting in therapy. Let's use a psychosocial problem among Hispanics as an example to demonstrate the different levels at which one can intervene and set goals in therapy. Mental-health professionals are very concerned about the high school dropout rate among Hispanics (Padilla & Ruiz, 1973). Some theorists believe that eradication of poverty is necessary for reducing this high dropout rate. Poverty, they suggest, leads to a feeling of futility, and this futility translates into negativism about school. Students feel that success in school is unlikely or that it is not even a meaningful goal, since success in life as a whole seems improbable.

Other theorists believe that the schools must be held responsible for the educational problems of Hispanic children. Discrimination by teachers and tracking systems that place Hispanics in classes for slow learners are presented as causes of high dropout rates among Hispanic students (Carter, 1970). Others hold that the basis for school disinterest can be traced to the home. An extensive government survey in the mid-1960s listed various home factors, such as how many books there are in the home or whether there are one or two parents in the home, as causes of school dropout (Coleman, Campbell, Hobson, McPartland, Mood, Weinfeld, & York, 1966). Still others (such as Heller, 1966) maintain that Hispanic ethnic traits are adverse to success in Anglo-oriented schools. The more individualistically oriented theorists (for example, Price-Williams, 1975) have posited a number of personal factors, such as poorer self-concept, as the cause of poor school performance. If the therapist assumes an individualistic approach, therapy may be directed toward increasing the positive self-concept of the student. If, on the other hand, the therapist ascribes to a more culturological view, intervention may be aimed at facilitating family and/or school relations.

The personality-mediation approach $(C_1 \rightarrow P \rightarrow C_2)$ is the position that we, the authors of this book, have taken. We will demonstrate how an understanding of individual and cultural variables can facilitate the growth of a constructive therapeutic relationship and offer guidelines for client change. This orientation implies that neither individual nor cultural dynamics *alone* are important. Rather, the focus is on the interaction of the two and the ways in which each changes as a consequence of the interaction.

If one accepts the tenet that, in part, culture affects and determines individual personality, a second question follows logically: does culture affect us in a patterned way so that individuals in a particular culture exhibit a pattern of personality types? As we said earlier, theorists who equate culture and personality have been interested in exposing national character or modal personality types. Studies employing participant observation (that is, the method of explicitly observing the behavior of people with whom the observer is interacting) and psychological testing have generated evidence that certain personality traits are associated with particular cultural groups. A good example can be seen in an early study by Kaplan, Rickers-Ovsiankina, and Joseph (1956). In this study the researchers used Rorschach protocols obtained from Mormon, Hispanic, Navajo Indian, and Zuñi Indian informants (Kaplan, 1955). Six protocols from each cultural group were used. Two judges performed a series of sorting tasks with the 24 records. One judge, who knew which cultures were represented and had personal experience with all four, had considerable success in sorting Rorschach records into the correct cultural groups. The judge who was informed only that the Rorschach protocols could be sorted into distinct categories and who had no knowledge of which groups were involved was unable to sort the records according to cultural group. On the basis of this finding the researchers conclude that they have provided modest support for the idea that cultures manifest "modal-personality" patterns. Rorschach responses from one Spanish-speaking group are "unique" and "homogeneous" enough to be discriminated from the other three groups. This research demonstrates the possible applicability of the modal-personality concept.

Exploration of modal-personality traits can be a way of developing sensitivity about individuals in a culture; however, various social scientists warn that modal-personality constructs may be of limited value in therapy (Opler, 1967). Each individual within a culture has been affected by unique experiences as well as by common cultural experiences. Thus an individual's personality will be unique. Overemphasis on the modal-personality approach can lead to overgeneralizations and stereotyping that mask the individual's unique needs.

In this book, as we sketch personality characteristics common to Hispanics, it is important to remember that these modal characteristics are mere guidelines. The reader, as therapist, must be sensitive and alert to determine the degree to which these modal traits apply to any one client.

MENTAL HEALTH AND MALADJUSTMENT

From a pluralistic perspective, mental health and good human relations occur concomitantly. Although norms for psychological functioning are difficult to determine, it can be said that the mentally healthy individual maintains open communication with people from all walks of life. Further, the mentally healthy individual is one who can (1) establish and enjoy many lasting friendships and love and be affectionate with close friends; (2) treat all persons with appropriate respect; (3) seek to contribute to the general welfare; (4) be concerned with personal welfare without exploitation of others; (5) alternate work with play; (6) be dependable, truthful, open-minded, and instilled with a philosophy that includes a willingness to grow, improve, and achieve wisdom; (7) be creative, spontaneous, happy, and free; and (8) be able to fulfill social responsibilities and work toward social change when necessary.

According to the pluralistic perspective, the parameters of mental health are determined by a particular culture. For example, in some African cultures it is mentally healthy to exhibit a ceremonial neurosis characterized by frenzied activity, laughing, and crying. This state is voluntary and reversible and serves a socially sanctioned purpose of designating a leader to the tribe (Wallace, 1970). In the United States it is considered mentally healthy to lament over the death of a significant other. Bereavement serves a personal purpose of catharsis and a social purpose of gaining solace from others. In other cultures stoicism and rejoicing are the mentally healthy responses to another person's death. The death is a signal for reaffirmation of life among the survivors. Thus, to the extent that an individual's creativity, spontaneity, and happiness fulfill social expectations, that individual will be viewed as mentally healthy within the culture.

Of course, social roles and personal aspirations are not always congruent. This is especially true in large, complex societies in which individuals may find themselves caught between conflicting social roles.

Such conflict has two general and mutually exclusive results: it may be the impetus for positive personal growth and enhancement, or it may result in maladjustment and behavior that is no longer appropriate to the culture and the time (Burger, 1974). The first of these is usually ignored or not given serious attention. An individual who turns a conflict situation into a growth experience is considered well adjusted and mentally healthy. It is the maladjusted response to conflict that is of concern.

Maladjustment, like adjustment, serves cultural functions. The maladjusted individual can admit social wrongdoing, receive help, and minimize punishment. The suspension of logic and the emphasis on emotion that are characteristic of many maladjusted individuals provide a feeling of escape from intolerable situations (Burger, 1974). Symptoms provide some personal organization while the individual attempts to develop more efficient ways of thinking and behaving (Opler, 1967). Finally, the symptoms may motivate others to help the maladjusted individual reenter society (Burger, 1974).

Maladjustment occurs in all cultures; however, the pattern of symptoms varies across cultures, and what constitutes maladjustment is culturally determined. A few classic syndromes investigated by anthropologists illustrate this point. The Algonkin Indians of Canada suffer *windingo*, which is characterized by cannibalistic impulses. In Southeast Asia and Indonesia the maladjusted may show symptoms labeled *latch*, involving a startle reaction followed by obsessive/compulsive behavior. In Northern Japan women in particular are susceptible to *emu*, an obsessive/compulsive syndrome. A disturbance in a certain Kenyan tribe is *saka*, a convulsive attack associated with hysteria. The Eskimo of Greenland suffer *pibloktog*, in which excitement is followed by convulsions, heavy sleep, and amnesia (Barnouw, 1963). Hispanics speak of **susto,** which is marked by restlessness during sleep and, during waking hours, by listlessness, loss of appetite, disinterest in dress and personal hygiene, loss of strength, depression, and introversion (Rubel, 1964).

On one level of abstraction, symptoms of maladjustment are the same cross-culturally. For example, across cultures the maladjusted are unable to function effectively within their group, and a common symptom of severe maladjustment is hallucinations. On another level of abstraction, symptoms are culturally specific. For example, the specific content of hallucinations varies across cultures. Some experiences, such as hearing voices, may be indicative of maladjustment in one culture and a common and accepted experience in another (Torrey, 1972).

The differentiation between normality and abnormality is also culturally determined. Critical cues to this discrimination include nonconformity to appropriate social patterns, exaggeration of norms, and unusual behavior (LeVine, 1973; Wallace, 1970). In the United States treatment and hospitalization are considered indices of maladjustment. Only a few societies have followed this Western pattern of hospitalization for mental illness (Wallace, 1970). In the Western world therapists have become "moral legislators, social engineers" (Burger, 1974, p. 66). In the United States, for example, the American Psychiatric Association wields an uncanny amount of power in defining the parameters of normal and abnormal behavior. A good example of how this power is used, positively or negatively, can be seen in the APA's decision to drop homosexuality as a diagnostic category, declaring in doing so that homosexuality was no longer a disease or mental illness.

Classification of maladjustment syndromes varies by culture, and a culture's conception of causation fixes its system of classification. In the Western world maladjustment is attributed to biological and psychosocial factors and is thus categorized as either organic or functional in origin. Many other cultures believe that there are three causes of maladjustment: biological, psychosocial, and metaphysical. Maladjusted behaviors may then be classified as due to organic or functional causes or to witchcraft or other supernatural forces (Torrey, 1972).

Even though the definition of maladjustment is culturally specific, members of one culture cannot be considered more or less adjusted than members of another culture. Wallace (1970) states that it is a contradiction in terms to consider an entire culture as maladjusted, although one culture may be more proficient than another in its control over the environment. Maladjustment is the inability to function within a group. If a culture survives over time, then it is adaptive and healthy. Only those individuals who cannot cope within the culture can be considered disturbed. Labeling a culture as having neurotic or psychotic tendencies can be a political maneuver for sanctioning discrimination. For example, the effort of Black slaves in the United States to run away to gain freedom was considered a serious symptom of basic pathology by their slave masters (Wallace, 1970). In similar fashion the patriarchal structure of Mexican culture has been reported to instill serious neurosis in Mexican women, fostering the concept that the Mexican woman is inferior to the man (Diaz-Guerrero, 1975). Descriptions of culturally specific syndromes of emotionl disturbance do not imply that a group itself is ineffective but, rather, that, when an individual experiences stress, it is likely to be expressed in culturally specific ways.

In general, mental health involves a realistic acceptance of self, a clear perception of the world, open relationships with others, and the ability to handle stress and crisis. The overall processes of mental health and maladjustment are universal attributes of culture. The specific events creating stress and the behavior manifestations of disturbances are culturally defined.

CULTURAL DETERMINANTS OF THERAPY

Throughout the world contact occurs between socially sanctioned healers and individuals seeking help. The therapist, witch doctor, **curandero,** spiritualist, and sorcerer all assist their clients to achieve subjective comfort while functioning within their society. However, it is inappropriate to assume that emotional healers throughout the world perform the same functions simply because they are called by the same label. Each establishes goals and employs techniques appropriate for the cultural milieu (Torrey, 1972).

The goals of therapy are specific to the cultural definition of mental health. For example, Morita therapy, a popular treatment in Japan, involves bed rest and discussion with the therapist of a daily diary. Concepts of Zen Buddhism are introduced in these discussions. Morita therapy directs a patient toward an Eastern conception of mental health—an inner-directed life of peace and meditation (Opler, 1967). Goals for therapy in any culture can range from removal of symptoms to attitude change, behavior change, insight, improved interpersonal relations, personal efficiency, social effectiveness, and preventive health (Torrey, 1972).

The techniques of therapy are also culturally based. For example, the preferred treatment of *saka*, a form of hysteria found among women of the Wataita tribe in Kenya, involves having the woman drink water in which a man's lower garment has been washed or having her suck some of her husband's blood. Sometimes the ritualized drinking is followed by a public dance in which the women wear bright garments saved for such occasions, a red fez or a man's felt hat, bandoliers, and a man's belt around the waist. The dance continues until the stricken female is "danced out" and presumably free of further attacks. The stress precipitating *saka* is often the woman's envy of the more powerful role held by men within this Kenyan culture. Therapy enables the woman to act out her tensions and to reenter society with socially sanctioned behavior (Barnouw, 1963). Without belaboring the point, it should be noted that this "therapy" does not "cure" the basic inequality that created the stress. In an analogous sense, it is on a therapeutic par with "treating" an ethnic-minority-group member in the United States to accept passively a subordinate socioeconomic role. There are, then, culturally sanctioned techniques and goals for therapy, but the fact that they are culturally sanctioned does not mean that they are adequate or appropriate. A point we will discuss in more detail later is that in pluralistic counseling the therapist must be ready to examine culturally sanctioned therapeutic practices and alter his or her orientation if these practices are either irrelevant and/or inadequate for the client.

Therapy procedures fall into four main categories. Many are control strategies such as confession, indoctrination, hellfire sermons, and commands (Wallace, 1970). Symbolic acts such as voodoo and sacrifice provide socially sanctioned ways of expressing aggression. Drugs are another control strategy, and sedatives are commonly used throughout the world (Torrey, 1972). Whether a particular drug socializes or dissocializes is culturally determined. Thus excessive drinking sets an individual apart from the group in some cultures but is a form of camaraderie in other cultures (Burger, 1974). Still other therapeutic techniques bind anxiety in institutional functions. For example, ceremonial rites of passage aid adolescents in dealing with anxiety associated with assuming adult responsibilities. In some cultures the maladjusted are ceremonially made shamans and thus reinstituted into their society (Wallace, 1970). A third category is milieu therapy. Hospitalization is a common therapeutic technique in the Western world (Torrey, 1972). In day treatment, which is also common in the United States, patients meet daily from early morning until late afternoon for therapy, resocialization, and in some cases vocational training. A fourth approach involves cathartic strategies. The release may be overt and orgiastic (for example, socially sanctioned orgies for religious reasons) or sublimated through a wide range of activities that are cathartic in nature. Such activities include the arts (music, drama, dance), games and sports, exercise, feasts and parties, mourning rituals, hypnosis, and verbal therapy (Wallace, 1970).

In the United States, therapy is generally oriented toward improved personal and social efficiency. Psychoanalytic, insight, or behavioral therapy, psychopharmacology, and occupational therapy are effective tools for achieving these goals. In other cultures, different goals and techniques are appropriate. Thus therapy processes are cultural artifacts determined generally by the overall functioning and structure of the culture and specifically by the characteristics of the maladjustment syndrome.

CULTURES IN CONTACT

In many parts of the world people who do not share the same cultural values, beliefs, and traditions coexist side by side. Sometimes the coexistence is friendly and uninterrupted by conflict. More often, however, when cultures are in contact, there is misunderstanding and domination of one group by another. The United States is a good example of a country whose history is marked by people with different cultural orientations living in close contact with one another. Further, the sociopolitical climate of the United States forces people to comply with the majority culture. The "melting-pot" philosophy that has guided educational and social policy has profoundly affected the lives of children and adults who do not share the cultural orientation of the majority culture. Although there have long been attempts by various ethnic-minority communities to maintain their ethnic heritage through private schools, after-school language classes, and ethnic community enclaves, it is only recently that many minority groups, in an upsurge of cultural pluralism, have called out to members of the majority to respect cultural diversity and to members of the minority community to manifest pride in their cultural roots.

One of the central issues that ethnic-minority-group members must deal with is their perception of their own ethnic or cultural identification. Identification refers to a process by which an individual assumes a pattern of behavior characteristic of other people in his or her environment. Although identification clearly refers to the totality of self-experience, the term *cultural identification* refers to that part of the self that includes those values, attitudes, and standards that constitute cultural-group membership.

When cultures are in contact, it is possible to identify with more than one culture. The child who comes from a Spanish-speaking home and must speak English at school may experience dual culture identification. In many cases this dual identification results in conflict and chronic anxiety, especially in that person who is only marginally familiar with the norms of one or the other of the cultures. Stonequist (1937) has used the term *marginal* to describe the person who has bicultural membership combined with the relative inability to form dual ethnic identification.

WHY IS PLURALISTIC THERAPY COMPLEX?

The marginal person may experience particular difficulties that lead him or her to seek therapy. A person may see the relative benefits of acculturating to the values of the dominant group while feeling pressure from family members and friends to remain ethnically "loyal." The degree to which the individual should acculturate or should remain a part of the minority group may be a major question in therapy. Such problems of dual cultural membership make pluralistic therapy challenging. The therapist must integrate an understanding of the dual cultural experience into the therapeutic process. At the same time the therapist must allow for each client's individual differences. The therapist must determine with the individual how much cultural separatism and/or acculturation to the majority group will facilitate personal growth.

Opinions about the degree to which ethnic groups should remain distinct vary greatly. Some people perceive full assimilation as positive and inevitable. Others postulate continued conflict, and still others envision an eventual balance between assimilation and pluralism (Dashefsky, 1976). In pluralistic therapy it is important that therapists not make decisions that will affect the client's position or role in either culture. For example, the therapist should not conclude that the client's problems would be resolved if he or she broke off relations with intimate family members and adopted a more "positive" attitude about acculturating to the majority group. Such decisions must be made jointly by both the therapist and the client.

It is also important for the therapist to understand the cultural concepts of adjustment and maladjustment in order to be able to work within the client's cultural framework. Knowledge about environmental factors that operate to encourage good mental health or to produce emotional problems is also critical. For instance, stability of income is an important factor in minimizing psychopathology among ethnic-minority-group members. Similarly, the effects of rapid acculturation and intergenerational conflict affect adjustment. Majority-group therapists may have little empathy for a situation in which Hispanic children are educated in English, acquire a life-style that differs from that of their parents, and, as young adults, are trained for jobs that then are not available. Traditional values are upset, intergenerational conflict may ensue, and no economic advantage results.

We have outlined only a few of the problems that make pluralistic therapy complex. Our purpose is to highlight these complexities through a thorough examination of the life situation of one American ethnic minority group, the Hispanic. We wish to reiterate, however, that the points to be discussed throughout this book are not specific only to Hispanics. It is our contention, rather, that many of the problems reviewed and solutions offered are applicable to other ethnic-minority-group members as well and that our approach can be used by the pluralistic therapist in working with minority-group members other than Hispanics.

QUESTIONS ABOUT PLURALISTIC THERAPY

We have now laid the foundation for pluralistic therapy. The therapist does not overgeneralize but looks for individual meanings against the context of culture (Opler, 1967). The therapist helps the individual develop an appropriate pattern of behavior and motivation that can be generalized to social situations apart from therapy (Wallace, 1970). The therapist must strive to work against the traditional approach that universalizes correlates of illness, because this approach tends to universalize treatment modalities also. If this occurs, clients are forced to fit existing treatment approaches and therapy may not fit clients' needs (Giordano, 1973), a situation that has all too often worked against the culturally different client. By pinpointing cultural differences, we are better able to assist clients' effective adjustment within their chosen environments.

Despite the broad groundwork that has been laid concerning pluralistic therapy, critical questions remain:

How extensive are the psychological differences among cultural groups? The differences may be large or small depending on a number of factors. For instance, the Hispanic immigrant may demonstrate a pattern of behavior that differs from majority-group behavior to a greater extent than does that of a third- or fourth-generation Hispanic American. Differences also depend on age and educational attainment of the individual. As more is known about the range of differences, better therapeutic plans for ethnic clients can be designed.

How much separatism should cultural groups in the United States maintain? We need to know whether pluralism, assimilation, or some balance of the two will fulfill the needs both of mainstream society and of the individual. The pluralistic therapist must decide where his or her ultimate responsibility lies—with the client or with society.

What principles can we employ to design pluralistic therapy appropriate for specific cultural groups? When this question is answered, the impact on the training of therapists will be tremendous. At present these principles are still evolving, and other important issues evolve from this basic question. Are there attributes of good therapists that cut across cultures? How should we measure effectiveness at pluralistic therapy? What environments maximize the effectiveness of pluralistic therapy?

What is the future direction of pluralistic therapy? Pluralistic therapy is a budding field, and practitioners as well as theorists must assume responsibility for determining the most productive direction. Continued research is needed to enhance our understanding about pluralistic therapy.

Answers to these questions may be sought in a number of ways. Theoretical evaluation is one possibility; existing data can be reexamined; and new investigations can be conducted. Our approach will be to investigate these questions theoretically after summarizing old and new evidence from a particular ethnic group.

FOCUS ON THE HISPANIC

The Hispanic population in the United States can be broken down into four different groups on the basis of ethnic origin. Figure 1-1 presents a population breakdown of these groups. Fifty-nine percent of Hispanics claim descent from Mexico. Some Mexican-American families have resided in the United States for centuries; for example, some in New Mexico trace their ancestry back to the original Spanish colonists. Others are recent immigrants to the United States and have taken up permanent residence, in some cases illegally. Some Mexican Americans prefer to call themselves **Chicanos,** signifying both pride in their admixture of Indian and Spanish blood (McWilliams, 1968) and a declaration of political separation (Rendon, 1971). This group of Hispanics of Mexican ancestry is itself diverse. Most Mexican Americans reside in the Southwestern states—California, Arizona, New Mexico, Colorado, and Texas (U.S. Bureau of the Census, 1977). Another 16% of the Hispanics have come from Puerto Rico; most of the Puerto Rican population reside in the Eastern states of New York, New Jersey, and Connecticut. Another sizable population of Hispanics (6%) has immigrated to the United States from Cuba. They have settled mainly in Florida, although there are large Cuban communities in New York and New Jersey. Another three-quarters of a million Hispanics have immigrated to the United States from Central and South America. These Hispanics with roots in Chile, Argentina, Colombia, Guatemala, and El Salvador as well as other countries are dispersed throughout the United States (U.S. Bureau of the Census, 1977).

It has always been difficult to estimate the Hispanic population in the United States, but, according to the 1970 Census (U.S. Bureau of the Census, 1973), there were 9.6 million such persons in the United States. The 1975 Current Population Reports (U.S. Bureau of the Census, 1975) raised the number to 11.2 million, which can be considered the most

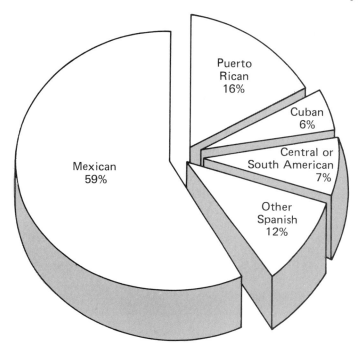

Figure 1-1. Percentage distribution of Hispanic groups in the United States by country of origin. (U.S. Bureau of the Census, 1977.)

conservative base figure for the Hispanic population. Currently there are four different estimates of the number of Hispanics in the United States (Macías, 1977):

1. The 1975 Census estimate of 11.2 million.
2. An estimate proposed by Hispanic leaders that accounts for Census undercount, increase due to births, and a certain amount of legal immigration. This figure is 16.0 million.
3. An estimate that includes the number of undocumented immigrants (approximately 7.4 million) added to the 1975 Census figures. This estimate is 18.6 million.
4. An estimate that adds the number of undocumented immigrants to the number proposed by Hispanic leaders. This is the most liberal estimate and places the number of Hispanics currently living in the United States at 23.4 million.

By any of these estimates it is apparent that Hispanics have become a significant segment of the American population. Furthermore, they are the fastest-growing ethnic group in the nation. As with the population estimate, there are different estimates of the growth rate:

1. The rate of natural increase estimated by the U.S. Bureau of the Census is 1.8% per year.
2. Estimates proposed by Hispanic leaders utilize other sources in addition to Census figures (for example, state school figures). The most conservative of these estimates is 3.5% per year.

The four base figures and the two estimated growth rates yield eight projections, which are presented in Tables 1-1 and 1-2. It can be seen that the projected number of Hispanics by the year 2000 ranges from a low of 17.5 million (using the base figure of 11.2 million and a growth rate of 1.8%) to 55.3 million (using the 23.4 million base figure and a 3.5% growth rate). In either case, the overall increase will be greater than that for the general population, and even by moderate estimates Hispanics are likely to be the largest minority group in the United States by the year 2000 (Macías, 1977).

Table 1-1. *Projections of the Spanish-origin population of the U.S. to the year 2000 at 1.8% annual rate of natural increase.*

| Year | Population Estimates (in Millions) | | | |
	1*	*2*	*3*	*4*
1975	11.2	16.0	18.6	23.4
1980	12.2	17.5	20.3	25.6
1985	13.4	19.1	22.2	28.0
1990	14.6	20.8	24.3	30.4
1995	16.0	22.9	26.6	33.4
2000	17.5	25.0	29.1	36.6

*Base (1975) figures for the four columns of projected population are from the following sources:
  Column 1: 1975 Current Population Reports.
  Column 2: Hispanic leaders' estimate of Spanish-origin population.
  Column 3: 1975 Current Population Reports plus estimate of the undocumented Hispanic population.
  Column 4: Hispanic leaders' estimate· plus the undocumented Hispanics.
  From "U.S. Hispanics in 2000 A.D.—Projecting the Number," by R. F. Macías, *Agenda: A Journal of Hispanic Issues,* 1977, *7*(3), 18. Copyright 1977 by the National Council of La Raza. Reprinted by permission.

In the following chapters, we will explore the cultural variables of each Hispanic group. We will note historical differences in time of arrival to the United States, and we will discuss reasons for immigration —exploration, colonization, economic opportunity, and personal liberty.

Table 1-2. *Projections of the Spanish-origin population of the U.S. to the year 2000 at 3.5% annual rate of natural increase.*

Year	Population Estimates (in Millions)			
	1*	2	3	4
1975	11.2	16.0	18.6	23.4
1980	13.3	19.0	22.1	27.8
1985	15.8	22.6	26.2	33.0
1990	18.8	26.8	31.2	39.2
1995	22.3	31.8	37.0	46.6
2000	26.5	37.8	44.0	55.3

*Base (1975) figures for the four columns of projected population are from the following sources:

    Column 1: 1975 Current Population Reports.
    Column 2: Hispanic leaders' estimate of Spanish-origin population.
    Column 3: 1975 Current Population Reports plus estimate of the undocumented Hispanic population.
    Column 4: Hispanic leaders' estimate plus the undocumented Hispanics.

From "U.S. Hispanics in 2000 A.D.—Projecting the Number," by R. F. Macías, *Agenda: A Journal of Hispanic Issues,* 1977, 7(3), 18. Copyright 1977 by the National Council of La Raza. Reprinted by permission.

Further, we will elaborate on intracultural differences where they exist. Significant genetic differences—Caucasian, indigenous Indian, **Mestizo,** and Black—will be discussed, since they are critical to a complete understanding of the psychological forces underlying Hispanics' world view and ways of coping with the environment. Our study of Hispanic culture will enable us to address ourselves to the major questions of pluralistic counseling.

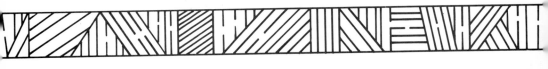

Chapter 2 Evolving Life-Styles

HISTORY OF HISPANIC IMMIGRATION

How much history must we know about a cultural group in order to be effective at pluralistic counseling? The adage "A little learning is a dangerous thing" applies well to this situation. We need to delve deeply into the history of a group in order to avoid overgeneralization. In the case of Hispanic history, this means that we must look back at least 400 years, to the earliest Spanish colonization of the New World along the Rio Grande Valley.

In the historical account that follows, we will discuss the variety and complexity of the Hispanic culture. We will explore the commonality of all Hispanics—that their homelands were colonized by Spain and their lives infused with Spanish culture and language. This account can serve as a background for interpreting the history of a particular Hispanic client, but, of course, precisely how culture and personality interact for a given client must be ascertained by the therapist within the therapeutic setting.

Mexican Americans

The first Hispanics to settle in the United States were of Spanish or Mexican extraction. The Spaniards first settled in territory that is now New Mexico, establishing the town of Santa Fe in 1598. In the 1600s they extended their settlements into Texas (Marden, 1952). In the 1600s and 1700s, 21 mission towns were founded in California through the works of Franciscan missionaries (McWilliams, 1968). Thus many Hispanics were born in what is today U.S. territory. They intermarried with native Indians and established themselves in the southwestern part of the United States.

The American West and Southwest were controlled by Mexico until 1848. Spanish was the primary language, and Spanish-Mexican culture flourished. During the first half of the 19th century, the United States instituted its policy of Manifest Destiny, and expansion into the Southwest gained momentum with the extension of the Santa Fe Trail through the territory in 1820. The drive by the United States for land led to war with Mexico in 1846. The war came to an end in 1848 with Mexico surrendering territory roughly equivalent to the present-day states of New Mexico, Colorado, Utah, Nevada, Arizona, and California.

The indigenous Mexicans in this territory automatically became citizens of the United States, and their rights were in principle protected through the Treaty of Guadalupe Hidalgo, executed on February 2, 1848 (McWilliams, 1968). Under this treaty, Mexico ceded a large amount of land, including California, Arizona, New Mexico, and other territory, to the United States and also approved the prior annexation of Texas. According to McWilliams (1968, p. 51):

> All citizens of Mexico residing within the ceded domain were to become citizens of the United States if they failed to leave the territory within one year after ratification of the treaty. Only a few thousand Mexican nationals, perhaps not more than 1,500 or 2,000, took advantage of this provision; the rest became citizens-by-default. The treaty also provided specific guarantees for the property and political rights of the "native" population and attempted to safeguard their cultural autonomy, that is, they were given the right to retain their language, religion, and culture.

As McWilliams points out, however, no provisions were made in the treaty to integrate the "native" people into the general mainstream of society. Granted cultural autonomy but denied access to mainstream institutions, these people were forced into an inferior social position. They lost their land through a series of land schemes, were forced to do "stoop" labor, were denied equal educational opportunity, and were discriminated against on every social indicator imaginable (McWilliams, 1968).

One might expect that the subjugation of and discrimination against these Mexican Americans would have deferred any other Mexicans from immigrating to the United States. However, Mexico was experiencing great political upheaval and economic difficulty in the late 19th and early 20th centuries, and hundreds of thousands of Mexicans crossed the border into the United States in search of political freedom and economic stability. Many crossed the Rio Grande carrying their only possessions on their backs. The illegal Mexican-American immigrants became known as **"wetbacks"** (Alford, 1972).

The burgeoning businesses in the United States gladly hired the Mexican immigrants, whether legal or not, as a cheap labor force for chopping brush, building railroads, mining copper, and picking cotton (Moore, 1970). Since 1880 more than 70% of the section crews and 90% of the extra gangs on the principal railroad lines of the West have been Mexican Americans (McWilliams, 1968). In 1900 these workers labored from early morning to night for only a dollar a day and were forced to live in boxcars (Bryant, 1912).

With increasing urbanization of the United States in the 1900s, some "wetbacks" began to find work in industries: tanneries, packinghouses, restaurants, dry cleaners, and trucking firms. At present approximately 85% of Mexican Americans reside in urban centers (U.S. Bureau of the Census, 1977); yet typically their work has remained seasonal, and Mexican Americans are often paid less than Anglos performing the same duties (McWilliams, 1968). Other Mexican Americans continued to live as migrants, constituting a significant part of the cheap labor force that built the railroad, sugar beet, grape, and cotton-picking industries (Burma, 1954).

Mexican Americans, although paid poorly, were able to find employment except during times of economic hardship. During the depression of the 1920s approximately 400,000 Mexican Americans and Mexicans were deported to Mexico.

During World War II, the United States was desperately short of labor. Mexican citizens were imported as a source of cheap labor, through an agreement between the two countries. In 1942, 42,000 Mexican laborers were imported. By 1944, 110,000 more Mexicans were welcomed to the United States (Bustamante & Bustamante, 1969). Like other minority groups, these Mexicans were hired quickly for low-paying jobs and fired just as speedily in times of economic trouble. With the recession following World War II, 16,000 Mexicans and Mexican-American citizens were forced to return to Mexico, even if they strenuously opposed this deportation (Burma, 1954).

Historically the Catholic Church has played a vital role in Mexican culture. Mexican Catholicism is a blend of Spanish and Indian beliefs (Kramer, 1962). The most revered figure in the Church is the Virgin of Guadalupe, who revealed herself to a simple Indian peasant near Mexico City. In early Mexican-American history, lack of funds and a shortage of priests made it difficult for the Church to plan programs beyond narrow ministerial functions (Kitano, 1974). Immigration in the early 1900s brought thousands of nominal Catholics, further limiting the pastoral functions of the Church (Moore, 1970). After World War I, the Church attempted to foster Americanization through religious services and the establishment of parochial schools. Contrary to the Church's goal, however, the schools may have furthered cultural identity by unifying the Hispanics (Moore, 1970). Today a small number of Hispanics ascribe to Protestant sects such as the Southern Baptist Convention and the Methodist Church (Wagner, 1966).

Despite historical and economic factors limiting the Catholic Church's power in Hispanic communities, Catholicism certainly has influenced the life-styles of many Mexican Americans. For many Catholic Mexican Americans, social activities center in the church, and the priest is a primary confidant. He is asked to resolve many personal and family crises (Padilla, Carlos, & Keefe, 1976). To the extent that a Mexican American subscribes to Catholic tenets, daily activity is influenced by a belief that events are controlled externally (God's will) and by a belief in an afterlife. Several researchers (Bronson & Meadow, 1968; Peñalosa, 1968; Peñalosa & McDonagh, 1966) have attempted to relate degree of religiosity among Hispanics to their adaptation in the United States. Results of this research have been conflicting, however, suggesting that religiosity does not affect the Hispanic's adjustment and acculturation in a consistent manner.

The history of Mexican immigration to the United States since 1880 illustrates the dramatic discrimination against the immigrants and the ways in which Mexican Americans were locked into poverty. Peasants fled poverty and revolution in Mexico only to find themselves limited to stoop labor in the United States. In many cases their culture, language, and families were their only vital possessions. It is important for therapists to remember this facet of American history; the client's family may have been rooted for many centuries in the United States, and recognition of early Mexican-American history will help the therapist understand why many Chicanos feel that they have been robbed of their land and power in the United States (Valdez, 1971). Such beliefs are not grandiose ideas that need to be rectified by therapy.

Mexican Americans have been stereotyped as lazy and unwilling to assimilate into American society. History reveals that discrimination, the **Bracero** program, and poor wages have operated to maintain poverty among many Mexican Americans, thus preventing their upward mobility in American society (Sanchez, 1966). Thus many problems brought to the therapist may reflect economic strains rooted in historical discrimination rather than intrapsychic factors.

Puerto Ricans

Since the early 1920s the Spanish-speaking population in the United States has increased through the settlement of Puerto Ricans on the continent. When Puerto Rico was colonized by Spain in the 16th century, the island was inhabited by Tainos Indians. The island lacked natural wealth, and the Tainos had never developed to the advanced level of civilization found in Mexico. The natives were outnumbered and absorbed by the Spanish conquistadors (Fellows, 1973). Gradually Black slaves were imported from Africa to work plantations, but, since Puerto Rico was more a garrison than an agricultural center, it never became totally dependent on slaves. Because of their small numbers, slaves were not so segregated as in the United States and eventually intermarried with the Spaniards and indigenous Indians. Today as many as 85% of Puerto Ricans claim both Negroid and Caucasian origin (Longres, 1974).

Control of Puerto Rico was ceded by Spain to the United States in 1898. At the termination of the Spanish-American War, the island was assigned an ambiguous status that did not allow statehood because its citizens were considered "racially inferior" (Longres, 1974). The prolonged period of colonization has provoked resentment among some Puerto Ricans toward Anglos (Vasquez de Rodriguez, 1973).

With the Jones Act of 1917, Puerto Rico became a Commonwealth Territory of the United States. Puerto Ricans could move freely from the island to the continent without an immigration check. Like the Mexicans, Puerto Ricans traveled to the United States in search of better jobs. Most of the islanders who moved in the early 1900s settled in New York City because it was cheaper to travel to New York than to almost any other city in the continental United States. Later Puerto Ricans continued to settle in New York because they felt welcomed by family and friends in New York's Puerto Rican enclave (Burma, 1954).

In 1947 the United States initiated Operation Bootstrap to industrialize Puerto Rico. Machinery and metal industries were established, and sugar (which had been a staple of the economy) became of secondary importance. Industrialization created dramatic economic and social changes; the standard of living rose, but the discrepancy between the upper and lower classes also increased, with concomitant social upheaval. Puerto Rico was no longer economically autonomous but was instead intimately tied to the mainland economy. With each successive economic recession, migration to the mainland increased (Fellows, 1973). In 1950 about a thousand Puerto Rican islanders a week migrated to New York to escape recession on the island and to fill a need for cheap labor on the continent. Responding to the need for factory workers, the Puerto Ricans moved gradually westward to New Jersey, Philadelphia, and Chicago. Today about 60% of the Puerto Rican labor force is employed in semiskilled positions. About 20% work as service attendants in hotels and restaurants. Because the Puerto Rican population is young compared to other ethnic groups in the United States—about 45% are under 20 years of age—there are relatively more children and consequently fewer employed persons per household in this Hispanic group than in any other (Abad, Ramos, & Boyce, 1974).

Puerto Ricans migrating to the United States are of diverse socioeconomic backgrounds; they include sugar-cane workers, coffee growers, and middle-class urbanites. The sugar-cane workers come from the coastal regions of Puerto Rico, and, because of a short growing season for this crop, there Puerto Ricans generally work only four to five months per year. Few own their own land, poverty is common, and unemployment has very little stigma attached to it. Coffee is grown in the interior of Puerto Rico on small farms, and coffee-farming families tend to maintain a traditional, rural way of life. The urban dwellers include government officers, small-store owners, and teachers. These people are possibly more oriented toward improving their economic and social positions than are rural Puerto Ricans, and the women exercise considerably more autonomy than do women in rural settings (Abad et al., 1974). The Puerto Rican immigrants may maintain values associated with their previous island life-styles. Today second- and third-generation mainland Puerto Ricans can be found in all major northeastern urban areas. These later-generation Puerto Ricans differ in life-style and in cultural orientation from their island relatives.

This historical sketch of the Puerto Ricans highlights several crucial points for therapists. First, Puerto Rican clients, particularly Black Puerto Ricans, may face discrimination because of their skin color. Second, the Puerto Rican clientele is a relatively young population, whose primary counseling needs may be for occupational and vocational guidance (Pollack & Menacker, 1971). Third, the open travel between the continent and the island may cause instability in assimilation (Preble, 1968), and therapy therefore may need to focus on how and how much the client wishes to adapt to Anglo culture. Fourth, the therapist should be aware of cultural differences between mainland and island Puerto Ricans.

Cubans

The southeastern tip of the United States has been populated by Hispanic people of a third national origin. When Cuba was colonized by Spain in 1511, the native Tainos Indians were almost annihilated. Many were killed or died of diseases brought by the Spaniards. Those Tainos who survived were treated like slaves; they were forced to till the land and mine the fields for their colonizers. In the 1700s Black slaves were imported to Cuba, and, as in Puerto Rico, the workers and Spaniards intermarried, so that today Cubans display the full range of genetic makeup from Caucasian to Negro.

Spain clung tenaciously to Cuba as its last stronghold in the Western Hemisphere. With the aid of the United States, Cuba won independence from Spain in 1898 and developed an agricultural and tourist economy that was dependent on American dollars for its survival. A small entrepreneurial class controlled most of the wealth.

The Cuban revolution of 1959, led by Fidel Castro, received support from people in many sectors of Cuban society who had become disenchanted with the government of the dictator Batista. At first only individuals directly connected with the Batista government were forced to flee. However, as the revolution continued, the new communist-oriented regime depended more and more on support from the lower classes, and large numbers of upper-class Cubans decided to leave the country.

Cuban immigration to the United States can be divided into six main phases: The first period was shortly before and after January 1959, when Castro seized power. About 3000 members of the elite Batista power structure escaped to the United States, and many managed to bring their considerable wealth with them. The second phase occurred during 1959 and 1960, when many upper-class owners of farms, ranches, and businesses decided to leave. Many were able to bring some personal property and money with them. By the end of 1960, a third phase of immigration began. Many middle-class Cubans, including professionals, managers, technicians, heads of companies, and stockholders, immigrated as their wealth was about to be seized. The fourth phase began after the Bay of Pigs operation in July of 1961. Castro announced that immigrants could take only necessities with them; they were allowed to take five dollars and a few clothes. Later they were not allowed to take any money. During this fourth phase, the wealthy continued to immigrate, but more middle- and lower-class office workers, and skilled and semiskilled workers also moved to the United States. An average of 1600 to 1800 destitute Cubans arrived each week during 1961 and 1962. The fifth phase of immigration began as a result of President Kennedy's quarantine of Cuba during the Missile Crisis. Castro blocked refugee air flights in October of 1962. Nevertheless, between then and December 1965, about 9500 Cubans escaped on small fishing craft. The sixth and final stage began in December 1965, when Castro and President Johnson reinstated the refugee flights (Rogg, 1974). When political channels were reopened and immigration reinitiated in 1965, 200 immigrants arrived in Florida every day for months (Alford, 1972). In addition to this direct immigration of Cubans to the United States, some 20,000 Cubans immigrated to Spain during the Missile Crisis and later entered the United States when they were able to obtain visas. These latter Hispanic immigrants have brought elements of the cultures of both Spain and Cuba to the United States (Klovekorn, Madera, & Nardone, 1974).

Miami-Dade County, Florida, was the first point of arrival of most of the Cubans. As this area became saturated with immigrants, the U.S. government developed a resettlement program (Rogg, 1974), and New York and New Jersey accepted a large proportion of the refugees. In fact, by 1968 Cubans constituted one-third to one-half of the population of New York City's West Side (Rogg, 1974).

The Cubans are an unusual immigrant group for several reasons. First, Cuban refugees on the whole represent a higher social class and are more educated than Hispanics who have immigrated from Mexico and Puerto Rico. Many Cuban Americans are skilled professionals, but they are often barred from practicing their professions because of differences in language and training (Alford, 1972). Thus Cuban immigrants express concerns about discrimination and lack of employment that are overtly similar to those of other Hispanics. A closer look reveals that many Cubans have been struggling to enter middle- and upper-middle-class American society, whereas a large proportion of Chicanos and Puerto Ricans are struggling to avoid poverty. Of course, one problem is not less serious than the other; each group of Hispanics is striving for a life of freedom and opportunity in the United States.

A second unusual characteristic about the Cubans is that they are primarily urbanites. Over 87% of Miami's Cuban population report having emigrated from a large city. Of the Cubans in New York's West Side, 41% emigrated from Havana and 25% from Las Villas, and over 56% report that their childhood home was a city (Rogg, 1974). As we will see later in this chapter, urbanites generally hold values and attitudes that are different from those of people accustomed to a rural or migrant life-style.

A unique characteristic of the Cuban immigrants is that many came to the United States with hopes of returning soon to Cuba, and this allegiance to Cuba appears to retard their acculturation to U.S. society. For example, as late as 1974 83% of a sample of Cuban children in New York's West Side reported having all or mostly Cuban friends. Only 40% of the adults in the community expressed a desire for U.S. citizenship. As it becomes more and more likely that life in Cuba as the immigrants knew it will not return, their knowledge of English, their use of English with their children, and their number of friendships outside the Cuban community have increased (Rogg, 1974). Recent research indicates that young Cuban Americans are acculturating at a much faster rate than their parents and that this discrepancy is resulting in a high degree of intergenerational conflict (Szapocznik, Scopetta, Kurtines, & de los Angeles Aranalde, in press).

The Cuban immigration itself was a unique experience in American history.

> Never before had the United States been a country of first asylum for refugees. The Cubans gave the Americans very little choice; they simply got on boats or airplanes and came. Many had no passports, no visas, or other papers necessary for legal entrance into this country. Many had to leave Cuba illegally. Visa waivers and other temporary measures were introduced by government officials in order to permit entry of these political refugees. Since it was believed that Castro could be quickly deposed more permanent measures seemed unnecessary at that time [Rogg, 1974, p. 7].

The United States was not fully prepared to provide needed help for resettlement. In a New York survey, only 10% of the respondents who were heads of households credited government agencies with helping them find jobs. Less than 2% of the women surveyed felt that the U.S. government had facilitated their adjustment (Rogg, 1974).

Perhaps because their immigration has occurred so recently, much less research has been done on the adjustment of Cubans in the United States than on that of Mexican Americans or Puerto Ricans. Nevertheless, the research findings that exist stimulate thought about effective pluralistic counseling for Cubans. A significant theme in therapy with older Cuban immigrants may be loss of social status in the move to the United States. Although the immigrants as a whole represent a middle-class population, the therapist needs to remember the phases of immigration from Cuba. It is important not to overgeneralize about Cuban immigrants lest their actual economic lot and values associated with social class be confused. Depending on when he or she fled Cuba, the immigrant will have escaped with more or less personal property. For some Cubans a central concern may be anger and despair over loss of rights and property. For Cubans who escaped with their wealth, a primary focus may be sorrow over loss of status and homeland. As we stated previously, many Cubans looked to the United States for only temporary asylum, and these Cubans may have feelings of mixed allegiance to both the United States and Cuba. Among the personal concerns they bring to therapy may be the degree to which they wish to acculturate to American society and the intergenerational conflict that this creates. Thus the cultural and socioeconomic backgrounds and the concerns of adjusting to life in the United States are both unique and varied among Cuban immigrants.

Other Hispanic Groups

Spanish colonization of South America was pervasive, second only to Portuguese colonization. The Spaniards conquered various Indian groups, and contact between the Spaniards and the indigenous groups resulted in hybridized ethnicities and cultures. Spanish domination continued through the 18th century. However, beginning in the 19th century, many parts of the Spanish colonial empire began to revolt against Spain, and ultimately South American countries won their independence. These countries share common cultural and religious beliefs arising out of common histories and face similar political, economic, and social problems. Despite geographic and historical similarities, however, the countries have distinct and varied economic, political, and social systems (Gunther, 1967).

There is a dearth of information about Hispanics who immigrate from Central and South America. We know that these Hispanics immigrate for varied reasons. Some leave their homelands because their political views have placed them in personal danger. They may leave family members and possessions behind, which, in turn, impedes their emotional adaptation to life in the United States. Many Central Americans immigrate to better their economic lot. To some extent, their adaptation may resemble that of many Mexican Americans and Puerto Ricans. Other South American immigrants are professionals who can best pursue their careers in the United States.

Because of their relatively small numbers in the United States and their varied historical backgrounds, Hispanics of Central and South American descent are seldom recognized as a distinct Hispanic subgroup. For example, Peruvians and Chileans in California are often assumed to be Mexican Americans, and Dominican Republicans on the East Coast are often considered Black or Puerto Rican.

Therapy with clients of Central or South American extraction is a largely undocumented domain (Thomas & Garrison, 1975). Much of the literature on counseling Mexican Americans, Cubans, and Puerto Ricans can be applied to Hispanics of South American heritage. Yet the therapist must be vigilant for possible differences in attitudes and behaviors from one Hispanic group to another.

LIFE-STYLES OF HISPANICS IN THE UNITED STATES

The Migrant Worker

Many Hispanics in the United States, particularly Mexican Americans, work as migrant field laborers. Most of these workers live in extreme poverty. Because of travel time and seasonal variation in crop quantity, they generally work less than 35 weeks a year. Families may live in company-owned housing projects that lack plumbing and other sanitary provisions. Lack of technical training and discrimination by the greater Anglo society prevent occupational mobility among this group (Scholes, 1966).

Contrary to general belief, most migrants claim a home base, usually in Texas, California, or Arizona. Those who have such a base usually own a *ranchito*, about half an acre of land, in an area known as a **colonia.** Many would like to live permanently in these homes but must travel in order to support their families (Scholes, 1966). They are the "currency of cheap labor, and like money . . . made to circulate" (Galarza, Gallegos, & Samora, 1970, p. 20).

In some cases, migrant workers hold special values associated with their way of life. For example, many express positive attitudes toward education but frustration with the schooling that is available to their children. Since migrant children travel with their families, their school year is often disrupted, and many fall far behind their peers in academic achievement (Manuel, 1965). Since the workers are paid by amount of harvest, parents may prefer that their children work in the fields rather than spend time and energy in an unsatisfactory school setting. The familial support system may differ between migrants and other Hispanics. Among migrants family interaction is usually limited to the nuclear family; their transient life-style precludes much interaction with extended-family members (Ulibarri, 1966). Some personality traits appear to be particularly functional for migrant workers. When 236 migrants and nonmigrants in Indiana completed a locus-of-control questionnaire, relative success—as indicated by higher IQ scores—was correlated with "outgoing" and "tough-minded" traits in migrant children. In contrast, success for nonmigrant children was associated with traits Henzlik (1974) labeled conscientiousness, social control, and low apprehension. Since they need great perseverance to satisfy even basic needs, it is not surprising that successful migrant children would be tough-minded and assertive.

The migrant population includes Puerto Ricans and other Hispanics as well. They usually work alongside Blacks in the citrus-growing areas of Florida and the South up through the northeastern agricultural areas. Little is known about this migrant population.

It is unusual for a therapist to encounter a migrant in therapy, since they usually live at some distance from cities, where most mental-health centers are located. If a therapeutic relationship with a migrant worker were established, it would be important to investigate the migrant worker's means of basic maintenance and to respect, if present, a relatively tough-minded attitude toward life.

The Rural Hispanic

The early Hispanic settlers were rural people. Mexicans established enormous ranches in the West and Southwest, but today few Hispanics live in the kind of gracious rural setting that their ancestors enjoyed. In fact, today rural Hispanics represent less than 15% of the total Hispanic population.

Rural Hispanics share the "traditional" values and attitudes that are characteristic of most Americans residing in rural settings. One such traditional value is a present-, rather than a past- or future-, time orientation. It has been suggested that the urban American tends to emphasize future goals, such as educational and vocational aspirations, whereas rural people, including rural Hispanics, stress present interactions, such as close relationships with family and friends. According to this view, rural people generally believe that future events will occur as they must or according to God's will and that the individual can exert only minimal control over future events. Since the future cannot be controlled, limited time should be spent planning for or worrying about tomorrow.

There is a joke about the Hispanic putting things off "until **mañana** (tomorrow)." What we should emphasize about the traditional Hispanic time orientation is not the tendency to procrastinate but, rather, the great importance attached to *present* experience. The ability to enjoy the present without fear about the future can add great joy to life. A mental-health professional who understands this present-time orientation can make use of it in therapy. A client from a traditional rural environment is more likely to adopt new behaviors and life goals if the immediate advantage of the changes or the real possibility of future changes is clearly apparent.

Traditional rural Hispanics have also been described as passive endurers of stress. Whereas urban dwellers may actively attack life's difficulties, traditionally oriented Hispanics believe that events are determined by forces outside their control, so they learn to cope with adversity rather than fight against it (Diaz-Guerrero, 1967). For example, in one game situation rural Anglos and Mexican Americans were less assertive than urban-middle class Anglos (Kagan & Carlson, 1975). In another study of assertiveness involving game simulation, semirural Anglo and Mexican-American children did not differ from each other in assertiveness, although both groups were more assertive than rural Mexican children (Kagan, 1973). Thus, both ethnicity (Mexican versus Anglo and Mexican American) and life-style (rural versus urban) affect degree of assertiveness.

Traditionally oriented rural Hispanics place much value on affiliation, the need for warm, mutually supportive relationships. Disruption of relationships can provoke great personal pain, and many life decisions revolve around maintaining interpersonal ties. In another game situation, Anglo children were more apt to play competitively than were Mexican-American children, although both Anglo and Mexican-American children played more competitively than did rural Mexican children (Madsen, 1971). Because of the importance attached to affiliation, traditionally oriented Hispanics tend to be more diplomatic and to avoid confrontation more than Anglos (Murillo, 1971). The Spanish words **hospitalidad** and **dignidad** emphasize the value of positive and proud relationships in Hispanic culture (Rothenberg, 1964).

For traditional rural Hispanics, the family is central to a good life (Marden, 1952). The family structure is usually patriarchal; the husband is the primary economic provider and decision maker (Burma, 1954), and he is expected to run the family in a strong but just manner (Murillo, 1971).

Much has been written about **machismo,** the tendency to assert superiority and dominance, among traditional Hispanic males. *Machismo,* as the term is commonly construed, expresses itself through multiple sexual conquests, sensitivity to insult, and a latent capacity for violence. This description is probably an exaggeration; in reality *machismo* may be related to the fact that the traditional Hispanic male has a more responsible, less restrictive social role than the female (Padilla & Ruiz, 1973). There are so many exaggerated and unsubstantiated beliefs about *machismo* that therapists must be very cautious not to incorporate fallacious ideas that could interfere with an effective therapist/client relationship. It can be damaging to a patient for the therapist to assume that the patient is stereotypically **macho**—for example, that he is involved in multiple sexual relationships simply because he is a Hispanic male.

Hispanic females are generally subordinate to the males, faithful to the Church, and committed to home and family (Burma, 1954). A mother is described in affectionate terms by both Mexican-American (Goodman & Beman, 1971) and Puerto Rican (Fernandez-Marina, Maldonado-Sierra, & Trent, 1958) children. The traditionally oriented female is sometimes hesitant to voice her opinions and rights, because she has been socialized to defer decision making to significant males, such as her father or husband (Murillo, 1971). Although she lacks social power relative to the Hispanic male, the Hispanic woman is much appreciated by her family (Fernandez-Marina et al., 1958; Marden, 1952). The therapist may face a critical conflict with traditionally oriented Hispanic women. If the therapist helps the woman become more assertive and powerful in her social interactions, her new behavior may cause strife in the traditional environment.

Children in the traditional rural setting are expected to be respectful and obedient to adults (Kluckhohn & Strodtbeck, 1961). The father/son relationship is generally distant but free of conflict. The mother, however, maintains close affectional ties with both sons and daughters (Peñalosa, 1968). Children are reared differently according to sex and birth order (Marden, 1952). The mother teaches the sons to be dominant and independent, and the eldest son usually has more authority than his younger male siblings (Kluckhohn & Strodtbeck, 1961). Siblings maintain close emotional ties, and parents discourage quarreling among them (Goodman & Beman, 1971). In accordance with the cultural emphasis on cooperation and affiliation, children are taught to be dependent on their parents and supportive of their siblings.

Family responsibility and love are not limited to the nuclear family. The traditional values of rural Hispanics include respect for elders; the older the person, the more respect due him or her. Familial ties are extended to include **compadres,** or godparents, as well (Murillo, 1971). Grandparents and godparents are highly influential, and children are encouraged to seek their advice (Goodman & Beman, 1971; Maldonado-Sierra & Trent, 1960). In one study (Komaroff, Masuda, & Holmes, 1968), adult Mexican Americans expressed significantly less fear about the death of a spouse than did Anglos or Blacks. The researchers concluded that Mexican-American extended family and community provide unusual support to their members, which aids them in grappling with such life crises as the death of a loved one.

Because of their values and because of limited opportunity for economic advancement, rural Hispanics often do not view power and prestige as realistic goals. Instead, they seek satisfaction through interpersonal relationships (Murillo, 1971). According to the traditional Hispanic value of **personalismo,** it is not ability but, rather, goodness and the quality of personal relationships that are important in life. The Hispanic trusts and relies on other Hispanics (Fitzpatrick, 1971); indeed, the traditional Hispanic may not seek financial help from public or governmental agencies, because of this strong tradition of mutual aid among family and friends (Marden, 1952).

The cognitive style of traditionally oriented Hispanics differs in some ways from that of urban, nontraditional Hispanics. Rural Hispanics are more *field dependent*; that is, they tend to interpret an object or an event in relation to its surroundings. Modern, nontraditional Hispanics are more *field independent*; that is, they tend to make interpretations about an object or an event by focusing exclusively on its features (Ramirez & Price-Williams, 1974). In one study with Mexican-American children, those living in traditional semiurban environments were more field dependent than those living in Los Angeles (Ramirez, Castañeda, & Herold, 1974). The therapist working with a traditionally oriented client should attempt to use the client's field dependence for therapeutic gains. For example, rather than focus directly on a client's inappropriate behavior, the therapist might illustrate the effect of the behavior on others.

Not all rural Hispanics, however, hold traditional values. For example, when Mexican-American students in Colorado and New Mexico responded to a questionnaire about value systems, there were no significant differences between urban and rural students. Both groups of subjects adhered to a dominant American value system (Romano-V., 1971). The pluralistic therapist needs to recognize that the traditional-versus-modern orientation is a significant dimension for understanding a wide range of values. Exactly where a particular client lies on this continuum must be established individually in the therapeutic setting.

The Urban Hispanic

With increasing industrialization, more and more Hispanics have moved to cities in search of better jobs, so that today 85% of these people are urban dwellers (U.S. Bureau of the Census, 1977). Industrialization has forced changes on Hispanics as it has on other Americans. Businesses often require their employees to move, living conditions are crowded, people face increased demands on their time, and a sense of alienation results. Individuals are shocked to discover that they must cope with conditions that they expected to occur many years in the future (Toffler, 1974). Recently, in urban centers, women have adopted more powerful roles outside the home, and, conversely, males have accepted less dominant positions. Residency in mainland cities by Puerto Ricans has been associated with a decrease in male dominance and in the power of the extended family (Preble, 1968; Recio-Andrados, 1975). Urban spouses tend to share in decision making and child rearing (Moore, 1971).

Urban Hispanics tend to have a more modern perceptual orientation. When Rotter's (1966) locus-of-control scale was administered to university students, Mexican Americans exhibited as much internal control as Anglos, thus indicating a modern orientation among both groups (Garza & Ames, 1974). In his review of the literature on Mexican-American value formation, Chandler (1974, p. 269) concludes that Mexican-Americans experience "the same cultural transformations that all people experience as a result of living in and attempting to cope with modern social trends."

It should be noted that urbanization does not mean that all vestiges of traditional society disappear. In a survey administered to a sample of urban Hispanics in California, the importance of the extended family was quite obvious (Padilla, Carlos, & Keefe, 1976). Moreover, city dwellers attempted to carefully shelter their children, chaperoning their activities and, when possible, accompanying them to school. Of course, children in the United States are not usually as closely watched as in traditional families in Mexico, Puerto Rico, or Cuba. It is interesting to note that, in a survey of Cubans residing in the West Side of New York City, 44.6% of the parents reported that they wished their children did not have so much freedom (Rogg, 1974). Although urban Hispanics may hold some traditional values, the problems and goals they bring to therapy reflect stress associated with fast-paced city life.

Many urban Hispanics live in ethnic enclaves called **barrios** and their life-style is usually somewhat different from that of rural Hispanics or non*barrio*-dwelling Hispanics living in an urban area. Some *barrios* are located near old plazas of early Spanish settlements (Moore, 1970); others are located near former labor-camp sites. The railroad companies built row houses along the lines and rented them to their employees; the large *barrios* in Kansas City, Los Angeles, and Chicago are outgrowths of such railroad camps. *Barrios* also developed where Hispanics worked as farm hands and as unskilled laborers (McWilliams, 1968). McWilliams (1968, p. 217) explains that these settlements are "invariably on the other side of something: a railroad track, a bridge, a river, or a highway." Most are located in unincorporated areas adjacent to a town. The site is determined by economic factors such as inexpensive land and cheaply built residences. In addition to the problems associated with poverty, *barrio* dwellers often must face disruption of their environment by interstate-highway construction and urban-renewal projects (Galarza, Gallegos, & Samora, 1970).

A minority enclave such as a *barrio* serves to insulate its residents from social subordination (Kramer, 1962). At the same time, it protects the majority from feeling threatened by the presence of minority people whom they may consider socially inferior. *Barrio* residents gain status by joining a cohesive group and accepting the *barrio* norms (Nava, 1971). Spanish is spoken frequently within the *barrio*, and, for many residents, recreation, work, and friendship center in the community (Burma, 1954).

Some *barrio* residents may maintain traditional values. Warmth and closeness within the family and perceived hostility outside may be elements of survival in poor, crowded areas. Many people in these urban enclaves adopt a mixture of traditional and modern values (Moore, 1970). Still others earn enough money to move out of the *barrio* and away from their traditional families.

As is common among adolescents, some Hispanic youths within the *barrio* have formed gangs. Investigations of Puerto Rican adolescent gangs in 1970 revealed that hostile aggression was minimal, although physical strength was a measure of status in the group. Many of the Puerto Rican gang members of the 1970 study held jobs or attended school (Gannon, 1970). Gangs appear to provide support for these adolescents as they attempt to find an appropriate balance between Hispanic values and Anglo norms (Alford, 1972). Attempts to diminish the Hispanic youth's association with the group (on the assumption that all gangs are potentially destructive social forces) could be quite detrimental to his or her mental health and work against the development of more socially acceptable behavior.

The impact of *barrio* life on Hispanics has led many researchers to recommend locating mental-health facilities within the Hispanic communities (Padilla et al., 1975; Scheidlinger, Struening, & Rabkin, 1970). A locally established mental-health team is more attuned to special *barrio* problems and can coordinate its efforts with those of other *barrio* institutions such as churches and schools.

CULTURE AND POVERTY

If you are poor in a technological society, how much choice do you have about improving your life? The poor may adopt more traditional values as the only realistic means of economic survival (Martinez, 1973). Many of the values ascribed to rural and *barrio* Hispanics may be related to their poverty.

Studies have shown a correlation between low socioeconomic class and traditional orientation. In one study of Mexican-American and Anglo 11th-graders, social class, more than ethnic group, was associated with locus of control (whether internal or external). Lower-class subjects, whether Anglo or Mexican-American, were more likely to perceive an external locus of control—to believe that external events rather than internal motivation directed life—than were middle-class subjects (Bender & Ruiz, 1974). In another study, social status overshadowed ethnicity in determining the nature of family functioning among Blacks, Whites, and Puerto Ricans (Geismar & Gerhart, 1968). Anglo and Mexican-American mothers of all socioeconomic strata were videotaped teaching their children cognitive and motor tasks. Mothers from the low socioeconomic class were found to be more passive than middle-class mothers (Stewart & Stewart, 1974). In a theoretical exposition, poverty was posited as a prime cause of outward docility among Puerto Rican islanders (Vasquez de Rodrigues, 1973).

Lower-class status may contribute to frustration with institutions for health care and for schooling. Lower-class individuals may lack the power and the economic base to establish institutions appropriate to their needs. Institutions established by the majority culture may appear impersonal or alien. In poor districts, school buildings are dilapidated, instructional materials are inadequate, and classrooms are overcrowded. Parents and children may turn away from the schools toward the familiarity of community life (Kramer, 1962).

Poverty may account for a fatalistic attitude and rejection of institutions (Casavantes, 1970). Poverty disrupts living.

> . . . Like, they don't really experience what you go through staying all night in a freezing apartment or watch the rats go along your books and stuff like that . . . the roaches—and you have to stop doing your work and kill the roaches before they eat your home [Palomares, 1971a, p. 92].

Opler (1967, pp. 395–401) presents a case of a young Puerto Rican that illustrates how social disruption associated with poverty can result in maladjustment. Ramon's psychological problems began during his early childhood in a Puerto Rican slum and magnified when his mother moved the family to New York City during Ramon's pubescence.

THE CASE OF RAMON. Ramon was partly colored. His father, also partly colored, had abandoned the family. The mother and four children promptly moved to the worst slum of San Juan, and on the few occasions when

the father visited the city, the parents fought violently.
Ramon remembers his father beating the mother brutally
and once trying to kill her with a gun. As a child, both
parents punished him mercilessly, the father using his
belt and the mother her broomstick. Ramon, whose lot
fell with the mother ultimately, felt that she showed him
no vestige of real affection.[1]

As we see, Ramon grew up in an environment that was certainly
conducive to psychological maladjustment. Of course, severe family
problems exist at all socioeconomic levels. Yet Ramon's lot was worsened
because his mother was frustrated by her own bondage to poverty.
Moreover, Ramon was subjected to tremendous psychological stress on
the ghetto streets.

. . . the slum was recalled as a place where "we were
brought up among savages." Killings and beatings forced
the young men to join gangs of hoodlums for survival.
When baseball or swimming seemed boring, sadistic
sports were substituted. One game involved being
thumped on the back with a stick as long as one could
bear the pain. Today, Ramon's brother is hospitalized
and under treatment for mental disorder, following
several aggressive and assaultative episodes.

Ramon incorporated healthy values from Puerto Rican culture, but
he also developed emotional problems, a fear of loneliness, and an
expectation of hostility from his life of poverty.

. . . Ramon impressed one immediately as a tense,
overactive individual, looking younger than his given age
and overly concerned about his health and sexual
identity. Ramon's fears and emotional constriction were
early developed. Hostility toward frankly rejecting
parents could not be expressed. Far from being merely
callous, Ramon was afraid to be alone and terrified of
being ridiculed. He learned to avoid punishments, tried
to escape parental tongue-lashings, but developed a
lengthy covert set of fears including high places, strange

[1]From *Culture and Social Psychiatry*, by M. K. Opler. Copyright 1967 by Aldine
Publishing Company. Reprinted by permission.

people, drunkards, food poisons, and being cut. The stern expectations of his mother bred in him a feeling that things should be done perfectly, that one should not show emotions to others, and that one should always be guarded with people. The introjection of these rules, based upon suspicion and hostility, he recognized as being far from Puerto Rican values. Yet Ramon preferred to keep such opinions to himself and to trust no one.

Fear of poverty became a theme in Ramon's life. He feared it because he knew the awful pain of a life of destitution.

... Generally, in this group, the acting out of lower-class persons is franker or more overt than in the class above. Here the mother, obese and overeating, ostensibly because of Island food deprivations, states that she is "rotten inside" because of constant suffering. For the most part, she and her children had always been hungry and deprived. Her son reported hunger in Puerto Rico that had even robbed him of sleep, and he recalled feeling at such times the most unhappy person in the world. The boys begged food from neighbors and learned to steal. In this period of the lean years, Ramon's oral concerns and resentments grew.

As is true of many poor people, Ramon saw no avenues for moving out of a life of poverty. For example, his mother perceived education as a way to achieve occupational mobility, but lack of suitable clothing prevented Ramon from attending school. Ramon was relatively dark-skinned, and prejudice against dark skin color was yet another barrier preventing his upward mobility.

... Ramon was mulatto and open to her [the mother's] further rejection, especially after they had moved to New York. On the mainland, the ethnic discriminations led Ramon to feel doubly stigmatized, both as lower-class Puerto Rican and as mulatto. The mother reinforced the social rejection, taunting him with the knowledge that in their tenement he was at first not allowed into the building, ostensibly for racial reasons.

Ramon spent several years in psychoanalytically oriented therapy. He gained insight about his diffuse anger toward both parents, and he progressed enough to be able to work successfully at blue-collar jobs. He did not develop successful heterosexual relationships, however, nor was he able to dissipate the core of his emotional distress or extinguish his phobic behaviors. He could not eradicate the effects of constant belittling and rejection associated with being poor and a minority person or the effects of having disturbed parents who were themselves frustrated victims of poverty. He achieved some degree of acculturation in the United States, but childhood trauma and present discrimination continued to distress him.

> . . . His personality integration and emotional balance have not progressed far beyond that of his starved childhood—of being the "unhappiest person in the world."

The Emerging Middle Class

A number of studies suggest that middle-class Hispanics and Anglos hold similar values. When Mexican Americans in Albuquerque, Los Angeles, and San Antonio responded to a value questionnaire, poor Mexican Americans held more traditional values, whereas middle-class Mexican Americans and Anglos had similar, more modern values (Moore, 1970). Studies of locus of control among university students in Texas reported no significant difference between Anglos and Mexican Americans (Garza & Ames, 1974).

In another study, Mexican-American and Anglo seventh- to tenth-grade children of blue-collar families expressed more fatalism than did Anglo and Mexican-American children of white-collar workers (Schwartz, 1971). When Mexican Americans in Lubbock, Texas, were interviewed by a Mexican American in the language of their choice, many expressed traditional orientations; yet, the younger Mexican Americans with higher-level jobs and more education did express some modern values. Although adoption of modern values correlated with age, education, and occupational status, it did not correlate with a host of other variables such as geographical mobility, number of children, marital status, and sex (Chandler, 1974).

Among Puerto Rican college students, a trend of decreasing influence of the father's authority was noted (Fernandez-Marina et al., 1958). Similarly, in middle-class Mexican-American homes, the male is apparently becoming less dominant, with more sharing by husband and wife of decision making and child rearing (Moore, 1970). Hispanics in the middle class are more likely to live in single-family homes and use birth control than are Hispanics from the lower socioeconomic classes (Moore, 1970). For the middle-class Hispanic, material comfort, recreational interests, type of employment, and educational achievement may be very typically "American" (Sheldon, 1966).

Some values differentiate middle-class Hispanics from other middle-class Americans. Generally, Hispanics want their children to speak Spanish (Sheldon, 1966). Middle-class Hispanics may not believe in *compadrazgo* as much as traditionally oriented Hispanics; yet the institution of *compadrazgo* may still function among them. For the middle-class Hispanic, *compadrazgo* may imply a bond of friendship rather than a religious bond of coparenthood where good friends are selected as baptismal sponsors for children. This extends the familial network. All females are referred to as **comadres** and males as **compadres.** Middle-class Hispanics are probably *compadre* or *comadre* with at least several other families (Carlos & Sellers, 1972).

This view of the Hispanic middle class points out the need for flexibility on the part of the therapist who is counseling Hispanics. Very likely, a rise in socioeconomic status is associated with the adoption of increasingly modern values. Sensitivity by the therapist is required to ascertain the extent of traditional- and modern-value orientation as this relates to goal setting and the therapeutic process.

IMPLICATIONS FOR PLURALISTIC THERAPISTS

The Hispanic immigrants from 1860 to the present experienced many hardships. Whereas early Spaniards conquered in search of gold and silver, recent Mexican, Puerto Rican, Cuban, and Central and South American immigrants settled in the United States with the tenuous hope for a better life. Many of the more recent immigrants from Puerto Rico and Mexico begin life in the United States as very poor transients, and they are usually unskilled at speaking, reading, and writing English. Social groups and individuals tend to develop values that are functional within their environment. In an environment of discrimination and prejudice, Hispanics have developed life-styles and associated values that maximize positive experiences in the United States. If a therapist is to assist clients in perfecting their adaptation to the environment, he or she must be aware of the clients' values. Yet the values of the Hispanic cannot be classified simply; because they are a highly pluralistic group, they represent a range of values. These values will vary among the Mexican Americans, Puerto Ricans, and Cubans according to their social history within the United States.

In this chapter, we have delineated two major value orientations —traditional and modern—of Hispanics in the United States. As indicated in Figure 2-1, we can schematize a number of factors that contribute to adoption of either set of values. Figure 2-1 shows that many Hispanics express modern values, as listed in the circle on the right; others adopt more traditional attitudes, presented in the left-hand circle. The arrows on the top and bottom of the diagram show forces that tend to keep these spheres of values separate. The forces on the sides of the circles exert pressure for fusion of these values.

Of course, modern values have evolved to promote effective functioning in our technological society. The modern-value system offers guidelines for personal advancement and adjustment to a rapidly changing society. Yet traditional values offer survival advantages too. Traditionally oriented Hispanics have an advantage over other ethnic groups by maintaining extended-family ties. They do not measure responsibility in terms of productivity or power but, rather, in terms of fulfillment of commitments to family and friends. The warmth and meaning they derive from their relationships may buffer these Hispanics against the destructive forces that Toffler (1974) describes in *Future Shock*. The extended family provides personal support and facilitates sharing (Murillo, 1971).

Present-time orientation associated with traditional values also may offer certain advantages. Gestalt psychologists believe that many people lose much of the intensity and beauty of life by spending excessive energy designing the future. Gestaltists explain that an emphasis on potentialities creates anxiety. The future-time-oriented individual broods about events that he or she cannot control (Perls, 1971). In contrast, traditionally oriented Hispanics emphasize "here-and-now" awareness. In doing so, they experience more joy than do future-oriented people (Murillo, 1971).

There is increasing evidence that a high drive to "fill up time"—to assess one's value in terms of production per hour—is detrimental to physical and emotional well-being. A tendency toward heart attacks has been associated with a set of personality traits characterized by an emphasis on time (Friedman & Rosenman, 1974; Northrop, 1971). The traditionally oriented Hispanic does not equate time with responsibility the way people with a more modern orientation do. Meaning in life is

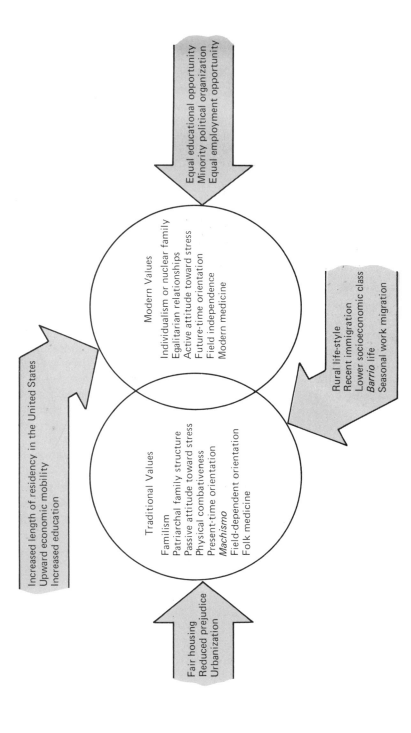

Figure 2-1. Traditional and modern values and the external forces that contribute to the adoption of one or the other set of values or of a combination of the two.

drawn from *being* (for example, being with people or being with nature) and not from *doing* (maximizing time in which to amass money, achieving recognition, or multiplying work). Many psychologists consider this traditional time orientation extremely healthy (Northrop, 1971).

> We discover that producing things, and living for things, and the exchange of things, is not the ultimate meaning of life. We discover that the meaning of life is that it is to be lived. . . . I am what I am, and at this moment I cannot be different from what I am [Perls, 1971, pp. 3–4].

There are also advantages in holding traditional attitudes about work. Many Americans are driven by the Protestant work ethic, believing that human worth is rooted in hard work. Some people work at such a high pace and for such long hours that exhaustion ensues and the joy in performance of the task is lost. On the weekends, these "workhorses" seek recreation so that they can "re-create" themselves in preparation for the next week's work. Industrial advances have created more jobs involving repetitive tasks. It is difficult to gain satisfaction and meaning from such tedious work, and the Anglo who places much value on work may find industrial jobs very demoralizing. Recent technological advances are also deflating the number of available jobs, and the typical Anglo American suffers extreme feelings of worthlessness when not employed (Jourard, 1971). For the traditionally oriented Hispanic, work is necessary for survival, but it does not have value in itself. It may be this attitude that allows these Hispanics to adapt to changing work roles in this technological age with little personal discomfort, while many other Americans find much of life's meaning eroding with their changing work roles.

Any individual, because of idiosyncratic values and because of changing life-styles, may hold mixed values. The adoption of traditional, modern, or mixed values can be evaluated only within the context of each individual's cultural and personal goals.

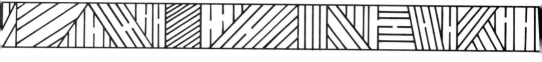

Chapter 3 Aspects of the Hispanic Dilemma

LANGUAGE

Language is perhaps the most powerful transmitter of culture (Farb, 1974). The great number of Spanish-speaking people in the United States attests to the viability of Hispanic culture in this country. Many new immigrants who speak only Spanish arrive every year. Moreover, large numbers of Hispanics, particularly those living in *barrios*, continue to speak Spanish in their homes after residing in the United States for many years and even generations.

Few Americans are bilingual. In a government survey, nine out of ten persons reported that they had no second language. Of those who did have a second language, the majority said that it was Spanish (U.S. Bureau of the Census, 1976). Among the Hispanic population, 70% report that Spanish is their mother tongue, and more than half speak "primarily" Spanish while at home (U.S. Bureau of the Census, 1971). Further, even many Hispanics who are bilingual prefer to use Spanish when speaking to family members and friends. This is particularly true among later-generation Hispanics. Difficulty with English was reported by 54% of those whose primary language was Spanish.

The fact that Hispanics can speak English does not ensure that they can express themselves fully in English. Many expressions cannot be directly translated from Spanish to English and vice versa. For example, the English word *chaperone* refers to an older and mature person who watches over young people, both male and female, to maintain propriety at social gatherings. The closest Spanish equivalent to *chaperone* is **dueña**. A *dueña* is an older woman charged with the responsibility of guarding over the reputation, and particularly the sexual behavior, of a younger woman. Thus, the meaning of *dueña* is much less general than that of *chaperone*. Another example of this difference can be seen in the

45

verbal expression of strong affection. In English, we use the verb *to love*. In Spanish, nurturant love can be expressed by either **te amo** or **te quiero**. *Te quiero* translates literally into English as "I want you" or "I need you." This expression has a connotation of ownership when it is translated into English that is not present in Spanish when it is used to express affection.

Bilingual children whose primary language is Spanish respond more positively when spoken to in Spanish than when spoken to in English. In one study, second-grade Chicano children who were considered fluent in English by their teachers were more likely to comply with the teachers' requests when the teachers spoke Spanish than when they spoke English (Brand, 1974). In another study, two adults worked with groups of bilingual Mexican-American first-graders. Again, the response level of the Hispanic children was higher when the experimenters spoke Spanish (Garcia & Zimmerman, 1972).

Some Hispanics speak a hybridized language consisting of Spanish and English. This hybridized form of speech has variously been called "Spanglish," **pochismo**, Chicano Spanish, and, more recently, code switching or linguistic switching (Lindholm & Padilla, 1978). The sociolinguistic study of code switching has demonstrated that a hybridized language is a natural linguistic occurrence where two cultures meet (Valdés Fallis, 1976; Weinreich, 1963). Read the following excerpt from a recorded conversation between one of the authors and a third-generation Mexican-American woman who is describing her feelings about being Mexican American. Observe her use of a mixture of English and Spanish to express her emotions. Her speech is characteristic of a very large number of Hispanics.

> Moderator: Okay, we were talking last time about . . . you know . . . how you identify . . . and you said you identified as a Mexican American, right?
>
> Interviewee: Um-hum.
>
> M: Okay, and we talked about why you don't identify as a Chicana?
>
> I: Why do I?
>
> M: Why *don't* you . . .
>
> I: Cause I'm not born in Mexico (pronounces "Mechico") . . . born here.
>
> M: The Chicanos are . . . should be born in Mexico?
>
> I: (Pause) I don't know . . . they full-blooded over there probably . . . because *tan de a tiro* full-blooded Chicanos . . . *aquí está puro* mix, you know.
>
> M: Aha.
>
> I: And me, you know . . . I'm part *gabacha* . . . you know, so I'm not full-blooded, what you call, you know? But you're not Mexican, I consider myself a Mexican, and I don't deny it, you know.

M: Um-hum . . . but you identify yourself as Mexican American?

I: Yeah, I'm Mexican American.

M: Okay, why don't you identify yourself as a *Mexicana*?

I: Why don't I? (Pause) I . . . well, I do sometimes, you know, I *cómo te digo*, how can I tell you . . . when they ask me, what are you, Mexican or (pause) I'll say *Mexicana*. . . . *Yo nunca digo que . . . que soy . . .* you know . . . I rarely use Mexican American when they ask me.

M: Oh, really, you really use Mexican more often?

I: I used to just say Mexican, you know? When I . . . in my applications *te pongo* Mexican.

M: Mexican?

I: Um . . . *nunca pongo* . . .

M: Mexican.

I: Mexican American, you know.

M: So you identify more with Mexican.

I: Yeah, Mexican.

M: Than Mexican American?

I: Yeah.

M: Okay, why don't you identify yourself as American?

I: Why don't I?

M: Just American.

I: I don't know, *Porque, soy más pa' acá que pa' allá . . . más* Mexican (laughter).

This excellent example illustrates several important points. First, the language of the interview is English, except for those occasions when the interviewee switches to Spanish to emphasize a point about her ethnicity. Second, the interviewee switches to Spanish when referring to her "Mexican-ness." Finally, the switches to Spanish serve to convey meaning that cannot be expressed accurately in English. For instance, the interviewee's final statement is "I don't know, *porque, soy más pa' acá que pa' allá . . . más* Mexican," which translates as "I don't know, I guess because I'm more on the side of Mexican than on the side of American." This is as literal a translation as can be given of the interviewee's statement about why she doesn't identify herself as American. It is also interesting to see how her language switching underscores her confusion concerning ethnicity.

Some researchers and teachers are critical of *pochismo* or code switching, claiming that it is not a pure language. They note that Hispanics do poorly in high school Spanish classes, and they conclude that many Hispanics do not speak either English or Spanish with confidence (Gonzales, 1965). It should be recognized that language is always in flux as it mirrors cultural changes. To criticize *pochismo* is to criticize the cultural changes of Hispanics as they adapt to the majority culture.

The following story portrays the difficulty that a Puerto Rican youngster experiences because of the bias toward "pure" Castilian Spanish.

THE CASE OF PEDRO.[1] The principal found out that Pedro was listening to the radio until late in the evening and thus oversleeping. His teachers reported that he was now extremely involved in elongating his final *s*, to the point where his peers ridiculed him for his "funny way of talking," and called him "collector of *s*'s."

After one incident, Pedro was brought to the principal with two girls who had made fun of him. Investigating the incident, the principal found that Pedro had said to one of them while trying to be friendly, "¿Cómo estáss?" The girls had mocked him by repeating, "¿Cómo estáss, cómo estássss?" He had broken down and tried to hit one of the girls.

Pedro's mother was worried and his father could not understand his behavior. They punished him for listening to the radio too much and for being late for school by forbidding him to listen to the radio.

The new principal was curious about this "Cómo estássss" phenomenon. It was a challenge to the rudimentary bilingual program that she had initiated, and it could not go unexplored.

"Why do you stretch your *s*'s so far?" she asked the boy.

"I want to say things right; one is supposed to pronounce the final *s*, you know?"

Why did he listen to the radio so much? "What I listen to is a Spanish station, because they speak right; they don't speak like my folks do." Further inquiry elicited that, "I did hear some teachers saying, 'They don't know how to speak real Spanish.'"

Behind all this was the bilingual teacher's bias in favor of her own high school Spanish, a slow-paced Castilian version with emphasis on not chopping the final *s*, as Puerto Ricans do routinely. Pedro was intent on being as soft-spoken and as correct and precise about the final *s* as his well-meaning teacher. In the process, he became as incongruous to his Puerto Rican friends as his teacher was. Though he was a self-motivated learner, he had become so fully taken over by his teacher's elitist Spanish that he was an object of ridicule by his peers and was becoming alienated from his own family. Now that his family's Spanish was second-rate, he was increasingly in doubt as to what else about them was inferior.

Social scientists are concerned about the assets and liabilities of being monolingual Spanish or bilingual Spanish/English in the United States. Research suggests that speaking Spanish as a primary language is a handicap only to the extent that the majority society deals with the language difference inappropriately. Very often, Spanish-speaking adults are denied employment on the basis of language. Some are employed in middle-class jobs as clerks and sales people so that they can serve as liaisons with the Hispanic community, but the majority work as laborers (Simmons, 1961).

As early as 1940, it was recognized that Hispanic children's use of Spanish in school was the basis of much prejudice toward them (Tuck, 1946). For children entering school as monolingual Spanish speakers, academic achievement is virtually impossible until they learn English, if classes are conducted only in English. As these children begin to learn English, they find that they have an underdeveloped sense of English phonology; many Spanish sounds are not duplicated in English, and many English sounds are not present in Spanish. The monolingual Spanish-speaking child may not discriminate English vowel sounds if those sounds are not present in Spanish. For example, a hard /c/ and a soft /s/ are characteristic of English but not of Spanish. Thus, the Hispanic child learning English will experience difficulty discriminating words such as *watch* and *wash*. The consonant and vowel contrasts in the left-hand column below are not discriminated in Spanish and often present difficulties for the Hispanic learning English:

Consonant Contrasts	*Examples of Words Heard as Similar*
/ch/ : /sh/	watch/wash; witch/wish; catch/cash
/ch/ : /dg/	batch/badge; rich/ridge
/y/ : /j/	yellow/jello; mayor/major
/s/ : /th/	bass/bath; mouse/mouth

/t/ : /th/	bat/bath; boat/both
/s/ : /ks/	miss/mix; sauce/socks
/b/ : /v/	robe/rove; bail/vail
/d/ : /th/	den/then; day/they
/s/ : /z/	racer/razor; bus/buzz
/n/ : /ng/	sun/sung; ran/rang; scene/sing

Vowel Contrasts	*Examples of Words Heard as Similar*
/ē/ : /ĭ/	beat/bit
/ā/ : /ĕ/ : /ă/	bait/bet/bat
/ū/ : /o͝o/	Luke/look
/ŏ/ : /ŭ/	lock/luck

The words on the right may be difficult to recognize for a Hispanic child. If the child concentrates very hard to discriminate these sounds, he or she may miss the next sounds in a message; thus the effects may be cumulative. Without special assistance, the Hispanic child entering school with little or no knowledge of English will fall further and further behind (Matluck & Mace, 1973).

English-speaking people experience similar difficulties when trying to learn Spanish. Below are a few examples of problems encountered by English speakers who are learning Spanish:

/b/ : /v/   These sounds are not differentiated in Spanish; therefore English speakers may force a difference between words such as *botar* (to throw) and *votar* (to vote).

/d/ : /r/   These sounds are not differentiated in Spanish, leading many English speakers to hear no difference between *sed* (thirst) and *ser* (to be), for example.

/r/ : /rr/   In English there is no difference between these two sounds, which creates confusion in Spanish between words such as *pero* (but) and *perro* (dog).

/b/ : /p/   In Spanish the /p/ is not aspirated; rather, it has a soft sound similar to /b/. Thus words such as *besar* (to kiss) and *pesar* (to weigh) may be confused by the English speaker.

In many school districts, no special instruction is provided for Spanish-speaking children. Until recently, Spanish-speaking children frequently had to repeat the first grade until they had mastered English

(Kobrick, 1972). In some schools, Spanish-speaking children are seated next to bilingual children, and the bilingual children translate for their Spanish-speaking peers. Thus, monolingual Spanish-speaking children begin school with the burden of learning a new language while simultaneously attempting to learn academic material (Brand, 1974) and to establish friendships with non-Spanish-speaking classmates (Montal-vo, 1974). The result may be emotional problems such as those described in the case of Domingo.

THE CASE OF DOMINGO.[2] Domingo sleeps barricaded by pillows and likes to draw ghosts and nothing else. He is seclusive and shy. Since he entered fifth grade, shortly after arriving from Puerto Rico, his mother has been worried because whenever she asks about his day in school or his friends, he stands quietly or leaves.

It took only a few interviews to discover that, in addition to the many family pressures triggering Domingo's behavior, he lives under a very peculiar arrangement: His helpful counselor checks with his teachers about his work every single day and talks with his mother weekly to "review his progress at home and at school."

How did this intensive supervision begin? Shortly after he was singled out as talking too much to the Spanish speakers around him, it became somehow important to find out more about him. It was then discovered that he smoked in the bathroom and that he disregarded the teacher. Because of a desire to assist him "before things became worse," a program for constant checking of his behavior both at home and at school was established between mother and counselor. But the school forgot that it was routinely requesting that he speak English and not Spanish during room changes. Somewhere during this period Domingo began to bundle up almost as to shield himself from demands.

[2]Reprinted from "Home-School Conflict and the Puerto Rican Child," by Braulio Montalvo, *Social Casework*, February 1974, *55*, 100–110. Copyright 1974 by the Family Service Association of America. Reprinted by permission.

It took a new teacher, fresh to the situation, to realize that Domingo felt like a ghost. He felt transparent and trapped. Everyone could "see through him" and "get to him." She saw that having deprived him of Spanish contact during classroom changes was destructive. He needed breathing space and a refuge. He needed contact with someone in his best, most familiar way, in Spanish. To her, his behavior seemed natural, not a step backward, and certainly not regressive, as the counselor had considered it. . .

The new teacher reached the counselor and helped him to loosen his tie with the mother. She was also instrumental in changing the school's unspoken policy about not speaking Spanish during room changes. She helped free Domingo from much pressure, and with some accompanying help from therapy he dropped his shield and began to learn.

Bilingualism should not interfere with academic accomplishment. Many studies comparing competency of monolingual and bilingual speakers fail to control for age, sex, and degree of bilingualism (Hernandez, 1973). In one study in which overall social adjustment variables were controlled, no correlation was reported between bilingualism and intellectual functioning (Henderson & Merritt, 1968). Adjustment was a stronger predictor of school language achievement than was specific knowledge of English words for a group of Head Start children (Stedman & Adams, 1972). In another study, English competency was associated with success in English class at school for a sample of Mexican-American junior high school students. Although English versus Spanish speaking in the home affected English-class performance, it did not affect math competency (Evans & Anderson, 1973). In one well-controlled study of French Canadians, bilinguals achieved higher IQ scores than monolinguals (Peal & Lambert, 1962). In yet another investigation, Spanish/English bilingual children performed better than monolinguals in object-constancy and naming tasks. Facility with two languages was advantageous because the sense of meaning, as a function of use, was more refined in bilinguals than in monolinguals (Feldman & Shen, 1971).

Many of the difficulties of monolingual or bilingual students could be ameliorated through bilingual programs (Sanchez, 1966). In a true bilingual program, a child is first taught school skills in Spanish.

Gradually the student is introduced to English via foreign-language instruction techniques (Ortega, 1971). The Hispanic child is drilled for understanding, not memorization, of English sounds (Manuel, 1965). Finally, English becomes the medium of instruction along with Spanish (Ortega, 1971). Elements of Hispanic culture are introduced wherever possible. Bilingual programs facilitate educational attainment of Hispanic children by teaching them about their culture as well as their language. In addition, such bilingual programs broaden the experience of Anglo students (Anderson, 1969).

Some schools have initiated special short-term programs to assist Hispanic children in English-language acquisition. Participation in such a program may not affect the children's tested achievement competency (Zimmerman, Steiner, & Pond, 1974) or may effect only short-term changes (Plant & Southern, 1972). It is understandable that children may be unable to learn all the intricacies of English syntax in a short program. Short-term intervention, such as summer programs before the start of school, cannot be equated to true bilingual education (Ortega, 1971).

The language factor affects the therapeutic process. As we have suggested, some experiences will be interpreted differently in Spanish than in English. Thus, concepts of mental illness may vary among Hispanics depending on whether Spanish or English is spoken. In one study, 444 Mexican-American residents of Los Angeles were asked to complete a questionnaire about eight vignettes describing people suffering from psychotic disorders. The 260 respondents who answered in Spanish differed from the 184 who responded in English on about 25% of the items. The Spanish-speaking respondents were more likely to perceive mental illness as inherited. They were more cautious in applying the label "mental problems" to descriptions of seriously disturbed individuals than were the English-speaking subjects. The Spanish-speaking subjects tended to use the label "nervous condition" to describe several serious cases. The Spanish-speaking subjects were less tolerant of delinquency described in the vignettes; whereas English speakers often recommended treating the delinquent child with love, the Spanish speakers often responded that harsher discipline was needed (Edgerton & Karno, 1971). As this study illustrates, therapists must recognize different conceptions of illness associated with each language in order to evaluate cases accurately.

Cognitive and psychological liability can result when Hispanic clients are compelled to speak only English. One study suggests that psychotic patients may appear more disturbed if required to speak English rather than Spanish. In a New York hospital, ten schizophrenic patients were interviewed in English and Spanish. Four psychiatrists rated the patients' degree of pathology. Bilingual patients were judged to be more pathological when speaking in English. These results occurred even if the patient's vocabulary was greater in English than in Spanish (Marcos, Alpert, Urcuyo, & Kesselman, 1973). The patients expressed themselves more slowly, paused more frequently, and exhibited speech disturbances more often when speaking English than when speaking Spanish (Marcos, Urcuyo, Kesselman, & Alpert, 1973).

Exactly how language use affects the counseling process is not easily determined. In another study, with prison inmates, those interviewed in Spanish appeared more psychologically disturbed than those interviewed in English. In this situation, inmates who appeared psychologically disturbed were more likely to be removed from the prison to a more therapeutic setting. Perhaps those speaking in Spanish were more skilled at portraying the image needed in order to be released from prison (Del Castillo, 1970).

Finally, some researchers (Marcos, 1976; Marcos & Alpert, 1976) have argued that fluency in two different languages can complicate psychotherapy with the proficient bilingual client. They show that, if only one of the languages is used in therapy, some aspects of the patient's emotional experience may be inaccessible to treatment; if both languages are used, the patient may use language switching as a form of resistance to affectively charged material.

At the minimum, an Anglo therapist needs familiarity with some basic Spanish vocabulary and phrases. Some basic phrases are listed below in Table 3-1. A dictionary of Spanish terms used in this book can be found in the Glossary. If the therapist can speak only English, he or she should speak slowly. Laconic responses from the Hispanic client should not be interpreted as evidence of withdrawal or uncooperativeness, and, clearly, disrupted speech in a bilingual client should not be considered prime evidence of psychopathology.

A therapist's fluency in Spanish can facilitate understanding of and communication with the Hispanic client. Hispanic researchers agree that more Spanish-speaking mental-health professionals are a necessity for effective community-mental-health care (Olmedo & Lopez, 1977; Padilla et al., 1975).

> As counselors, we have tendencies to experience our frustration in communicating with persons from divergent racial and ethnic groups as largely *their* fault. We have blamed the lack of genuine communication on those whom we counsel. It is time to force our attention on ourselves as prime causes of miscommunication and prejudicial evaluation [Palomares, 1971c, p. 144].

STEREOTYPING

Tuck (1946) stated that the injustice done to Mexican Americans was done "not with a fist . . . but with the elbow"—that is, not through direct confrontation but through neglect and stereotyping. Some stereotyping may be unavoidable, but generally more differences exist within groups than between them (Pollack & Menacker, 1971). Therefore it is important to keep stereotypes flexible and to modify them when appropriate.

Stereotypical attitudes among Anglos toward Hispanics develop as early as age four (Johnson, 1950). The extent to which stereotypes direct behavior is not fully understood, but negative stereotyping of Anglos and Hispanics perpetuates problems in ethnic relations (Casavantes, 1969). Although Anglos may state that they believe in equal rights, certain stereotypes provide justification for discrimination against Hispanics (Simmons, 1961). Some common stereotypes about Hispanics are that they are "all the same"; they are unclean; they are alcoholics; they are criminally inclined and deceitful; they are not intelligent; they are not friendly or good-natured (Carter, 1968; Rudolph, 1972; Simmons, 1961). Other stereotypes characterize Hispanics in a more positive fashion but are nevertheless undocumented: Hispanics are musical; they love flowers; they are romanticists rather than realists (Simmons, 1961). Social scientists have been accused of changing their negative stereotypes of Hispanics very little in the last 100 years (Romano-V., 1971).

The media are guilty, too, of perpetuating many ethnic stereotypes. Martinez (1971) analyzed a number of television commercials that depict the Hispanic in stereotypical—and negative—ways. For example, the "Frito Bandito" in the commercial for Frito Lay corn chips portrays the Mexican as shrewd. In one commercial for Camel cigarettes, a "typical" Mexican village is shown; everybody is sleeping. The implication is that all Mexicans are lazy. An Arrid deodorant commercial shows a Mexican "bandito" spraying his underarms, and we are told "If it works for him, it will work for you." Mexicans, the commercial suggests, smell bad.

Such advertising may create a set, a "collective preconscious," that leads the public to expect negative traits in Hispanics (Morales, 1971b). Although caricatures are frequently harmless and sometimes amusing, they are potentially damaging when they are associated with ethnic groups. For instance, Figure 3-1 depicts a caricature that appeared in a major newspaper in a large metropolitan area where many Hispanics live. The advertisement concerned a business that was closing several of

Table 3-1. *Basic phrases in English and Spanish with a pronunciation guide for the Spanish.*

English	Spanish	Pronunciation of the Spanish*
Good morning.	Buenos días.	*Bway*-nos *dee*-as.
My name is . . .	Mi nombre es . . .	Mee *nom*-bde es . . .
What is your name?	¿Cómo te llamas?	Ko-mo tay *ya*-mas?
Let's speak English/Spanish.	Vamos hablar inglés/español.	Ba-mos a-*blad* ing-*glace*/es-pan-*yol.*
I speak a little Spanish.	Hablo un poco de español.	A-blo oon *po*-ko day es-pan-*yol.*
I don't speak Spanish.	No hablo español.	No *a*-blo es-pan-*yol.*
I understand it a good deal, but I don't speak it.	Lo entiendo bastante, pero no lo hablo.	Lo en-tee-*en*-do bas-*tan*-tay, *pay*-do no lo *a*-blo.
Speak slowly, please.	Hable despacio, por favor.	A-ble des-*pa*-seeo, pod fa-*bod.*
What can I do for you?	¿En qué puedo servirle?	En kay *pway*-tho sed-*beed*-lay?
Can you tell me?	¿Puede usted decirme?	*Pway*-thay oo-*steth* day-*seed*-may?
I think (so) (not).	Creo que (sí) (no).	K*day*-o kay (see) (no).
What do you think?	¿Qué le parece a usted?	Kay lay pa-*day*-say a oo-*steth?*
You know what I mean.	Usted sabe lo que quiero decir.	Oo-*steth sa*-bay lo kay key-*e*-do day-*seed.*
How do you say that in Spanish?	¿Cómo se dice eso en español?	Ko-mo say *dee*-say *e*-so en es-pan-*yol?*
What is this for?	¿Para qué es ésta?	P*a*-da kay es *es*-ta?
Do you understand me?	¿Me entiende usted?	May en-tee-*en*-day oo-*steth?*
I understand when you speak slowly.	Le entiendo cuando habla despacio.	Lay en-tee-*en*-do *kwan*-do *a*-bla des-*pa*-seeo.

English	Spanish	Pronunciation
Of course.	Por supuesto.	Pod su-*pwes*-to.
Excuse me, but I didn't understand you.	Perdón, pero no le entendí.	Ped-*don*, *pay*-do no lay en-ten-*dee*.
Please repeat the question.	Favor de repetir la pregunta.	Fa-*bod* de rray-pay-*teed* la pday-*goon*-ta.
Now I understand.	Ahora sí entiendo.	A-o-da see en-tee-*en*-do.
You are welcome.	No hay de qué.	No eye day kay.
How are you getting along?	¿Cómo le va?	*Ko*-mo lay ba?
Very well, thank you.	Muy bien, gracias.	*Moo*-ey bee-*en*, *gda*-see-as.
How is your family? wife? husband?	¿Cómo está su familia? esposa? esposo?	*Ko*-mo es-*ta* su fa-*meel*-ya? es-*po*-sa? eo-*po*-so?
Are you happy today?	¿Está contento(a) hoy?	Es-*ta* kon-*ten*-to (ta) oy?
You seem more relaxed today.	Parece más tranquilo(a) hoy.	Pa-*day*-say moss tdan-*key*-lo (la) oy.
That upsets you a lot.	Eso le molesta mucho.	*E*-so lay mo-*les*-ta *moo*-cho.
I would like you to talk to: your social worker your husband (wife)/child your teacher your family your doctor your priest your parole officer.	Quisiera que hablara usted con: su trabajador(a) social su esposo(a)/hijo(a) su maestro(a) su familia su doctor su sacerdote su oficial de palabra de honor.	Key-see-e-da kay a-*bla*-da oo-*steth* kon: soo tda-ba-ha- thod (*tho*-da) so-see-*al* soo es-*po*-so (sa)/*ee*-ho (ha) soo my-*es*-tdo (tda) soo fa-*meel*-ya soo dok-*tod* soo sa- sed-*do*-tay soo o-fee-see-*al* de pa-*la*-bda de on-*od*.
What we say here is confidential.	Lo que digamos aquí es confidencial.	Lo kay dee-*ga*-mos a-*key* es kon-fee-den-see-*al*.
I charge according to what you can pay.	Yo cobro de acuerdo a lo que usted pueda pagar.	Yo *ko*-bdo de a-*kwed*-tho a lo kay oo-*steth* *pway*-tha pa-*gad*.

Table 3-1, continued.

English	Spanish	Pronunciation of the Spanish*
Our next appointment will be . . .	La próxima cita va a ser . . .	La *pdo*-gsee-ma *see*-ta ba sed . . .
What medication are you taking?	¿Qué medicamento está tomando?	Kay me-dee-ka-*men*-to es-*ta to-man*-do?
Have you taken your medicine?	¿Ha tomado usted su medicina?	A to-*ma*-tho oo-*steth* soo me-thee-*see*-na?
Where do you live? For how long?	¿Dónde vive? ¿Por cuánto tiempo?	*Don*-de bee-bay? Pod *kwan*-to tee-*em*-po?
Who lives with you?	¿Quién vive con usted?	Key-*en bee*-bay kon oo-*steth*?

*a—ă, as in lot, stop
ay—ā, as in pay
e—ĕ, as in let, step
ey; ee—ē, as in bee
o—ō, as in lone, cone
oo—u, as in moon, soon
s—soft, as in say
th—as in *these*, *this*
d,t—pronounced with tongue just behind teeth, rather than on roof of mouth.
d,t,p,b,k—softened without release of puff of air, like the d in *ladder*, p in *steeple*, b in *hobby*, k in *ticket*.
r is pronounced by tapping the tongue against the roof of the mouth, as in *ladder* or *glider*. Here it is written with the letter d.
rr—is trilled, although, if this can't be done, the tap may be close enough.

its stores and reducing the price of much of its merchandise. This type of advertisement illustrates clearly the negative stereotyping of Hispanics.

Figure 3-1. An unfavorable caricature that appeared in a major newspaper in a large metropolitan area where many Hispanics live. The negative stereotype is obvious.

INSTITUTIONAL RACISM

When stereotyping and consequent prejudice are broadly sanctioned, discrimination is formalized within institutions. Padilla and Ruiz (1973, pp. 119–120) explain that, once racism is institutionalized, it is self-perpetuating.

> After all, if people are "inferior," they don't warrant the expenditure required for an adequate education; if people are poorly educated, they will hold menial positions with low income. When family finances are restricted and schools are of poor quality, children will tend to drop out early and seek gainful employment, however humble, to supplement family income. And, of course, there is the ultimate non sequitur: If people are poorly educated and menially employed, they are obviously "inferior," and their children don't want or need adequate schools.

Let's look at some of the specific ways discrimination against Hispanics is institutionalized.

Economics

The standard of living for Hispanics is well below the national average. In general, a very small proportion of Hispanics with income in 1975 had high incomes, and a substantial proportion had low incomes. Only 1% of all Hispanics with income had incomes of $25,000 or more, whereas about 50% had incomes below $5000 (U.S. Bureau of the Census, 1977).

Among Hispanics with income, there were marked differences between men and women. For instance, 39% of Mexican-American men had incomes below $5000; yet about 75% of Mexican-American women had incomes at that level. Furthermore, the median income for these men was $6500, and for the women it was $2800. Among Hispanics of Puerto Rican origin, men had a median income of $6700 compared to $3800 for women. Men of Cuban origin had a median income in 1975 of about $7100, while the median income of Cuban-origin women was substantially lower at $3400 (U.S. Bureau of the Census, 1977).

As these figures indicate, some variation in income occurred among the Hispanic subgroups. Although the median income of Puerto Rican-origin men was not significantly different from that of Mexican-origin men, the median income of Puerto Rican-origin women was about $1000 higher than that of Mexican-origin women. Figure 3-2 shows the median income in 1975 of Hispanics age 16 and over, by ethnic subgroup and sex.

Economic discrimination against Hispanics dates back to the earliest encounters between Hispanics and Yankee settlers. High taxes waged against the Hispanic ranchers forced them to sell their large landownings in the West (Valdez, 1971). Once the wealth and power of the early Hispanics diminished, Anglo industrialists controlled wages by manipulating the size of the labor force. In times of labor shortage (when Hispanics would be able to press for higher wages), monitoring of illegal immigration of Mexicans decreases. From 1951 through 1964, Public Law 78 allowed the recruitment of Mexican nationals, *braceros*, as field hands, thus further diminishing the bargaining power of the Hispanic laborers. During economic recessions, many Mexican-American citizens, wet-backs, and *braceros* have been forced to return to Mexico, and the stability of Hispanic communities is disturbed further (Galarza, Gallegos, & Samora, 1970).

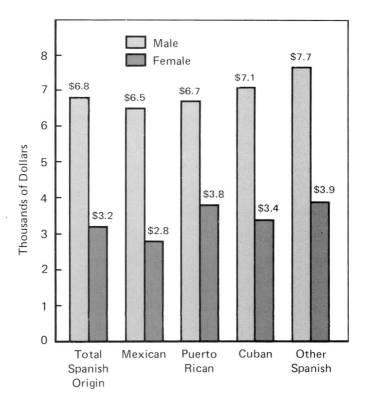

Figure 3-2. Median income of Hispanics age 16 and over, by subgroup origin and sex. (U.S. Bureau of the Census, Current Population Reports, 1977.)

Much of the struggle for Hispanic economic equality has consisted of efforts to achieve full participation in the job market. In the past, socioeconomic barriers have discouraged many Hispanics from acquiring the education and training they need to gain access to stable, well-paying jobs. Over the past decade, slow but measurable progress has been made toward breaking down these barriers, but serious disparities continue to exist.

The economic progress of the Hispanic community will depend greatly on the progress they make in the job market. A broad overview of job-market trends will clarify the economic situation of Hispanics today and the directions in which they must move in order to advance into the mainstream of the economy.

According to the U.S. Bureau of Labor Statistics in late 1976, there were 3.9 million Hispanics in the labor force. They held 3.4 million jobs, and 462,000 were unemployed. At the same time, the civilian labor force totaled 96.0 million; total employment was 88.4 million, and 7.5 million workers were unemployed. Thus, in 1976, Hispanics comprised 4.1% of the civilian labor force, 4.4% of the employed, and 11.8% of the unemployed. The unemployment rate of Hispanics is consistently 1.5 times the national rate.

In addition to the 7.5 million persons unemployed on the average during 1976, 914,000 persons outside the labor force wanted work but were not seeking jobs because they had concluded that none was available for them. Approximately 60,000 of those persons were Hispanics.

There were also 4.2 million people in 1976 who wanted jobs but were in school, were temporarily ill or disabled, had family responsibilities, or had other reasons for not looking for work. Of these, nearly 300,000 were Hispanics. In the same year there were 5.45 million employed heads of household who had not earned enough in the prior twelve months to raise their families above the poverty threshold, and it is estimated that 627,000 were of Spanish origin.

During 1976 an average of 3.3 million persons worked part-time involuntarily because full-time jobs were not available, and roughly 450,000 were Hispanics. Also, over half of all unemployed were young people between the ages of 16 and 24, and this ratio held true for Hispanics.

Yet the labor-force participation rate—that is, a percentage of the total population who are employed—declined in the 1970s from 62.0% to 59.0% among Hispanics, while rising from 59.5% to 62.2% among total Anglos. This trend reflected lower labor-force participation for men and higher participation for women, with Hispanic men leaving the labor force at a faster rate than Anglo men and Hispanic women ent ring at a slower rate than Anglo women. Throughout this period, the proportion of Hispanic women at work or seeking jobs was consistently lower than the proportion of employed or job-seeking Anglo women.

Since the turn of the century, Hispanics have moved slowly toward increasing participation in the economic mainstream. Statistics on the foreign-born population of Texas, New Mexico, and Arizona show that, in 1900, about half of all Mexican-born workers were employed in agriculture. They also constituted the majority of the work force in railroads and mining. Up to 70% of the workers on section crews of the large Western railroads between 1880 and 1930 were Mexicans (McWilliams, 1968).

Mexican immigrants were also employed in other low-skill occupations in the early 1900s. From 10 to 25% of the domestic-service work force were Mexican immigrants employed as waiters and waitresses, carpenters, laundry workers, and retail-trade employees (Fuller, 1928). A tradition of hard physical labor was established by the early immigrants who worked in irrigation development, canning and food packing, and construction.

The 1920s saw significant numbers of Mexican-American workers recruited for the burgeoning industries of the Northeast. They worked in Chicago's steel and meat-packing industries, in Detroit's automobile factories, in Kansas City's meat packinghouses, and in the steel mills of Ohio and Pennsylvania (Moore, 1970). Over 150,000 Puerto Ricans migrated to the United States during the 1920s, and most of these immigrants were in pursuit of jobs in the large urban areas of the Northeast. The net migration for the decade was 40,000 after discounting those who chose to return to Puerto Rico.

The economic advances made by Hispanics during the first third of the century were virtually wiped out by the depression of the 1930's. Hispanics in manufacturing industries were hit especially hard as rising unemployment took its toll among thousands of semiskilled and unskilled workers. Similar setbacks struck Hispanics and other workers in the building-construction industry. In the early 1930's Chicano males were still employed predominantly as laborers—35% on farms and 28% in nonfarm work. Only 7% were employed in white-collar jobs in 1930 (Fogel, 1966).

The employment situation for Hispanics did not improve until World War II, when increased production in defense-related industries such as airplane manufacturing and ship building created numerous employment opportunities. The number of Hispanics in civilian jobs increased by an estimated 300,000 between 1940 and 1944, in addition to an estimated 225,000 who entered military service (Romero, 1977).

Throughout the 1940s, Hispanics moved upward into semiskilled and skilled positions. The number who worked in manufacturing rose from 150,000 to 330,000; those in trade rose from 100,000 to 206,000; and those in professional and semiprofessional occupations increased from 60,000 to 120,000. These increases were accompanied by a marked decline in the number of Hispanic agricultural workers (Romero, 1977).

Large-scale Puerto Rican migration to the U.S. mainland occurred after World War II. Between 1940 and 1970, about 750,000 Puerto Ricans left the island to seek opportunities in the United States. By 1975 the total number of Puerto Ricans in the United States had reached 1.7 million, located in practically every major urban area in the country.

Like their Mexican-American counterparts, Puerto Ricans are primarily employed in low-skill, blue-collar jobs. Employment data for 1950, 1960, and 1970 show only marginal increase in occupational representation in the high-skill, white-collar jobs. Like other Hispanics, Puerto Ricans who managed to penetrate the white-collar occupations between 1950 and 1970 remained near the bottom of the earning scale. Those in professional positions were primarily technicians. Puerto Rican managers and administrators were mostly in wholesale and retail trade, rather than manufacturing. In sales, they were mostly retail clerks, rather than insurance or real estate agents. In the clerical field, they were usually clerks and typists, rather than secretaries (Report of the U.S. Commission on Civil Rights, 1976).

Much of the progress made during the 1940s was reversed between 1954 and 1960 when a sluggish economy and changing patterns of industrial employment resulted in decreased economic opportunities for Hispanic workers. The unemployment rate among Hispanics rose from a low of about 4.0% in 1950 to a peak of 8.0% in 1960 (Romero, 1977). At the same time, industries such as durable-goods manufacturing and construction, which employed large numbers of Hispanics in well-paying jobs, grew at a much slower rate than industries such as retail trade and services, which employed relatively fewer Hispanics at generally lower wages. Also, semiskilled manufacturing jobs were located increasingly in suburban areas, outside the cities and thus beyond the reach of large numbers of Hispanic workers residing in *barrios* or immediately adjacent to inner cities.

Despite some gains, the Hispanic worker continues to be restricted to lower-range occupational fields. For example, although there were significant increases in the number of Hispanic professionals, in 1975 most Hispanic professionals—both men and women—were social workers and school teachers. The proportion of Hispanics employed as engineers, accountants, managers, and sales people was much smaller. than the proportion of Hispanics in the total labor force. Similarly, among Hispanic women in clerical jobs, there were five times as many clerks as bookkeepers (Romero, 1977).

Among men in craft jobs, Hispanics continued to be concentrated in the trowel trades, such as masonry and cement finishing, and were less well represented among electricians, machinists, and pipefitters. Still, in comparison with their occupational distribution in 1960, Hispanics have made some headway into higher-paying, more secure jobs and have broadened the scope of their occupational experience (Romero, 1977).

In general, institutional racism against Hispanics is expressed economically, by controlling the size of the labor market, binding salaries, and preventing Hispanics from entering higher-status positions. A therapist may encounter many Hispanics who are unemployed or underemployed or who feel that their efforts to improve their economic lot are futile. The therapist, and the client, must ask "How much choice does a person have when locked into poverty by economic racism?"

Education

According to the U.S. Bureau of the Census (1977), about 19% of Hispanics 25 years old and over had completed less than five years of school and about 61% were not high school graduates (see Figure 3-3).

However, younger-generation Hispanics are rapidly raising their educational-attainment level; for example, the proportion of adults with less than five years of school was only 5% for those from 25 to 29 years of age, as compared to 51% for those age 65 and over.

In addition, significant differences in educational attainment existed among the subgroups of Hispanics. About 24% of Hispanics of Mexican origin 25 years old and over had completed less than five years of school; the corresponding proportion for Hispanics of Puerto Rican origin was 19%. Statistics about Cuban-origin Hispanics underscore this difference in educational attainment. People in this group have a relatively high educational level compared to those of Mexican or Puerto Rican origin; for example, only 10% of Cubans 25 years old and over had completed less than five years of school, and about 52% of all Cubans in that age category had a high school education or more (U.S. Bureau of the Census, 1977).

There is a misconception that Hispanics are uninterested in academic achievement. In fact, however, a review of ten surveys of Hispanic attitudes toward education reveal that they hold as high educational aspirations as Anglos do (see Table 3-2). As many Hispanic as Anglo high school students plan to attend college. Hispanic parents express great interest in their children's education, and Hispanic children

Table 3-2. *Summary of research on Hispanic attitudes toward school.*

Investigators	Population	Methods	Student Attitudes toward School
Anderson and Johnson, 1971	163 junior high school Anglo and Mexican Americans (foreign and U.S. born).	Questionnaire.	
Barberio, 1967	342 Anglo and Mexican-American eighth graders.	N-ach., or achievement orientation through stories written about pictures; IQ controlled.	
Carter, 1970	Hispanics throughout Southwest.	Interview and questionnaires.	Students develop defensive techniques so they can function in class-room in which prejudice exists.
Coleman, et al., 1966, and Mayeske, 1968	Cross-ethnic study conducted throughout U.S.	Largest federal demographic survey.	
Demos, 1962	Stratified sample of Mexican-American and Anglo 7th- through 12th-graders, matched on sex, grade, socioeconomic status, age, and IQ.	Survey.	Differed in six out of 29 issues —one with more favorable school attitudes expressed by Mexican Americans; five with more favorable attitudes expressed by Anglos; all students agreed on the remaining 23 issues.

Table 3-2, continued.

Students' Educational Aspirations	Parent Attitudes toward School	Factors Associated with High Educational Aspirations
Mexican-American students expressed stronger desire to get high grades; U.S.-born Mexican Americans had much higher aspirations.	Anglo and Mexican-American children report same degree of support from parents.	Background of father, whether American or foreign-born; English spoken at home.
N-ach. was the same for Anglos and Mexican Americans.		
Hispanics desire to go to high school and college as much as Anglos.	Parents may hold unrealistically high expectations for children's achievement.	English spoken at home; parent's aspirations for the children.
Hispanics desire to stay in school and attend regularly; planned to go to college as often as Anglo children; and held high occupational aspirations.		Family background most important single factor related to student achievement; teacher characteristics most important school factor associated with achievement.

Table 3-2, continued.

Investigators	Population	Methods	Student Attitudes toward School
Logan, 1966	Anglo, Mexican-American, and Mexican college males.	TAT; auto-biographical and value survey.	
Ramirez, Taylor, and Peterson, 1971	300 Mexican-American and 300 Anglo junior high and high school students.	Stories written to sets of pictures; attitude survey.	Mexican Americans expressed less favorable attitudes toward school.
Rogg, 1974	Cuban high school students in west New York City.	School records; questionnaire to parents	
Ulibarri, 1966	65 migrant and nonmigrant Hispanic children in New Mexico and Colorado.	Interview.	Timidity about school.

state that they receive as much support from their parents about their educational pursuits as Anglo children do.

Other stereotypes suggest that Hispanic children do not complete as much schooling as Anglo children because they lack aptitude. Clearly, data are lacking to support this assertion. Many tests purported to measure intelligence of minority children are biased in favor of Anglos (Mercer, 1973). The language in which the test is administered will significantly affect results (Chandler & Plankos, 1969). One investigator studied Anglo and Mexican-American children of the lower socioeconomic class who had been classified as retarded according to one verbal intelligence scale (Jensen, 1961, 1969, 1973). When reexamined with individually administered performance tests, the Anglo children performed poorly compared to the Mexican Americans. It was concluded that the original IQ measure was not an accurate indication of the intellectual aptitude of the Mexican-American children. Although a

Students' Educational Aspirations	Parent Attitudes toward School	Factors Associated with High Educational Aspirations
Mexican American students had the highest achievement motivation, by autobiographical survey.		
Mexican Americans express lower N-ach.	Students felt parents were interested in their school achievement.	Correlated positively with achievement.
	83% of the parents wanted their children to complete college.	
	Parents were concerned about children's education but preferred the children to drop out of school rather than to continue struggling with it.	

disproportionate number of Hispanics have been classified as retarded, few score within the lower range of retardation on intelligence scales (Carter, 1970; Mercer, 1973). These findings probably reflect sociocultural differences rather than actual intellectual retardation (Garcia, 1977; Mercer, 1973).

If lack of motivation and lack of competence do not explain the poor academic performance of Hispanic children, what factors do explain it? A number of studies suggest that racism and lack of regard for Hispanics' needs contribute largely to the poor academic performance rate of young Hispanics. Many teachers favor Anglos or English-speaking Hispanic students over bilingual or monolingual Spanish-speaking students. In an extensive study of teacher behavior in 494 urban and rural fourth-, eighth-, and twelfth-grade classrooms throughout Texas, California, and New Mexico, it was found that teachers favored Anglo students over Hispanic students in the following ways: they praised them more; they

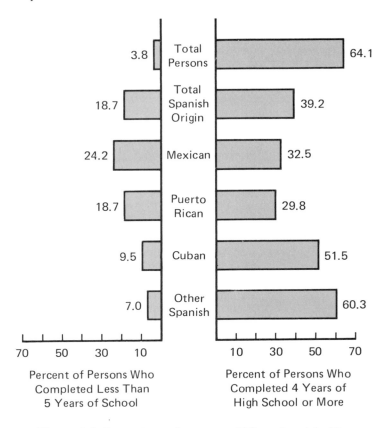

Figure 3-3. Percentage of persons of Hispanic origin 25 years old and over, by years of school completed and Hispanic subgroup origin. (U.S. Bureau of the Census, Current Population Reports, 1977).

were more accepting of their ideas; they gave them more positive feedback; and they more frequently engaged in general conversation with them (Jackson & Cocsa, 1974).

In many schools attended by Hispanics, all teaching is done in English; monolingual Spanish-speaking children will not understand instruction in these classrooms. Also, there are relatively few teachers of Hispanic background in public schools. Special techniques for teaching reading to bilingual children do exist, but these are not always employed. In addition, Hispanic culture and history are not academic subjects in many schools, and Hispanic students may feel that their identity is not considered as important as that of Anglo students (Carter, 1970). Much of the material taught may seem irrelevant. Children of migrant workers, whose lives revolve around farming, nature, travel, and the family, may have difficulty seeing the relevancy of many academic issues. It is understandable that many Hispanics would perceive school as another part of the establishment that does not meet their needs.

In vocational counseling, it is important to recognize that Hispanics have broad concerns about education. In some cases, short-term assistance, such as "rap groups," short-term career counseling based on vocational inventory results, scholarships, and other financial assistance, can raise academic performance (Cornett, Ainsworth, & Askins, 1974; Locascio, Nesselroth, & Thomas, 1976; Stedman & McKenzie, 1971); in many cases, more than short-term intervention is needed (Reeves, 1974). A school counselor or social worker can assist Hispanic children by working with school personnel to develop culturally pluralistic programs that capitalize on students' cognitive and communication styles. For example, programs stressing cooperation are more effective with Hispanics than those that stress individual competition (Castañeda, 1974). The story of Luciano illustrates a number of ways in which a counselor can assist the Hispanic student. The counselor recognized Luciano's aptitude and helped him find relevant school programs. With the counselor's help, Luciano did not become a school-dropout statistic.

> *THE CASE OF LUCIANO.*[3] Luciano Garcia is a young
> man of Mexican American descent now age eighteen.
> Luciano's parents have had little formal education. They
> came to Chicago when he was five. His father is a
> manual laborer, and his mother works part-time as a
> seamstress. He has three younger sisters and a younger
> brother.
>
> The Garcia family lives in a neglected tenement in
> the center of the city, where much of their neighborhood
> has been torn apart to make room for an expressway.
> Their three-room apartment for seven people is well-kept,
> but the building is without adequate lighting and is in
> need of many repairs. Recently a fire took the lives of
> two people in an apartment on the floor. The Garcias got
> out of the building just before the fire spread. The entire

[3]From *Spanish-Speaking Students and Guidance*, by E. Pollack and J. Menacker. Copyright 1971 by Houghton Mifflin Company. Reprinted by permission.

family is worried about living where they do, and they are looking for an apartment, but the rentals are usually beyond their reach.

Mr. and Mrs. Garcia speak little English, even after living in Chicago for thirteen years. Luciano has served as the family interpreter since he was a youngster. He was fortunate to be able to learn enough English at a young age to help the family with some of the contacts which were necessary to have with Anglos. Partly because of the parents' inability to speak English, their combined income is very low, and they have had little opportunity to earn more money.

Luciano attended public school near his house for eight years. He was very shy and soft-spoken as a child and had great difficulty in looking at people when they spoke with him. He was very submissive and obedient in school. This was the stance he adopted, and it worked well enough for him to be able to plod his way through. Most of his elementary school teachers were Anglos. The one Mexican American teacher he had was a young male who was very punitive with the children and demonstrated his dislike for them in a variety of ways. Luciano described this teacher as quiet and even meek with adults, but as a power hungry tyrant with the children. The principal of the school recognized Luciano's latent abilities and recommended him for entrance after graduation into an experimental part-time program for inner-city boys, sponsored by the Ethical Humanist Society of Chicago. Luciano met the criterion of being a student who had more ability than his school achievement showed.

The experimental program was basically designed to help students complete high school. The first summer he participated in the program was immediately after elementary school graduation. He was exposed to a variety of new experiences, such as going away for two weeks to a camp outside of the city. This was the first time he had ever been away from home and his immediate neighborhood for any length of time. At the camp Luciano engaged in formal language study in Spanish in the Ethical Society's "Horizons" program, along with activities in art. He surprised those of his teachers who thought he was slow because of his achievement record and his seemingly poor abilities. He excelled at the non-verbal creative work developed by the staff, and he became more outgoing in his relations with other people. He even had a short-lived fist fight during a baseball game. Luciano said he never had had a fight before that time.

After that initial intensive summer in the Horizons Program, Luciano entered a parochial high school. He continued to avail himself of the tutoring help offered him by Horizons. The high school was co-educational, but very traditional. Luciano described some of his teachers as very nice people, but several in particular were extremely biased, in his view. His United States History teacher stereotyped Mexican Americans and taught her students that the Mexicans were "the bad guys" in the Mexican-American War, and particularly in the Battle of the Alamo. Many of Luciano's classmates resented this as did he, but no one spoke out against this type of teaching.

The Horizons Program helped Luciano overcome some of these biases by exposing him to tutors who helped him learn the truth about his cultural heritage and by taking an interest in him and his school work. Luciano's attendance record in high school was near perfect, and his grades were very good. The one time he was marked tardy in four years was the day after Chicago was blanketed with 27 inches of snow during the winter of 1968. This was but one example of the rigid type of school he went to and what he could expect in school. The school's counselors were interested only in those students who received the top grades, and Luciano reported that it was difficult for any student to see a counselor at any time unless he was "qualified."

At the end of his third year of high school, Luciano was selected to go to a six-week Encampment for Citizenship sponsored by the American Ethical Union. This was held outside of New York City. Luciano combined study with recreation and benefitted greatly from his experience there. He met students from other parts of the United States and other countries, and he spoke glowingly of the friendships he developed at the camp. The experience did broaden his horizons, and he came back to Chicago and successfully completed his last year of high school.

His counselor in the Horizons project helped Luciano to prepare for college entrance tests and helped him select a university. Luciano was admitted to the College of Liberal Arts and Sciences at the University of Illinois at Chicago. A well known university in the West announced it was looking for Mexican American students, but Luciano turned down the offer. He said he would not want to go to a school of higher learning which could let them brag that they were doing something for the Mexican American community by giving special consideration to Mexican Americans when in fact they were not. The person assigned to this university to recruit Mexican Americans used xeroxed form letters which merely invited students with top grades to consider matriculation. Luciano felt it was a white-wash. The person chosen had a Mexican American name, but after several correspondences, Luciano decided that it was mere tokenism.

Luciano qualified for financial assistance because of his parents' income. At one point he was about to lose this aid because he did not send back his application with the seal of a notary public, as was required. Luciano did not know, nor did his parents, what a notary public was. The counselor who worked for Horizons went to the University and saw the Director of Financial Aid, who was persuaded to re-open the file and give Luciano another chance. Soon after, the Director communicated with counselors all over the city, and told them to advise their students on what a notary public is and where to find one.

Luciano is half way through his first year at the University of Illinois. His financial assistance enables him to spend all of his time at his studies, and one of his strongest subjects in school is Spanish.

The guidance of one such youngster took a great deal of effort on the part of several people, but it has already paid off handsomely to this student and to society.

The case of Luciano demonstrates a number of principles about the importance of vocational counseling. Luciano's family and school experience is not uncommon. As the case illustrates, Luciano did not have models for success in American society. His teachers were Anglo, and his parents were unable to provide direction. Without the assistance of a counselor who cared, Luciano would probably have dropped out of school. The counselor's input was important not only for the support he offered but also for the new possibilities he helped open up for Luciano. It is important for counselors to be aware of programs such as "Horizons" and to encourage the participation of Hispanic students in those programs. Luciano's story exemplifies the need for long-term intervention with some Hispanic clients. Although the amount of individualized support and assistance Luciano received is not feasible in all cases, the example demonstrates that, given the right kind of help, Hispanic students may be academically capable of more than they or others would predict.

Housing

Discrimination in housing can be seen in the failure of city and state agencies to improve conditions in the *barrios*. In 1970, 35% of the occupied dwellings in East Los Angeles were classified as unsound and dilapidated. In a poverty tract in Houston, 90% of the residences were built before 1939. Many residents of Guadalupe, Arizona, lived in dwellings that lacked indoor plumbing (Galarza, Gallegos, & Samora, 1970). The fact that little or no public aid is provided to alleviate these conditions attests to the lack of regard for Hispanics' right to a decent standard of living.

Mass housing relocation is a frequent by-product of urban renewal, highway construction, the growth of "model cities," and public-housing or slum-clearance projects (Stoddard, 1973). Often these projects benefit society in general but not the Hispanic resident. Many Hispanics cannot afford to rent in the multiple-story apartments that replace their tract houses. Often reimbursement from the government for their dwellings does not begin to cover the cost of purchasing new residences. Furthermore, relocation programs often have the intention of improving living conditions for Hispanics but overlook such critical factors as proximity to grammar schools or a family's general financial condition (Stoddard, 1973).

Ironically, while urban redevelopment scatters the Hispanic community, at the same time discriminatory real-estate practices prevent Hispanics from moving into better neighborhoods. Hispanics may be strongly discouraged from living in certain neighborhoods. Real-estate brokers have been known to hang up the phone when called by a potential client who speaks with a Spanish accent (Glick, 1966).

Health Care

Good health is a basic social need. It is valued by all people, yet health-care services are not uniformly distributed. In the United States, majority-group members enjoy better health than do people from ethnic minorities. For instance, infant mortality in Colorado is three times as high among Mexican Americans as among Anglos. In Colorado, Mexican Americans die younger, at about 56.7 years of age, than Anglos, whose average life span is 67.5 years. In San Antonio, Texas, Mexican Americans have a higher death rate than Anglos, up to age 75, and infant mortality is 28.2 deaths per 100,000 Mexican Americans, whereas it is 21.3 deaths per 100,000 Anglos. Illness and death due to tuberculosis, pneumonia, and diabetes are more frequent among Hispanics than among Anglos (Ellis, 1962; Moustafa & Weiss, 1968). Clearly, the Hispanic community needs health-care services.

Despite this critical need for health care, there is a higher incidence of *untreated* physical and psychological ailments among Hispanics than among Anglos (Moustafa & Weiss, 1968; Padilla & Ruiz, 1973). In California, Mexican Americans report a lower physician-visitation rate per person per annum (2.3) than Blacks (3.7) or Anglos (5.6). Similarly, the annual hospital-admission rate is lowest for Mexican Americans (76 per 1000 persons), higher for Blacks (82 per 1000), and most frequent for Anglos (95 per 1000) (Moustafa & Weiss, 1968).

Responsibility for this health-care crisis is placed typically on the minority groups themselves. By using stereotypes, one can conveniently explain that Hispanics simply do not take advantage of available medical facilities. Recently, however, evidence is emerging that Hispanics have positive attitudes toward health care. In Orange County, California, Mexican Americans and Anglos expressed similar preferences for receiving health care from private physicians and hospitals (Weaver, 1973). In a study in Nebraska, distrust of modern medicine was not correlated with ethnicity (Welch, Comer, & Steinman, 1973).

In actuality, the critical health-care needs of Hispanics are associated with racism in health and social-service institutions. Health-care facilities are generally established outside Hispanic communities. The costs of health care are often prohibitively high, and, since most

Hispanics are poor, they are often denied service. Since medical staff are seldom minority-group members or bilingual, Hispanics may feel uncomfortable and unwelcome (Weaver, 1973). In some health-care agencies, Hispanics' needs are attended to more slowly than those of Anglos. Hispanics generally receive short-term care, whereas Anglos may receive long-term intervention for similar problems. Less money is spent to rehabilitate Hispanic disabled citizens than their Anglo counterparts (Rivera, O. A., 1974). In a subsequent chapter, we will focus on specific deficits within mental-health-service agencies serving Hispanics. The main point here is that insufficient health care is another form of discrimination that retards the adaptation of Hispanics within the United States.

Political and Legal Representation

Through a number of political maneuvers, Hispanics have until recently been denied fair representation in government. First, their voting patterns have been manipulated. The Hispanic vote has been divided by gerrymandering so that it has less impact. Second, poll taxes have prevented poor Hispanics from voting. Third, employers have threatened to fire workers unless they vote certain ways. Fourth, many poor workers lack transportation to polling booths, and employers may provide transportation for only those workers voting for particular candidates. These factors have successfully limited the number of pro-Hispanic or Hispanic candidates who have been elected to political office (Acuña, 1972).

The political power that Hispanics can wield if they are mobilized to go to the polls and vote for Hispanics can be seen in the redistribution of political power in Crystal City, Texas (Miller & Preston, 1973). This small Texas town was completely dominated by Anglos until 1963, when the "ruling establishment was deposed by five relatively uneducated Mexican American city council candidates" (Miller & Preston, 1973, p.776). With this turn of events, Crystal City received national and international publicity. The town has since become the focal point of political activism, and *La Raza Unida* party was founded in 1970 to foster political "self-determination" among Chicanos. Unfortunately, there have been few other examples of sustained political activism in other Hispanic communities, even though in recent years Hispanics have won election to city councils, school boards, mayoral seats, and, in two Southwestern states, even governorships.

Another long-standing abuse of Hispanics' political rights is their limited representation on grand and petit juries. Hispanics are rarely on venire lists for potential jurors. They have been kept from serving on juries if they cannot read English, even in states where the constitution specifies that jurors need only understand spoken English (Hernandez, Haug, & Wagner, 1976).

Legal representation for Hispanics is poor. There are few Hispanic lawyers, and there are very few Anglo lawyers willing to defend Hispanic clients (Acuña, 1972). Public defenders are generally not knowledgeable about Hispanic culture. Many trials involving Spanish-speaking clients are conducted with unskilled interpreters or no interpreter at all. Hispanics are poorly represented throughout the law-enforcement and legal systems, from the police to judges (Hernandez et al., 1976).

Police/Community Relations

Inadequate political and legal representation may lead to easy abuse by police. Police protection in Hispanic communities tends to be sparse (Hernandez et al., 1976). Because of racism within the judicial system, there is a high potential for violence between Hispanics and police. The case of Judge Chargin, below, although not common, illustrates our point.

THE CASE OF JUDGE GERALD S. CHARGIN: A PUBLIC RECORD

IN THE SUPERIOR COURT OF THE STATE OF CALIFORNIA IN AND FOR THE COUNTY OF SANTA CLARA JUVENILE DIVISION

Honorable Gerald S. Chargin, Judge	Courtroom No. 1

In the Matter of (Name deleted), a minor	No. 40331

STATEMENTS OF THE COURT

San Jose, California	September 2, 1969

APPEARANCES:

For the Minor:	FRED LUCERO, ESQ., Deputy Public Defender
For the Probation Department:	WILLIAM TAPOGNA, ESQ., Court Probation Officer
Official Court Reporter: September 2, 1969	SUSAN K. STRAHM, C.S.R. 10:25 A.M.

STATEMENTS OF THE COURT

The Court: There is some indication that you more or less didn't think that it was against the law or was improper. Haven't you had any moral training? Have you and your family gone to church?

The Minor: Yes, sir.

The Court: Don't you know that things like this are terribly wrong? This is one of the worst crimes that a person can commit. I just get so disgusted that I just figure what is the use? You are just an animal. You are lower than an animal. Even animals don't do that. You are pretty low.

I don't know why your parents haven't been able to teach you anything or train you. Mexican people, after 13 years of age, it's perfectly all right to go out and act like an animal. It's not even right to do that to a stranger, let alone a member of your own family. I don't have much hope for you. You will probably end up in State's Prison before you are 25, and that's where you belong, anyhow. There is nothing much you can do.

I think you haven't got any moral principles. You won't acquire anything. Your parents won't teach you what is right or wrong and won't watch out.

Apparently, your sister is pregnant; is that right?

The Minor's Father: Yes.

The Court: It's a fine situation. How old is she?

The Minor's Mother: Fifteen.

The Court: Well, probably she will have a half a dozen children and three or four marriages before she is 18.

The County will have to take care of you. You are no particular good to anybody. We ought to send you out of the country—send you back to Mexico. You belong in prison for the rest of your life for doing things of this kind. You ought to commit suicide. That's what I think of people of this kind. You are lower than animals and haven't the right to live in organized society—just miserable, lousy, rotten people.

There is nothing we can do with you. You expect the County to take care of you. Maybe Hitler was right. The animals in our society probably ought to be destroyed because they have no right to live among human beings. If you refuse to act like a human being, then, you don't belong among the society of human beings.

Mr. Lucero: Your Honor, I don't think I can sit here and listen to that sort of thing.

The Court: You are going to have to listen to it because I consider this a very vulgar, rotten human being.

Mr. Lucero: The Court is

indicting the whole Mexican group.

The Court: When they are 10 or 12 years of age, going out and having intercourse with anybody without any moral training—they don't even understand the Ten Commandments. That's all. Apparently, they don't want to.

So if you want to act like that, the County has a system of taking care of them. They don't care about that. They have no personal self-respect.

Mr. Lucero: The Court ought to look at this youngster and deal with this youngster's case.

The Court: All right. That's what I am going to do. The family should be able to control this boy and the young girl.

Mr. Lucero: What appalls me is that the Court is saying that Hitler was right in genocide.

The Court: What are we going to do with the mad dogs of our society? Either we have to kill them or send them to an institution or place them out of the hands of good people because that's the theory—one of the theories of punishment is if they get to the position that they want to act like mad dogs,

then, we have to separate them from our society.

Well, I will go along with the recommendation. You will learn in time or else you will have to pay for the penalty with the law because the law grinds slowly but exceedingly well. If you are going to be a law violator—you have to make up your mind whether you are going to observe the law or not. If you can't observe the law, then, you have to be put away.

STATE OF CALIFORNIA
COUNTY OF SANTA CLARA

I, SUSAN K. STRAHM, do hereby certify that the foregoing is a true and correct transcript of the STATEMENTS OF THE COURT had in the within-entitled action taken on the 2nd day of September, 1969; that I reported the same in stenotype, being the qualified and acting Official Court Reporter of the Superior Court of the State of California, in and for the County of Santa Clara, appointed to said court, and thereafter had the same transcribed into typewriting as herein appears.

Dated: This 8th day of September, 1969.

Judge Chargin was censured for his comments and forced to retract and publicly apologize. Yet it is important to note that he was reelected in 1972. Running unopposed in 1966, Chargin obtained 158,362 votes. In

1972, after his censure and running opposed, he received 143,235 votes, while his closest opponent received 71,079 votes (Hernandez et al., 1976).

Efforts by Hispanics to organize politically have resulted in violence, as during the **"Zoot Suit"** riots of 1942. In Los Angeles, several delinquent acts were committed by a gang of Mexican-American teenagers, who, characteristically, dressed in flashy zoot suits. Newspapers dramatized the incidents highly. With police support, soldiers on leave from nearby military installations entered the Mexican-American community and attempted to quell the disturbances. Instead, they catalyzed further frustration (Burma, 1954). Finally, when the police attempted to control the situation, they instead caused riots (Morales, 1971a). In the days that followed, hundreds of Zoot Suiters and other Mexican-American citizens were beaten and arrested, and similar riots erupted in San Diego, Philadelphia, Chicago, and Detroit (Burma, 1954). Recently, a play opened in Los Angeles based on the cultural role of the "Zoot Suiters" during the 1940s. The play represents the first major effort in "legitimate theater" by Chicanos to portray the social injustices encountered by Chicano youth.

Police have been cruelly assaultive to Hispanics. In the so-called "Sleepy Lagoon Murder" of 1942, a young Mexican American was slain as a result of interethnic rivalry. Twenty-four Mexican Americans were arrested and beaten by police. Fifteen were convicted unfairly, and the conviction was not overturned for two years (Burma, 1954). In 1966, two days of rioting ensued in Chicago's Puerto Rican community after a policeman shot a Puerto Rican youth who allegedly had attacked him. (Fitzpatrick, 1971). There are frequent allegations that police use excessive and discriminatory force with Hispanics, discriminate against Hispanic juveniles, impose harsh penalties on Hispanics for traffic offenses, and stop Hispanics frequently on grounds of "suspicious activity" (DeBlassie, 1976; Morales, 1971a).

Hispanics have little recourse in such situations. Their complaints must be made to the police, the very agency employing the accused officer, and few attorneys will accept cases of alleged police abuse against Hispanics. For example, Hispanics have not been able to obtain redress for the death of Ruben Salazar, a well-known Chicano newspaperman who exposed the injustices perpetrated against Chicanos by Los Angeles police (Acuña, 1972). Police report the shooting as accidental, but it has never been adequately explained why police entered a bar with their weapons drawn and why only Salazar was killed.

Once arrested, Hispanics may experience further abuse of their rights. The bail is sometimes excessive, or the right to bail may be withheld. It is reported that, in agricultural regions, bail has sometimes been manipulated so that local farmers pay bail at a discount during harvest season. Hispanics, however, are not told of this discount (Hernandez et al., 1976).

Anger and disappointment are appropriate reactions to discrimination by politicians and police. The frustration caused by such discrimination is well described by a Puerto Rican youth who stated during an interview (Palomares, 1971a, p. 95):

> . . . We become a statistic . . . you know, of Puerto Ricans, 7.21 kids in the family, 8.6 are . . . you know . . . like you are just a number and a statistic. Every time they attempt to deal with you it's in relation to that number and statistic instead of trying to find you out. Like they are afraid of you or something. Like they only want to study you. Yes, and they will observe you and they will watch you but then they don't use any of the information except in formula-like facts and figures.

The pluralistic counselor must recognize all the diverse forms of institutional racism experienced by Hispanics. A lifetime of these experiences can create frustration and rage in the individual. Further, such experiences can make Hispanics suspicious of institutions and agencies as well as of well-meaning non-Hispanics who want to help. This distrust of strangers and institutions is a normal and adaptive response to a prejudicial society. The therapist who works with Hispanics must be careful not to mislabel behavior as pathological until all the facts are known about a client's background, community, and perceptions of the majority group and institutions.

EFFECTS OF RACISM

Self-Concept

Social scientists have predicted that discrimination creates negative self-concepts in Hispanic children. Evidence about this thesis, however, is contradictory. Several researchers report that Mexican Americans perceive themselves unfavorably. In one study with eighth-grade Mexican-American and Anglo students, a greater disparity between real self and ideal self was exhibited by the Mexican Americans (Peterson & Ramirez, 1971). In unstructured doll play with 4- and 5-year-old Mexican Americans, Werner and Evans (1968) reported that, by age 5, Mexican-American children generally showed a preference for the White doll. The results of the Werner and Evans study, however, are suspect; some researchers contend that the dark-skinned doll used in the study was too dark to be representative of Mexican Americans (Padilla & Ruiz, 1973).

A number of researchers, using a variety of questionnaires, report that Hispanics do not perceive themselves less positively than Anglos perceive themselves (Albright, 1974; Anderson & Johnson, 1971; Carter, 1968; Healy & DeBlassie, 1974; Muller & Leonetti, 1974; Rice, Ruiz, & Padilla, 1974). When the California Psychological Inventory (Gough, 1957) was administered to Mexican-American and Anglo junior high school students, Mexican Americans scored higher than Anglos on social responsibility, tolerance, and intellectual fluency (Mason, 1967). With a semantic differential, Mexican Americans scored as high on intellectual power, goodness, and happiness as Anglos (Carter, 1968). Some disadvantaged children may develop greater ability to assume responsibility and independence (Soares & Soares, 1969). Since many Hispanics are from poor backgrounds, they may possess positive self-concepts as a result of their struggle for self-preservation. One interesting study suggests that self-concept is rising among Mexican Americans. A questionnaire was administered to Mexican-American students in Los Angeles and Denver in 1963 and in 1968. In each case, the students perceived themselves as sensitive and emotional; but these traits were considered to be more positive by the 1968 sample (Dworkin, 1971).

Data concerning Puerto Rican self-concept are also inconsistent, but most of them reveal as high self-concept among Puerto Ricans as among Anglos. When Coopersmith's (1967) inventory of self-esteem was administered to Black, White and Puerto Rican children in Connecticut, Puerto Rican children exhibited the poorest self-images (Zirkel, Moses, & Gnanara, 1971). In contrast, Puerto Rican self-concept was as high as Anglo self-concept in two studies employing verbal questionnaires (Cruz, 1974; Soares & Soares, 1969).

Little research on Cuban self-concept is available. In one study comparing self-concepts of Puerto Rican, Dominican Republican, and Cuban children residing on the East coast of the United States, Cuban children perceived themselves most positively on trustworthiness and proper-behavior dimensions (Morris, 1974).

DeBlassie (1976, p. 116) concludes that the research is contradictory but that much "speculation and conjecture with respect to self-concept of the Mexican American . . . continue and perpetuate stereotypic notions and generalizations." A therapist working with a Hispanic client should not assume that his or her client has a poor self-concept just because of having ethnic-minority status. If the Hispanic client does have a poor self-concept, the therapist should consider discrimination and poverty as possible causes.

Denial of Ethnicity

Some Hispanics cope with racism by denying their ethnicity and overidentifying with the majority culture. They may devote much energy to democratic causes, such as volunteering for army duty during wartime. They may refuse to refer to themselves as Mexican American or Puerto Rican or Cuban. Instead, they will call themselves Spanish Americans or Americans of Spanish descent. Kitano (1974) states that these individuals are trying to prove to the larger society that they, too, are Americans.

Denying one's ethnic heritage can cause great emotional stress (Simmons, 1961). When the value systems of emotionally disturbed and emotionally healthy Mexican Americans were compared, 50% of the nonpatients and only 22% of the disturbed patients ascribed to clear-cut traditional or Anglo-American values. Patients expressed more mixed cultural values than nonpatients. Thus, confusion about ethnic identity and personal identity were correlated with emotional problems (Fabrega & Wallace, 1968). Such confusion in ethnic and personal identity is poignantly demonstrated in the story of Rodrigo, an "'All-American Boy' Imposter."

THE CASE OF RODRIGO.[4] At the time Rodrigo sought help, he was suffering from severe asthma and dermatitis. He was 24 years old, married, and the father of two children. His Mexican heritage was apparent in his physical features, especially his dark complexion. He was a good-looking, virile young man, endowed with superior intelligence. Despite all these graces, he loathed himself.

Rodrigo was the oldest in a family of seven children and considered himself the least favored by his mother. He grew up in a slum area in East Chicago which was populated mostly by what he called "crude, dirty, illiterate Mexicans." His father had been a worker in a steel mill for some 32 years. Rodrigo described him as a hard-working man who lacked the ability to make a dollar. He characterized his mother as a "whore," who

[4]From "The Impact of Dual Cultural Membership on Identity," by V. Sommers, *Psychiatry*, 1964, *27*, 332–344. Copyright © 1964 by the William Alanson White Psychiatric Foundation, Inc. Reprinted by permission.

always expected him to take care of the younger siblings or do chores around the house. He remembers, "I was never allowed to be a little boy. I was always plugging away at some job."

Rodrigo was very ambitious and interested in higher learning, although his mother wanted him to quit school and go to work. To have a college degree was very important to him. It meant rising above his environment and not being a "dumb Mexican kid."

After finishing high school, Rodrigo worked on the railroad in the daytime and went to college at night, hoping to become a business executive. As in his early childhood, he had no time for pleasure. His family often compared him to his paternal grandfather, an overseer on a Mexican ranch. He was remembered as a "feared and hated" man—a "brute," as he was often called. Rodrigo resented this comparison, although he admitted reluctantly that, at times, he did feel like a wild man.

Rodrigo had earned the equivalent of one year of college when he enlisted in the Marine Corps at the age of 21. Within a year of joining, he became a sergeant. He stated, "Although I felt cold and scared most of the time, I never let my emotions show. On the contrary, I acted like a daredevil. I volunteered wherever there seemed to be danger." He went on to say, "This was the one time in my life when I felt good and not depressed or guilt-ridden. It was the only time I felt, 'I'm just as good as the other guys.' Bullets do not discriminate between race and color." At this time he also was completely free of physical symptoms. Evidently, during the war his hostile-aggressive feelings found adequate expression. He was an "overseer," as his grandfather had been. At this point, his identification with his grandfather was very gratifying to him. He felt worthwhile; he had status and received social approval. The military situation not only *approved* but *demanded* his role as an aggressor, which he had then to renounce upon his return to civilian life. For a man who did not have a solid and merged identity, the shift in roles became very disturbing.

With his Marine discharge, the grim partners of his psychic turmoil, the asthma and dermatitis, from which he had suffered since infancy, returned. Viewed symbolically, it seemed as though Rodrigo was trying to scratch away his skin, that ever-present reminder which stigmatized him as a "dirty Mexican," a "second-class citizen." . . . He was not seeing himself as a person, as a human being, but only as a Mexican. He felt ashamed of his parents, ashamed of the Mexican people, and ashamed of himself for having so much prejudice.

New aspects of Rodrigo's inner self finally broke through when he brought out material involving his marital relationship. He revealed a strong yearning for closeness and tenderness which he had tried to shut out of awareness all these years. He confided that he engaged in sexual activities nearly every day, that he frequently masturbated after sexual intercourse, and that his need for sexual closeness, tenderness, and affection seemed boundless. He admitted that he felt very jealous of his wife, even of her love for their children. He also related how he enjoyed putting his head in her lap, sucking her breasts. Rodrigo himself became aware of his conflicting desires for *sucking* and *socking*.

In exploring his insatiable need for sex, love, and closeness, Rodrigo associated to his early childhood and his relationship with his mother. As a child, he had never felt wanted. As he put it, "I was not even wanted when I was born . . . I was never my mother's favorite. She cuddled only my brother Robert. He was a healthy baby."

. . . Rodrigo took great pride in his successes at emulating the "all-American boy." His very appearance bespoke the self-image he was trying to build—with his hair clipped in a crew-cut, and his athletic physique clad in sportswear. He savored his prizes—a collection of no fewer than sixteen letters in sports. He very nearly succeeded in imitating the model for this ego-ideal, the fictional Jack Armstrong. And the closer he came to his newfound identity, the all-American boy, the more he repudiated his early identifications. He moved into an Anglo neighborhood, became violently anti-Catholic, and gave up talking Spanish. It seemed as if he were murdering the past.

In the third year of therapy, Rodrigo finally succeeded in being promoted to an office job in the organization where for years he had been a warehouse man. This shift from a blue collar to a white collar identity made him feel even more self-conscious at first. He felt that he "didn't fit," that he was "much too conspicuous" in this "all-Anglo crowd."

. . . Rodrigo had anticipated rejection; he was prepared to fight. He felt bewildered when he found himself accepted and respected. He began to wonder whether "I'm the only one who really raises doubts in myself." He repeatedly asked, "How can others accept me if I haven't accepted myself? . . . I can see that I have changed my outer self, but I'm still a slave to my inner self."

As Rodrigo grew in his understanding of the distortions he had developed about himself, he also recognized his many distortions about his family and his cultural group. His more realistic appraisal and acceptance of his mother was expressed as follows: She couldn't have been an irresponsible mother. She has raised seven children and not one has been an alcoholic, a delinquent, or any other kind of misfit.

According to Sommers (1964), insights gained through verbal therapy enabled Rodrigo to let go of his defenses and develop new, adaptive ways of responding to personal and social stress. He became interested in the welfare of his ethnic group and attended city-council meetings to fight delinquency and to improve social conditions for Hispanics. "His goal now is clear—to extricate his downtrodden people from misery and to raise their culture, so that he may feel himself to be a better and more worthy person. With the gradual resolution of some of his intrapsychic and ethnic conflicts, he is no longer a caricature of the 'all-American boy'" (Sommers, 1964, p. 335).

Just as denial of ethnicity may precipitate emotional distress, conversely, ethnic identification may foster personal adjustment. When 30 Puerto Rican former psychiatric patients responded to a community-adaptation inventory, those who expressed Puerto Rican cultural values exhibited more effective community readjustment. For those former patients who retained Puerto Rican values and also lived with their families, the readjustment was facilitated further (Amin, 1974). Rodrigo's tortuous struggle to achieve emotional stability exemplifies the importance of a positive ethnic identity.

Many times a therapist must help the Hispanic client adapt to the majority culture, and the therapist's role, in part, may be to foster assimilation. The pluralistic therapist must recognize that the breakdown of ethnic identification may precipitate great emotional pain and loss of self-esteem. A primary purpose of pluralistic therapy is to help clients adapt to life in the majority culture without relinquishing their ethnicity.

If a therapist works with a Hispanic who denies his or her ethnic identity, a primary goal of the therapy may be to rekindle ethnic awareness. The therapist may recommend that the client join ethnic associations or read about Hispanic history. In general, therapeutic recommendations will incorporate Hispanic culture.

Subjective Discomfort

Many Hispanics do not deny their ethnicity or develop poor self-concepts because of discrimination. Nevertheless, they may experience tremendous personal discomfort by internalizing stress from racism. The subjective discomfort may be expressed as nervousness or psychosomatic illness. Sometimes the discomfort may become so intense that the individual retreats from society. Alcoholics, drug addicts, and vagrants are often people who have adopted retreatist postures because of their continued frustration with racist institutions (Kitano, 1974).

This subjective discomfort may result in expressions of aggression or direct retaliation. Hispanics may stereotype negatively and discriminate against Anglos. They have stereotyped Anglos as cold, phlegmatic, conceited, and inconstant (Simmons, 1961). High school Mexican Americans have perceived that Anglos would support the position that "it is good to mix only with your own kind" (Kaplan & Goldman, 1973), thus generalizing that most Anglos are separatists. Generally, stereotyping by Hispanics occurs after age 8, at an older age than among Anglos, who begin stereotyping at about age 4 (Johnson, 1950). In a study comparing stereotypes of Anglos by Mexican Americans born in Mexico with those of Mexican Americans born in the United States, negative attitudes toward Anglos correlated positively with length of stay in the United States, rather than with country of origin (Dworkin, 1971). Apparently, Hispanics' stereotyping of Anglos occurs as a reaction to the discrimination they feel. In addition to direct retaliation and stereotyping against Anglos, Hispanics may express anger through political writings and passive resistance.

A variety of symptoms and inappropriate behaviors may develop from the internalization of frustration about racism. In these cases, good mental health is fostered by reducing the impact of racism upon the individual. Sometimes, as explained in the next section, it is adaptive for the client to express the anger associated with this subjective discomfort.

THE RISE OF HISPANIC NATIONALISM

Ingrouping

One way in which Hispanics cope with discrimination is to combine their efforts to better their lives. Group cohesiveness increases optimism of the members by creating a sense of "interdependence of fate" (Guttentag, 1970). The group motivates its members to work toward their goals. When high school and college students in Los Angeles were asked whether or not they would adopt pro-Chicano positions on various issues, the Mexican Americans who identified with Chicano stands held higher educational aspirations than those who were not pro-Chicano (Leyva, 1975). Although this pattern did not hold true for college students aspiring to post-college work, the results point to growth in self-pride associated with ethnic cohesiveness.

Ingrouping can ameliorate personal crises. For example, the traditionally oriented Hispanic seldom seeks welfare assistance, because of the aid of family, friends, and neighbors (McWilliams, 1968). Ingrouping also stimulates social change. However, it should be emphasized that current-day Hispanic power movements are not the first efforts by Hispanics to change their socioeconomic situation. Hispanics have long struggled for their rights. The following historical record demonstrates that Hispanics have actively fought discrimination for nearly 150 years:

> In 1833 a strike was called by several hundred field workers in the Texas Panhandle under the leadership of Juan Gomez.
> In 1859 the "Cortina Wars" were staged by a Mexican-American rancher against a Brownsville sheriff for arresting several of his workers unfairly.
> In 1903 over 1000 Mexican-American sugarbeet workers called a strike in California.
> In 1930 a strike of Mexican-American coal miners spread through New Mexico.
> In 1933 an extremely large strike of agricultural workers shook the San Joaquin and Imperial Valleys in California.
> In 1934 a strike of sheepherders and pecan shellers occurred in Texas.
> In 1945 Gonzalez Mendez filed a case of discrimination and segregation against the schools in Orange County, California, and won.

These and many more protests have been valiantly staged. Until recently, Hispanics' efforts effected minimal change, because they lacked sufficient numbers to enforce their rights (Moore, 1970). Moreover, Hispanics have held few powerful positions in politics and the media, thus having only limited ability to make their needs generally known (Galarza, et al., 1970). Many protests have been quelled with violence and have ended in deportation (McWilliams, 1968).

Organization of Power

Hispanic labor and political parties have been plagued with many problems. Organization has been impeded by the diversity of the Hispanic groups (Galarza et al., 1970). Although a broad political stance allows Hispanic groups to support various political candidates who are sympathetic to the Hispanic cause, the diversity of the groups has prevented them from enlisting financial aid from larger labor and political parties.

Despite these difficulties, the number and strength of these Hispanic organizations has grown steadily since the early 1900s (see Table 3-3). They gained tremendous momentum in the late 1950s and 1960s when Hispanics learned to protest through walkouts. Hispanics walked out of schools and public meetings and even "walked out" of the Democratic party to draw attention to their cause (Acuña, 1972).

Migrant workers began organizing for better pay and improved working conditions around 1950. Cesar Chavez was hired to administrate the Community Service Organization (CSO) established to support Hispanic workers' rights in California. Chavez quickly gained the support of California migrants and extended the CSO into Arizona. The CSO did not provide the activist approach Chavez desired, so he reformulated the organization into the United Farm Workers Association in 1960. The first strike by this group was instigated by the gardeners' contingent in 1965. With this large number of workers finally organized, ¡**Huelga!—Strike!** —has become a call to Hispanics to improve their employment situations.

The present decade has seen the reaffirmation of their culture by many Hispanics. **Chicanismo**—Brown power—flourishes. Movements within Chicano, Puerto Rican, Cuban, and other Hispanic groups emphasize ethnic pride and identification, social change, strong respect for Hispanic heroes, and cultural rebirth (Leyva, 1975).

Chicanismo and concurrent pride in Puerto Rican, Cuban, and other Hispanic origins have been associated with the evolution of the new youth organizations. In 1967, David Sánchez organized the "Young Chicano Youth for Community Action" in Los Angeles. The group was initiated to support *barrio* youngsters in their struggles for economic mobility. After some problems with local police, the group reorganized with a more militant attitude, calling themselves the **"Brown Berets."** The social-action efforts of Hispanics are epitomized by the National Chicano Youth Liberation Conference held in Denver in 1969. The conference was attended by over 1500 Hispanics interested in actively pursuing the rights of Hispanics (Alford, 1972). In 1950 a group of young Puerto Ricans established the Puerto Rican Forum in New York to represent Puerto Ricans at various meetings. **Aspira** was developed in 1961 to upgrade the education of Puerto Ricans (Fitzpatrick, 1971). Originally the Lords of Chicago were just another urban gang, but in the 1950s this Puerto Rican gang negotiated with Anglo gangs to fight social injustices instead of each other. The Lords of Chicago have created better housing, free health clinics, a day-care program, and a children's park. In 1969 a young Lord's Party grew out of a gang in New York City and has been instrumental in increasing health-care and welfare services to mothers, as well as providing door-to-door lead-poisoning-detection tests.

There is often a mutually enhancing relationship between self-esteem and political activism. In Crystal City, Texas, Hispanics have developed a strong sense of identity and self-determination since they wrested political power from the Anglo minority in 1970 (Acuña, 1972). Students in Crystal City who identified as Chicano differed from those identifying as Mexican American. The students adopting *Chicanismo* are more likely to expect active legal action for equal rights, are more sensitive to discrimination, are more likely to engage in collective bargaining, and are more aware of their own possibility for success (Gutierrez & Hirsch, 1973).

It is often appropriate for a therapist to encourage the Hispanic client to join ethnic organizations. It could be helpful for a therapist to learn the location of local organizations and make information about these organizations available to interested clients. Recent immigrants might find the information particularly useful.

Several dangers of overidentification with various power movements have been noted. Some organizations might spur too great a release of anger among marginally adjusted individuals. In some cases, identification with a Hispanic organization can lead to such raised hopes that a sense of despair follows if goals are not reached. In a few cases, identification with an organization has led to the dogmatic rejection of all others who are not activists for Hispanic rights (Martinez, 1973).

A therapist should be alert to the possible dangers of organizations but recognize, as in the quote that follows (Negron, 1971, p. 112), that members of Hispanic political, labor, and social groups usually gain the energy and optimism needed to effect personal and social change:

> . . . There are 57 Aspira clubs in all of the high schools in New York City, and their main focus is on leadership development and a professional plan for each student for the future, as far as his career is concerned. There is

Table 3-3. *Hispanic labor and political organizations.*

Name of Organization	Founding Date	Description/Objective
Orden de los Hijos de América	1921	To support emerging middle-class Mexican Americans in assimilation.
League of United Latin American Citizens (LULAC)	1927	Originally, to aid assimilation; today to improve position of Mexican Americans, without violence.
Confederación de Uniones Obreras Mexicanas	1927	Southern California Labor Union; unionize agricultural workers.
Community Service Organization (CSO)	1947	Emphasized voter registration and articulation of community needs.
American G.I. Forum	1948	Urged political participation through voter registration; lobbied for Hispanic appointments at the local and state level.
Council of Mexican American Affairs	1953	Nonpartisan support for Mexican-American leaders.
Mexican American Political Association (MAPA)	1957	Active endorsement of Mexican-American political candidates and non-Hispanics sympathetic to Hispanic community needs (such as John F. Kennedy).

Table 3-3, continued.

Name of Organization	Founding Date	Description/Objective
Political Association of Spanish Speaking Organizations (PASSO)	1960	Same organization as MAPA but based in Texas.
United Farm Workers Union	1965	Campaign to improve the working conditions of Mexican American agricultural workers.
United Mexican American Students (UMAS) Mexican American Youth Organization (MAYO) Mexican American Student Confederation (MASC) Movimiento Estudiantil Chicano de Aztlan (MECHA)	1967–1969	Active rejection of traditional styles of political action; support of Chicano political candidates; educational opportunity; social justice.
Mexican American Legal Defense and Education Fund (MALDEF)	1968	Provide legal assistance to Mexican American population; lobby for civil rights; support students in law.
La Raza Unida Party (LRU)	1970	Political party that actively supports its own slate of candidates for local and state offices.
Congressional Hispanic Caucus	1977	Enact and support legislation that affects Hispanic population; confer with the President on Hispanic community issues.

involvement in the civic activities of the school and the general organization (G.O. as we call it). The kids also get involved in voter registration drives and become more aware of the needs of their community. They are really with it.

. . . Aspira's doing this, and fortunately, the present school system is beginning to emulate the work that Aspira has been doing for all these years. The reason that Aspira became a reality was because the school system was not doing its job. It wasn't in any way helping the Puerto Rican students. It was almost . . . creating a genocide of our children.

IMPLICATIONS FOR PLURALISTIC THERAPISTS

The language, customs, and physiognomy of the Hispanics make them easy targets for stereotyping. The American economy has required cheap labor for field and industrial work. By negatively stereotyping Hispanics, majority-group members are superficially justified in usurping Hispanic land, offering low wages, and sanctioning pathetic living conditions. Thus, negative stereotyping and discrimination grow side by side. Discrimination in the schools, social systems, and government retards social and economic mobility among Hispanics. Stereotyping and discrimination beget personal and social problems among Hispanics, which in turn reinforce the negative stereotyping and discrimination.

Clearly, issues associated with racism and discrimination will be central in pluralistic counseling with Hispanics. The therapist must be constantly vigilant to avoid stereotyping the Hispanic client. Differences among Mexican Americans, Puerto Ricans, Cubans, and other Hispanics, as well as individual differences, must be recognized. Therapists should evaluate their own ideas and behavior and the institution with which they are associated for possible prejudice and discriminatory practices. The therapist's open-mindedness is expanded by knowledge of the Spanish language and Hispanic cultures.

An effective therapist for Hispanics will have as a major goal the amelioration of personal distress caused by discrimination and institutional racism. The therapist can help the Hispanic client find appropriate outlets for anger and ways to direct that anger toward effecting social change. When necessary, the therapist will focus on enhancing the client's self-concept and appreciation of his or her cultural roots. In those clients who have dealt with racism by denying their ethnicity, the therapist will attempt to foster pride in Hispanic cultures. The therapist may direct the client toward Hispanic groups and organizations with which he or she can identify.

In order to help the Hispanic client deal fully with the emotional effects of racism, the therapist may need to be an agent for social change. Mental health for Hispanics requires the alleviation not only of the suffering caused by prejudice but also of the causes of prejudice. The therapist may help the client identify and deal with racism in employment, residential, or educational settings. The client may need help locating pro-Hispanic lawyers, interpreters, or physicians. It may be helpful for the therapist to educate school personnel about the values of bilingual teaching. The therapist may identify discriminatory practices within agencies with which the Hispanic client is interacting and assist the client in educating agency personnel about those practices. The therapist must also become involved in preventive mental health, teaching social and health agencies how to attract and aid Hispanic clients.

In general, the pluralistic therapist is nonprejudicial with clients and is a force in reshaping institutions toward nonprejudicial attitudes. Much of the therapist's power will be directed toward prevention of discriminatory practices. The therapist cannot avoid the issues of prejudice and racism. If the therapist does not become a social advocate for the client when it is necessary, he or she is sanctioning, through neglect, continued discriminatory practices.

Chapter 4 Stress and Maladjustment

The first step in planning mental-health intervention for Hispanics is determining the type and extent of maladjustment. Once this has been done, appropriate treatment services can be designed. The major focus of this chapter will be to review common types of maladjustment that occur among Hispanics and to suggest therapeutic interventions. Where information is available, we will contrast symptomatology observed among Hispanics with that observed in other American ethnic groups.

Opler (1967) discusses how psychological symptomatology reflects cultural factors. The case that follows is about Alberto, a 21-year-old Hispanic who sought therapy for acute anxiety and severe psychosomatic complaints, primarily chronic colitis.

THE CASE OF ALBERTO.[1]

Born and reared in Puerto Rico until his adolescence, Alberto, his mother, two sisters and his brother, Roberto, moved to New York City following his parents' marital separation.

The stage for Alberto's problems was set by cultural and familial factors that affected his parents' coping mechanisms, their style of childrearing, and ways in which they handled their marital difficulties. Alberto's father responded to family stress with agitated behavior and severe drinking bouts. As a reaction to her marital difficulties, Alberto's mother distorted the Puerto Rican cultural value of good housekeeping and, in doing so, set up a pathogenic environment for her children.

[1]From *Culture and Social Psychology*, by M. K. Opler. Copyright 1967 by Aldine Publishing Company. Reprinted by permission.

. . . Both mother and paternal grandmother laid great stress upon learning language through constant repetition of words. In this, as in every aspect of child care, the manipulative older woman and the rigidly strict mother vied and quarreled with each other. Disassociating himself from these female battles, Alberto's father would assume his most manly, decisive (and **guapo**) manner on the rare occasions when he was at home. Issuing orders in a deep, guttural voice, his decisions were preemptory and arbitrary. Often, he would side with his mother for no apparent reason or indulge in frequent fits of anger. In time, the sinecure on the police force led to illegal scrapes and shady deals, salted with a series of the extramarital liaisons sanctioned in this culture for males. The number of alcoholic sprees with boon companions increased. Alberto's mother salvaged her all-important marital status by rigid adherence to the routines of a meticulous housewife, becoming overly clean, orderly, and compulsive.

Environmental factors can increase certain types of culturally specific symptomatology. In Alberto's case, the epidemic frequency of worms heightened the mother's and Alberto's obsessive characters.

. . . He and his siblings also had their share of worms, the childhood plague of Puerto Rico. In addition, two siblings, both girls, were born when the patient was, respectively, five and six years old. With all siblings, the castor oil was administered to counteract *Worms* and *Constipation*, the twin evils, but since Alberto's bowel involvement was the greater, he drew the greater attention on both scores.

By age seven, when his female siblings required infancy care, his mother began to give him hot water enemas at least once a month. Later, at eighteen, during the acute onset of his schizophrenic illness, he tried to self-administer such an enema, but failed because he feared too much hot water, and complained, for the first time in his life, that his mother had given the children laxatives and enemas "when we didn't need them." To this was added, "it was done when father was away and he didn't care about the house anyway."

As a result of family pathology colored by cultural symptomatology and environmental stress of worms, Alberto developed an obsessive concern with cleanliness.

> . . . he early began to cater to his mother's phobic fear of "city dirt and disease." In the daytime, he never liked to sit on the floor as did most children; he wished to be bathed by his mother frequently; and he delighted her by constantly washing his hands.

By eighteen, his problem developed into full blown psychosis. Despite some culturally-specific situations leading to his condition, his psychotic symptomatology resembled that of a broad range of highly disturbed individuals.

> . . . Sexual life is described as beginning in adolescence, coincidental with the father's separation and shortly after arrival in New York. Masturbation occurred frequently in showers and toilets, either before or after bowel movements. Heterosexual excitements are claimed in New York's crowded apartments, but despite more talk of divorce and desertion than in San Juan, he himself had neither dates nor girl friends, and denies any homosexual experience. In late adolescence, masturbation began to evoke guilt. "It makes you dumb or dull and pimply." One should also know where to go for sex with women. His own busy life began to require his attendance at college in evening classes while working overtime as a clerk. The patient added that there was too much preoccupation with homosexuality in Puerto Rican neighborhoods, but he was, at first, unaware of his selective attention to this matter.
>
> Perhaps the most striking symptom on this score was the patient's compulsive need for having bowel movements in public toilets. At first, he was unaware of the homosexual motivations for this, but explained that he stopped several times at subway stations for this purpose. This pattern occurred about three times a week, with anxiety about going to work, and masturbation occasionally to lessen this anxiety.

Alberto's dreams exemplify fears characteristic of patients of varied ethnicities. In the following excerpts, dreams 1, 2, 3, and 6 rely on common symbolism to express heterosexual concerns. Through death metaphors, dream 5 expresses anxiety about death.

> . . . *Dream 1*: He dreamed he owned a horse, and
> stated, "You wake and find it's no horse." *Dream 2*
> reflected similar doubts of male potency, and concerned
> driving a car which magically transformed into a broom
> or stick incapable of motion. This dream was quickly
> associated, in frank Puerto Rican terms, with others
> about sexual intercourse. Alberto stated, "I think I need
> sex with a woman—dreaming of intercourse and waking
> up with night losses or wet dreams; the body must get
> rid of sperms because they accumulate." *Dream 3*
> concerned travel on a ship to Spain where he saw the
> Pyrenees covered with snow; it all changed to clouds as
> he awoke. In *Dream 4* an older nightmare was evoked;
> he was dying, and all the persons around him were busy
> nailing him into his coffin; he wished to tell them he was
> really alive, but could not speak. In *Dream 5*, he was
> breaking windows and doing this fearfully, but he could
> not run away like the friends with him. "I felt like I
> was nailed down to the floor." *Dream 6* had him married
> and settled down with a girl he knew back in New
> York; she was described as being brunette and small,
> and was a person occasionally seen in real life.

Treatment required sensitive integration of cultural concepts and understanding of psychodynamic etiology. Alberto was a latent homosexual, and many of the psychodynamic interpretations of this condition seem appropriate. Alberto's fear of homosexual impulses evoked particular pathos if viewed in terms of the Hispanic concept of *machismo* with its stress on male assertiveness.

The mother's and the patient's own perception of his illness were influenced by Puerto Rican cultural ideology. Thus, Alberto's mother viewed her son's problems as caused by nervous exhaustion (a common explanation for emotional distress according to traditionally-oriented Puerto Ricans), rather than personal or social dysfunction.

> . . . The mother, when visiting the patient in the
> hospital, proved to be an extremely attractive, carefully
> groomed woman of forty-one, with surface warmth and
> affability, who at the same time gave the impression
> of underlying coldness. Her icy manner developed in

discussions of the family, particularly the father's role
in family separation. There was distinct defensiveness
about the patient's illness of which she had no real
understanding. Her English was halting at times only
because of concern about the effect of her statements.
What emerged most clearly was the strong-willed and
rigid drive to be accepted and admired.

While the patient was aware of the seriousness of
his illness, the mother denied any understanding of what
had happened to him, being more concerned with her
expectations for him. In her eyes, the outlook was good
if only one realized he had been a good boy, clean in
childhood and abstemious with women and alcohol in
youth—in contrast to the uncontrolled behavior of his
father. She paraded his successful school career and
willingness to help her financially while working his way
through college as almost official reasons why nothing
serious could be wrong. True, the patient had complained
of being tired from combination of overtime work and
college attendance, but he slept well and possessed a
good appetite. Finally, to clinch it all, there was no
history of mental illness in the family and she was overly
vehement in denials of nervousness or tension in the
patient's entering service. Like most Puerto Ricans, she
preferred to describe mental illness as a simple matter of
bodily malfunction (nerves), possibly brought on by
overwork.

Psychoanalytically oriented therapy that included consideration
of culturally flavored symptomatology and cultural explanations of his
behavior assisted Alberto in overcoming his personal pain.

. . . The patient's future, however, is not bleak.
Disappearance of acute symptoms occurred rapidly with
insight. The family has learned that he cannot continue
to develop insight and alone carry the burdens of a
problematic family in a setting far different from that of
San Juan. His plans to travel are undoubtedly a means
of removing himself further from the strong maternal
control. Hostile and inwardly suspicious, he nevertheless
is able to perceive the blocks to further self-realization.
Alberto has learned to read the mapping of his own

symptoms—the passivity in hypochondriacal complaints, the earlier lack of firm identification, and the long-buried resentments and hostilities. With good intelligence, verbal facility, and growing insight into a traumatic past, Alberto is catching up with the half lost years.

DETERMINING THE EXTENT OF MALADJUSTMENT

Not only do symptoms vary between Hispanics and clients of other ethnicities, but also perceived symptomatology may differ between Spanish-speaking and English-speaking Hispanics. For example, Mexican-American and Anglo residents of Los Angeles were interviewed about eight vignettes describing persons suffering from psychiatric disorders. The vignettes described cases of a paranoid man, a suicidal woman, a delinquent teenage boy, and a teenage girl suffering an acute schizophrenic reaction. The Mexican Americans who preferred to be interviewed in Spanish agreed with the English-speaking Mexican-American respondents on about 75% of the items. On the other 25% of the items, the Spanish speakers perceived religion as important in their lives, labeled serious problems more often as "nervous conditions," tolerated delinquency less, and believed with greater frequency that mental illness was inherited than did the English speakers (Edgerton & Karno, 1971). Thus, we may conclude that Hispanics will respond differently to surveys concerning their emotional problems depending on their cultural and linguistic backgrounds. However, in addition to variance in symptomatology, this response variation may also indicate different language sets concerning socially desirable responses (Dohrenwend, 1966).

Another difficulty in analyzing the determinants of maladjustment among Hispanics is that poverty compounds cultural variation in symptomatology. Low socioeconomic status has been correlated with high frequency of mental illness in many studies investigating Anglo, Black, and Hispanic groups (Dohrenwend, 1966; Dohrenwend & Dohrenwend, 1969; Fabrega, Swartz, & Wallace, 1968; Malzberg, 1965). It is unclear whether social factors associated with poverty catalyze emotional illness (the "social-stress" model) or whether those who experience emotional problems tend to drift downward occupationally so that they are overrepresented in poverty milieus (the "social-selection" model). Thus, exactly how poverty interacts with maladjustment is not clear, but it is safe to assert that the poverty experienced by many Hispanics may be associated with a high frequency of emotional distress.

Despite the influence of poverty and varied cultural definitions of maladjustment, researchers have attempted to specify the degree of psychological distress among Hispanics. Several researchers report higher severity and frequency of emotional problems among Hispanics than among Anglos. When experimenters reviewed patients' records from all Texas psychiatric hospitals in 1970, more severe pathology was noted among Mexican Americans than among Anglos, even when education, marital status, and a host of other variables were controlled (Porknoy & Overall, 1970). A higher rate of first admissions in New York City psychiatric hospitals was noted among Puerto Ricans than among Anglos (Malzberg, 1956, 1965). In contrast, several studies report relatively low rates of emotional disturbance among Hispanics. One investigator surveyed records of all Anglos, Blacks, and Mexican Americans seeking psychiatric treatment in public institutions in Texas during 1951 and 1952. Anglos sought help most frequently, and Mexican Americans least frequently (Jaco, 1957, 1959). When a 22-item scale that screened for emotional disorders was administered to 1441 Anglos, Blacks, and Mexican Americans stratified on age and occupational level, Blacks and Mexican Americans revealed fewer pathological responses than Anglos (Antunes, Gordon, Gaitz, & Scott, 1974). Finally, in a Texas psychiatric hospital serving a Mexican-American catchment area, Anglos, Blacks, and Mexican Americans matched for age, sex, previous hospitalization, socioeconomic level, education, and IQ were rated on a brief psychiatric-disturbance scale, a nursing-observation scale, and the Holtzman inkblot projective test. Symptomatology was similar across all the groups. Hispanics did not display more severe pathology than Anglos or Blacks (Fabrega et al., 1968).

Considering the variation in these frequency studies, firm conclusions cannot be drawn concerning the exact frequency of maladjustment among Hispanics. Unmeasured intervening factors may explain some discrepancies in results. Some studies measured number of admissions to psychiatric hospitals, and others focused on severity of illness. Possibly, the frequency of disturbance differs across Mexican American, Puerto Rican, and other Hispanic groups; and subgroup differences have not been systematically measured. At this point, we can conclude only that emotional problems do exist in significant proportions among Hispanics; the exact frequency in relationship to Anglos and other minority groups has yet to be determined.

Emotional problems among Hispanics can be classified in different ways. One functional way is to categorize disorders according to the themes of personal conflict. It is also functional to scan the demographic variables, such as age and sex, that are associated with particular frequencies and syndromes of emotional distress. Still another way is to categorize the emotional problems of Hispanics according to the classification system established by the American Psychiatric Association and contained in the Diagnostic and Statistical Manual No. II (American Psychiatric Association, 1968). Since each of these approaches highlights points for therapeutic intervention, we will now consider each approach in detail.

THEMES OF PERSONAL CONFLICT

Economics

A common theme in the complaints of Hispanic clients is economic distress. In New York City, female and male Anglo, Puerto Rican, and Black psychiatric inpatients responded to a scale concerning needs they felt were unfulfilled. Economic complaints were most common among the young patients of all ethnicities and the recent Puerto Rican immigrants of all ages (Fitzgibbons, Cutler, & Cohen, 1971). The responses to a social-readjustment scale (which listed 43 significant life events, such as death of a spouse, divorce, or marriage) of Mexican Americans and Blacks were compared to the responses of middle-class Anglos. Mexican Americans perceived items related to economics as greater stressors than Anglos and Blacks did (Komaroff, Masuda, & Holmes, 1968). It is not surprising that the lower-class Hispanics expressed more economic concern than middle-class Anglos. It is also interesting that economic distress was higher among Hispanics than among Blacks of similar economic standing. A study of Puerto Rican and Black clients to a storefront center in the Bronx, New York City, yielded similar information about the differential effects of economic distress on these two groups (Lehmann, 1970). Puerto Rican clients went to the center with basic concerns about finances (mean annual income $2942) and family, whereas the Black clients' major concerns focused on employment (mean annual income $3145) and housing. But, as Lehmann (1970) states, the center was better able to assist Puerto Rican clients with their family and finance problems (often by helping them with their legitimate welfare claims) than the Black clients with their employment and housing problems. Consequently, Blacks were more likely to make a single visit, while Puerto Ricans made multiple visits to the center. Therapists working in mixed ethnic communities must be attentive to their clients' economic concerns and recognize the differential effects that these concerns have on their clients. The case of a Cuban woman illustrates how advice about economic rights combined with supportive therapy assisted her in minimizing her psychological complaints.

THE CASE OF A CUBAN WOMAN.[2] A. S., a 58-year-old, single Cuban woman, was referred by the medical clinic because they found no cause for her acute back pain. Two weeks before coming into the clinic, she had been notified by the Department of Social Security Benefits that she had exhausted her funds and was no longer entitled to benefits. She became depressed and agitated. Sleep and appetite were disturbed, and she complained of headaches and strange noises in her ears. For many years she had had asthmatic attacks, which were treated with Decadron. The patient was living with her 48-year-old unmarried sister in an unheated apartment infested with rats and roaches, and they did not mingle with others.

In the early group sessions, she was angry; angry with the Welfare Department for not supporting her, angry with the Latin population in New York for tolerating their substandard living conditions, and angry with the others in the group for not helping her. She met any advice from the others with contempt; when they talked about their own problems, she ridiculed them. It took the therapist several sessions to get her to see her own contribution to her isolation. Focusing on her behavior in the group, he showed her that her haughty attitude antagonized people. The whole group tried to convince her that they were not looking for faults in her but wanted to help her.

Slowly she began to understand that her way of behaving played a part in creating her problems. On their suggestion, she enlisted the help of the Union supervisor and succeeded in getting welfare assistance. She joined a Cuban club and made friends. She became more and more involved in the problems of the other group members and took great satisfaction, for instance,

[2]From "Brief Group Therapy to Facilitate Utilization of Mental Health Services by Spanish-Speaking Patients," by W. C. Normand, J. Iglesias, and S. Payn, *American Journal of Orthopsychiatry*, 1974, *44*, 37–42. Copyright 1974 by the American Orthopsychiatric Association. Reprinted by permission.

in helping one of them find an apartment. The more she became interested in other people, the more confident she was about dealing with her own affairs. She felt satisfied, ate and slept well, and had no more physical complaints. She started taking classes in English, and enrolled in training as a sewing machine operator.

Throughout the group program, the patient received amitriptyline (Elavil). On completion of the group experience, she was referred to the Mental Health Clinic for further psychotherapy.

This case demonstrates an interaction between poverty and maladjustment. As the therapist assisted the woman in dealing with her personal frustrations, she became better equipped psychologically to learn a trade and deal with the welfare agency, so that she could become economically independent. Further, her improved economic outlook fostered increased self-assurance and personal adjustment.

Marginality

A second common theme among Hispanics is concern about acculturation and/or dual cultural membership. Social theorists have long recognized that psychological stress is associated with coexistence in two cultures (Wallace, 1970). Stonequist (1937) identified the "marginal" person as one whose bicultural membership retards integration of ethnic and personal identity. Often, marginality is associated with poor communication skills, poverty, and seasonal migration for work, making personal adjustment even more difficult. It is posited that, as acculturation increases among Hispanics, they will experience increasing personal stress associated with the imposed cultural differences (Ruiz, Padilla, & Alvarez, 1978).

A number of studies attest to the adjustment difficulties associated with marginality. In one study, the value orientations of Mexican-American psychiatric outpatients were compared to matched nonpatients. A Mexican-American interviewer presented stories about social conflicts and asked these subjects to select one of several resolutions based on either traditional or nontraditional attitudes. The patient group was more apt to adopt a mixed orientation than the nonpatient group. About 50% of the nonpatients accepted mixed values, whereas 78% of the patients expressed a mixed cultural orientation (Fabrega & Wallace, 1968). A study conducted with Mexican-American high school subjects illuminates personal stress associated with acculturation. When subjects responded to an attitude scale of Mexican-American values and to an adjustment scale, those expressing "rebel" attitudes (rejecting their heritage) experienced more psychosomatic symptomatology, personal guilt, and self-derogation than those expressing traditional values. For many of the "rebels," their fathers no longer represented their ideal of manhood. The rebels believed that they must leave home to avoid conflict, but they felt guilty about rejecting their families and their ancestry (Ramirez, 1969). A study that involved Puerto Rican neurotics and matched non-neurotics revealed that the non-neurotics were more accepting of traditional Hispanic beliefs than the neurotics on responses to an adjective checklist (Maldonado-Sierra, Trent, & Fernandez-Marina, 1960). Similarly, in a Texas town, a therapist concluded from his clinical records that Mexican Americans adopting Anglo values were more likely to suffer from anxiety, fear, guilt, and somatic problems than were unacculturated Mexican Americans (Madsen, 1969).

In contrast to the personal distress that appears to be associated with marginality, several studies indicate that maintenance of Hispanic values is associated with strong coping abilities. When married Puerto Rican males of different middle-class occupations were interviewed, most mentioned a close relationship with the Puerto Rican community, pride in Puerto Rican identity, and a desire to instill Puerto Rican values in their children (Kelly, 1971). When Mexican-American high school students in Texas were tested concerning occupational aspiration, subjects with strong ethnic identity, as exemplified by their frequent use of Spanish, expressed high occupation aspirations (Kuvlesky & Pattela, 1971).

In only a few studies is the process of acculturation accompanied by increased adjustment. In one such study, Hispanic females between the ages of 18 and 55 responded to a verbal interview and two personality questionnaires. Those low on acculturation ranked higher on depression and obsessive-compulsive indexes (Torres-Matrullo, 1974). A second study revealed no correlation between acculturation and adjustment. When Mexican Americans randomly selected from various grade levels were tested with an acculturation index, a personality questionnaire, and an achievement test, self-concept did not correlate with level of acculturation (Pruneda, 1973). Clearly, more research is needed on the relationship between acculturation and possible psychological distress.

To give the pluralistic therapist some idea of the type of problem that acculturation may produce, let's examine the case of a Puerto Rican child who feels "tied in knots" as he watches his mother interact with members of the majority group.

THE CASE OF RICARDO.[3] Consider the more complex situation of Ricardo, a four-and-a-half-year-old who would not talk and who constantly tied and would not unfasten the female dolls in the school's doll corner and the psychologist's office. His mother had been recruited as a teacher's aide into a program to teach youngsters to become bilingual. The program was developed to enable children to make an easier transition into English, bridging the gap between school and family. The therapist accidentally discovered that the mother worked in the same school that the son attended, and occasionally worked in the same classroom.

What was the mother's experience in that classroom? She was supposed to help the children use the toilet, to change sneakers, and to carry out errands for the teacher. Discouraged from engaging the children in anything resembling teaching, she angrily felt like a maid. She was vocal about it at the dinner table, and the child could observe her in the classroom where she felt derogated by the teacher. The two adult dolls that could not be unfastened were his mother and this woman. The child saw them as tied together. He was not only mirroring the reality of the situation, but had also sensed his mother's strain and distance from this woman and may have wanted to see a genuinely friendly tie between them. When his mother dropped the school job, the child became more able to cope with the school situation and unfastened his dolls. He began talking, although haltingly and with a stutter.

This child was sensitive to a situation which demeaned his mother, and his symptoms revealed "offended dignity." He would not talk in a situation which deprecated his mother. But our story does not end there. The fact that the mother felt like a slave tied to the teacher required some attempt to work with the classroom and staff hierarchy. Yet when faced with this example, the principal said, "Well, my teachers wouldn't

[3]From "Home-School Conflict and the Puerto Rican Child," by B. Montalvo, *Social Casework*, 1974, *55*, 100–110. Copyright 1974 by the Family Service Association of America. Reprinted by permission.

have it; the aides are supposed to be aides and teachers are supposed to be teachers." At face value, this looks like a perfectly reasonable plea for job differences and professionalism in the school, but it reveals, as well, the process through which we may put down a culture precisely through a program which tries to respect it. Here again, in the name of good intentions, in a bilingual program meant to help the Puerto Rican mother and child, we have systematically undermined the culture.

Ricardo's school problems began as he observed how his mother was treated in her work situation and felt her discontent. His problems were enflamed further because he wanted to please his teacher, which caused a conflict between his mother's traditional Hispanic values and those of the school, which sought to acculturate students into the broader "American" culture. The result of this conflict was a child who had difficulty coping with his school environment. Montalvo (1973) continues by stating that:

The fact that an incident of this type can happen to a young child makes this situation particularly alarming. The child is caught in problems when he is most vulnerable, when he is testing whether the relationship style that made him safe at home will also yield safety outside. For many Puerto Rican children this process alone entails difficulties . . . Their relationship style calls for them to hover around the teacher, listening, watching, asking, with a search and research system that often hinges on a checking orientation, by asking the adult, because this is a required way to be respectful and to assemble a reliable knowledge. In school, this is often considered bad behavior, a sign of dependency that, with the best of intentions, must be modified. The gap between developmental expectations at home and at school often produces a stressful, dislocating situation for these children. Some of them solve the problem by intensifying their hovering around the teacher, only meeting further rejection. Going against their culture, which tends to call on them to check frequently with the adult, the school unwittingly heightens their conflict, demanding, from the moment they enter school, what to them is premature independence.

The profound effects of the marginality created in Hispanic children by school are even more apparent in our next case. Here we will quote from the autobiographical material of Richard Rodriguez (1974-75, pp. 15–21). The content of the autobiography is self-explanatory and serves nicely to highlight our discussion of marginality.

> *THE CASE OF RICHARD RODRIGUEZ.*[4] . . . I am the son of Mexican-American parents, who speak a blend of Spanish and English, but who read neither language easily. I am about to receive a Ph.D. in English Renaissance literature. What sort of life—what tensions feelings, conflicts—connects these two sentences? I look back and remember my life from the time I was seven or eight years old as one of constant movement away from a Spanish-speaking folk culture toward the world of the English-language classroom. As the years passed, I felt myself becoming less like my parents and less comfortable with the assumption of visiting relatives that I was still the Spanish-speaking child they remembered. By the time I began college, visits home became suffused with silent embarrassment: there seemed so little to share, however strong the ties of our affection. My parents would tell me what happened in their lives or in the lives of relatives; I would respond with news of my own. Polite questions would follow. Our conversations came to seem more like interviews.
>
> . . . Coming from a home in which mostly Spanish was spoken, for example, I had to decide to forget Spanish when I began my education. To succeed in the classroom, I needed psychologically to sever my ties with Spanish. Spanish represented an alternate culture as well as another language—and the basis of my deepest sense of relationship to my family. Although I recently taught myself to read Spanish, the language that I see on the printed page is not quite the language that I heard in my youth. That other Spanish, the spoken Spanish of

[4]From "Going Home Again," by R. Rodriguez, *The American Scholar*, Winter 1974-75, *44*(1), 15–28. Copyright © 1974 by the United Chapters of Phi Beta Kappa. Reprinted by permission.

my family, I remember with nostalgia and guilt: guilt because I cannot explain to my aunts and uncles why I do not answer their questions any longer in their own idiomatic language. Nor was I able to explain to teachers in graduate school who regularly expected me to read and speak Spanish with ease, why my very ability to reach graduate school as a student of English literature in the first place required me to loosen my attachments to a spoken language I spoke years earlier. Yet, having lost the ability to speak Spanish, I never forgot it so totally that I could not understand it. Hearing Spanish spoken on the street reminded me of the community I once felt a part of, and still cared deeply about. I never forgot Spanish so thoroughly, in other words, as to move outside the range of its nostalgic pull.

Such moments of guilt and nostalgia were, however, just that—momentary. They punctuated the history of my otherwise successful progress from *barrio* to classroom. Perhaps they even encouraged it. Whenever I felt my determination to succeed wavering, I tightened my hold on the conventions of academic life.

Spanish was one aspect of the problem, my parents another. They could raise deeper, more persistent doubts. They offered encouragement to my brothers and me in our work, but they also spoke, only half jokingly, about the way education was putting "big ideas" into our heads. When we would come home, for example, and challenge assumptions we earlier believed, they would be forced to defend their beliefs (which, given our new verbal skills, they did increasingly less well) or, more frequently, to submit to our logic with the disclaimer, "It's what we were taught in our time to believe . . . " More important, after we began to leave home for college, they voiced regret about how "changed" we had become, how much further away from one another we had grown. They partly yearned for a return to the time before education assumed their children's primary loyalty. This yearning was renewed each time they saw their nieces and nephews (none of whom continued their education beyond high school, all of whom continued to speak fluent Spanish) living according to the conventions and assumptions of their parents' culture. If I was

already troubled by the time I graduated from high
school by that refrain of congratulations ("Your parents
must be so proud . . . "), I realize now how much more
difficult and complicated was my progress into academic
life for my parents, as they saw the cultural foundation
of their family erode, than it was for me . . .

In recent years the problem of marginality, as described by Richard
Rodriguez, has been compounded by another issue. This issue has to do
with the role of minority students in institutions of higher education and
the fact that often students who have had to surrender cultural and
linguistic ties with their community are viewed by university officials as
representatives of this same community. Added to this conflict is the
self-doubt created in many Hispanic students that their achievements are
due solely to compliance with affirmative-action policies by institutions
of higher education rather than to their own intellectual ability. In his
autobiographical sketch Rodriguez makes this point exquisitely.

One college admissions officer assured me one day
that he recognized my importance to his school precisely
as deriving from the fact that, after graduation, I
would surely be "going back to [my] community." More
recently, teachers have urged me not to trouble over the
fact that I am not "representative" of my culture,
assuring me that I can serve as a "model" for those still
in the *barrio* working toward academic careers. This is
the line that I hear, too, when being interviewed for
a faculty position. The interviewer almost invariably
assumes that, because I am racially a Mexican-American,
I can serve as a special counselor to minority students.
The expectation is that I still retain the capacity for
intimacy with "my people."
This new way of thinking about the possible uses of
education is what has made the entrance of minority
students into higher education so dramatic. When the
minority group student was accepted into the academy,
he came—in everyone's mind—as part of a "group."
When I began college, I barely attracted attention except
perhaps as a slightly exotic ("Are you from India?")
brown-skinned student; by the time I graduated, my
presence was annually noted by, among others, the
college public relations office as "one of the fifty-two

students with Spanish surnames enrolled this year." By having his presence announced to the campus in this way, the minority student was unlike any other scholarship boy the campus had seen before. The minority group student now dramatized more publicly, if also in new ways, the issues of cultural dislocation that education forces, issues that are not solely racial in origin. When Richard Rodriguez *became* a Chicano, the dilemmas he earlier had as a scholarship boy were complicated but not decisively altered by the fact that he had assumed a group identity.

The assurance I heard that, somehow, I was being useful to my community by being a student was gratefully believed, because it gave me a way of dealing with the guilt and cynicism that each year came my way along with the scholarships, grants, and, lately, job offers from schools which a few years earlier would have refused me admission as a student. Each year, in fact, it became harder to believe that my success had anything to do with my intellectual performance, and harder to resist the conclusion that it was due to my minority group status. When I drove to the airport, on my way to London as a Fulbright Fellow last year, leaving behind cousins who were already hopelessly burdened by financial insecurity and dead-end jobs, momentary guilt could be relieved by the thought that somehow my trip was beneficial to other persons than myself. But, of course, if the thought was a way of dealing with the guilt, it was also a reason for the guilt. Sitting in a university library, I would notice a janitor of my race and grow uneasy; I was, I knew, in a rough way a beneficiary of his condition. Guilt was accompanied by cynicism. The most dazzlingly talented minority students I know today refuse to believe that their success is wholly based on their own talent, or even that when they speak in a classroom anyone hears them as anything but the voice of their minority group. It is scarcely surprising, then, though initially it probably seemed puzzling, that so many of the angriest voices on the campus against the injustices of racism came from those not visibly its primary victims.

In concluding this case, it is important to emphasize that, although Rodriguez himself does not express any serious psychological problems as a consequence of his minority status, he is the exception. Many Hispanic students caught in similar situations require counseling (Ruiz, Casas, & Padilla, 1977). In counseling with students, the pluralistic therapist must be alert to possible emotional problems associated with acculturation and marginality. In cases where acculturation stress is suspected, it may be helpful to encourage the client to define clearly values and roles with family, friends, and members of the dominant culture. The therapist may also need to know how the family reacts to the client and work with them to identify and resolve points of conflict. The client and the family may both need assistance in understanding the cultural gulf that has been created between them. Moreover, clients may require special help in recognizing that they still possess the skills necessary to interact meaningfully with family, friends, and the Hispanic community at large.

Skin Color

Another significant concern among Hispanics is skin color. Skin color is an especially emotionally laden subject among Puerto Ricans. Because their ancestors intermarried with Black slaves, many Puerto Ricans exhibit some Negroid characteristics, including dark skin color. In Puerto Rico, racial prejudice exists but not to the degree demonstrated in the mainland United States. In Puerto Rico, the primary source of identification is class, not color. On the mainland, it has been historically true that, if one possesses any noticeable trace of Negro ancestry, one is considered to be Black. This is not so in Puerto Rico, where the full range of skin coloration is observed and where distinctions in genetic makeup are not used to assign a person an inferior social position. On the mainland, even light-skinned Puerto Ricans are considered Black and discriminated against (Longres, 1974). This difference in evaluation of Puerto Ricans' skin color by islanders and mainlanders can precipitate personal distress, as described by Longres:[5]

> The writer was acquainted with a Puerto Rican student who was extremely active in campus and community politics. To many persons, the student was considered a radical militant. He was of medium to somewhat

[5]This and all other quotations from this source are from "Racism and its Effects on Puerto Rican Continentals," by J. F. Longres, Jr., *Social Casework*, February 1974, *55*, 67–75. Copyright 1974 by the Family Service Association of America. Reprinted by permission.

dark complexion, but with straight hair and relatively straight features. In no way did the student appear Negroid.

One night at a community function, I had the opportunity to meet his parents. However, before introducing me, the student nervously described his parents as white and added, "Most people think that because I'm dark my parents are mulatto." Later the student questioned me twice regarding my observations about his parents' racial ancestry; the student wanted to know if I thought they looked Black. Regardless of whether the student was of mixed racial ancestry, the fact that it was necessary for him to raise the issue of race in its American connotation was an indication of the student's own racial insecurity.

When a very light-skinned Puerto Rican migrates from the island to the mainland United States, his or her acculturation may be relatively easy, as in the following example (Longres, 1974):

> Once while teaching a course on minority groups during a summer session at a western university, the writer received a term paper from a young student who perhaps for the first time was admitting to anyone outside her immediate relatives that she was Puerto Rican. Her grandparents had migrated to Hawaii where they lived and raised their children in the small but downtrodden Puerto Rican community in Hawaii. The student's mother was Puerto Rican, but her father was not. She had lived her early life in Hawaii, but had been living on the continent for a number of years. In the term paper, she described an experience that took place on the continent:
>
> "In a game once, with my friends, we were telling what national background we derived from. Everyone was Scotch, German, French, or English. When it came my turn, I had a variety to pick from—Spanish, Indian, black and Scotch. So I said them all, emphasizing Indian because it was exciting and leaving off black because I didn't want to be ostracized. I left off black despite my mother's instruction to be proud of my heritage."
>
> Since I had not met the student, I wrote a note asking her to meet with me so that we might discuss our common backgrounds. The girl did come to see me—shy and small, and blonde and blue-eyed.

Dark-skinned Puerto Ricans who migrate to the mainland are especially susceptible to prejudice, as suggested above. On some occasions, these Hispanics react to the prejudice through rejection of family members. This extract is about a woman who has become defensive about her skin color after moving to the mainland (Longres, 1974):

> During a conversation with a Puerto Rican associate, I was told of a Puerto Rican secretary whose father was very light, but whose mother **"tenía su rajita"** (was racially mixed). The secretary was described as very

attractive but somewhat dark and with slightly kinky hair. Shortly after her arrival in the United States, she developed a deep inferiority complex concerning her racial identity: her behavior in the office became openly hostile when her white American boss married a Black American girl. "I can not understand why such an attractive man would marry such a woman." Of even greater consequence, she became hostile toward her mother and finally rejected her altogether.

Although total rejection of family members because of skin coloration is rare, therapists should be aware that it can occur. More common among dark-skinned Puerto Ricans are feelings of inferiority and alienation, and, interestingly, more dark-skinned than light-skinned Puerto Ricans return to the island (Christensen, 1975), again suggesting the powerful effects of mainland majority-group prejudice against dark skin color (Galli, 1975). It is possible for concern about skin color to escalate so greatly when a Puerto Rican migrates to the mainland that it brings on psychosocial problems that were previously nonexistent. In the case of a young Puerto Rican woman, the prejudice against dark skin on the mainland catalyzed family upheaval, a divorce, and the near abandonment of a child.

THE CASE OF A YOUNG PUERTO RICAN WOMAN.[6] A young Puerto Rican woman approached a public welfare agency with the desire to place her nineteen-month-old daughter in a foster home. She told the worker that she was alone in the United States with little means of support for herself and the child. She had obtained a factory job and felt that she would no longer have the time to raise her child properly. The woman was married, but she stated that her husband had deserted her and that she expected to get a divorce.

Through the course of several interviews, a quite different account of her difficulties emerged. Her migration to the United States had been encouraged by her brother and sister, both of whom had migrated much earlier and had achieved a modicum of economic success. Just before she migrated, she had married, but her brother and sister did not learn of the marriage until

[6]From "Racism and its Effects on Puerto Rican Continentals," by J. F. Longres, Jr., *Social Casework*, February 1974, *55*, 67–75. Copyright 1974 by the Family Service Association of America. Reprinted by permission.

after her arrival in the United States, when she could not hide her pregnancy. Her husband did not arrive until two months later because he stayed behind to take care of business matters.

His eventual arrival, rather than being a happy occasion, caused the problems which led to the dissolution of the marriage and the desire to place the child in foster care. The husband was very dark, and although she had realized that to marry him was somewhat of a step down even in Puerto Rico, there had been no great concern expressed by the rest of the family in Puerto Rico. Therefore, she had not anticipated the reactions of her brother and sister in the United States.

The brother and sister were vehemently opposed to the marriage. They claimed to have heard stories from their relatives in Puerto Rico that the husband was worthless and lazy and was using their sister to come to the United States and be supported by her. The real issue, of course, was the racial background of their new brother-in-law.

Upon their arrival in the United States, the brother and sister had learned quickly to take full advantage of their medium complexion and straight hair. They accepted the American definition of race and identified themselves strongly as white. Having a "Negro" brother-in-law awakened fears that they might also be considered Black, and they felt that their economic success and upward mobility in the United States would be jeopardized by his presence. Because of these feelings, they refused to visit their sister or to allow the sister to bring her husband to their homes. When they did see the sister, they spoke disparagingly of the husband. Furthermore, after the birth, they refused to act as godparents to the baby, thus, in essence, denying baptism to the child. It was not until the child was six that she was baptized.

The young woman, becoming aware of the advantages of being white in the United States, was susceptible to the stories told by her brother and sister . . . so intensely that she had left her husband and was now on the verge of rejecting their child.

The increase in ethnic identification among minority groups in the United States in the last ten years or so has ameliorated feelings of inferiority associated with dark skin (Brand, Ruiz, & Padilla, 1974). However, when prejudice and discrimination are evident and directed at dark-skinned individuals, significant personal despair can be provoked, as we have shown above. Before concluding this discussion, it should be noted that, although all the cases highlighted in this section on skin color were about Puerto Rican people, problems involving skin color are shared by all Hispanic groups. A large proportion of the Mexican-American population are dark skinned, for example, and share many of the same feelings of inferiority and/or alienation felt by Puerto Ricans. Although the factor of skin coloration is often discussed among Mexican Americans, there is as yet little research on the psychological effects of dark skin on Mexican Americans and other Hispanic people.

DEMOGRAPHIC VARIABLES

In the most important study to appear comparing Hispanics, Blacks, and majority-group members on admission rates to state and county mental hospitals, Bachrach (1975) has shown that Hispanics have lower admission rates than do the other groups. Among Hispanics as among other ethnic groups, males have higher admission rates than females. Discrepancy by sex reflects the large number of Hispanic males admitted for treatment of drug addiction. Perhaps Hispanic males are particularly subject to the stresses associated with living in two cultures. The male, more than the female, may attempt to maintain historic and cultural values and thus be more susceptible to marginality. Hispanic females, on the other hand, may interact less with the dominant culture or have more coping ability, thereby reducing stress. Because of the possible marginal status, the young Hispanic male may be more susceptible to emotional distress than young adult females (Bachrach, 1975).

The lowest admission rate for each ethnic group occurred among married persons, with somewhat higher rates for widowed persons and substantially higher rates for never-married persons and especially for separated and divorced persons. Among Hispanics the admission rate for separated/divorced persons (1056.3 for males and 321.5 for females per 100,000 population) was substantially greater than for married persons (148.2 for males and 74.3 for females per 100,000 population). Among Anglos the rate of admission for separated/divorced persons is even higher than among Hispanics when compared with married persons. By contrast, the rates for Black separated/divorced persons were closer to those for Anglos than those for Hispanics, with more separated/divorced individuals than marrieds requiring hospitalization. For many Hispanics, marriage is associated with emotional stability, and, although divorced or widowed status is an inducer of stress among Hispanics, it is less so than among Anglos or Blacks.

More Hispanics than Anglos and Blacks are admitted to county and state mental hospitals after the age of 65. For Hispanics, 278 out of 100,000 admissions are patients older than 65. Among Anglos, 127 per 100,000 of general admissions are elderly patients (Bachrach, 1975). This higher rate of admission for the Hispanic aged is important because it suggests that this population has therapeutic needs that have gone unrecognized until now. Our review of relevant literature failed to uncover many references to emotional problems among the elderly. Moreover, the common belief among Hispanics and non-Hispanics is that the Hispanic aged are better cared for than the non-Hispanic elderly because of the role of the extended family in serving as a support system for family members, but this belief may be fallacious. It is also important to note that the higher admission could be reflective of organicity; quite possibly poverty and substandard living conditions contribute to organic psychosis.

Pluralistic therapy for Hispanics requires recognition of special groups—widowed persons, divorced persons, young males, and the aged. More research is needed to determine the psychosocial factors contributing to adjustment difficulties within these demographic groups. Further research could assist in designing preventive mental-health programs for groups that are most vulnerable to stress.

PSYCHIATRIC NOMENCLATURE

We have looked at two ways of classifying maladjustment syndromes, by themes of personal conflict and by demographic variables. The third and final way to classify maladjustment that we will consider is the use of standard psychiatric nomenclature. Our review of themes of personal conflict and demographic variables has placed emphasis on interpersonal and social forces related to maladjustment. This review of the psychiatric schema places more emphasis on intrapersonal sources of maladjustment.

Therapists disagree about the relative value of psychiatric nomenclature. In addition to criticisms about its general usefulness, pluralistically oriented professionals argue that such nomenclature does not recognize cultural variation and symptomatology. However, we believe that when used appropriately psychiatric nomenclature can be helpful in planning treatment programs for the very disturbed. In the following sections we will discuss the special factors pluralistic therapists must consider when diagnosing ethnic-minority clients. We will discuss syndromes that are ethnic specific and demonstrate that the import of some symptoms varies across ethnic groups.

Neurosis

Researchers have been concerned about the relative frequency of neurotic disorders among Hispanics and Anglos. Three studies suggest that Anglos seek therapy for neurotic disorders whereas Hispanics are more likely to seek therapy for psychotic disorders. When Anglo, Black, and Mexican-American hospital patients (matched for age, sex, previous hospitalization, socioeconomic level, education, and IQ) were evaluated according to their responses on a psychiatric-rating scale, a nurse-observation scale, and the Holtzman inkblot test, Mexican Americans appeared somewhat more regressed than Anglos and Blacks (Fabrega et al., 1968). A review of intake records at a mental-health center in which the Mexican-American, Anglo, and Black patients were proportionate in number to the local population revealed more neurotic disorders among Anglos and more schizophrenic and thought disorders among Mexican Americans (Heiman & Kahn, 1977). Similar results were obtained from patient records of Mexican-American and Anglo children randomly selected from three child-guidance clinics. The Anglo children displayed the following neurotic symptomatology: anxiety, nail biting, nervousness, enuresis, poor social relationships, and lack of friends. Symptoms of the Mexican-American children indicated more serious affective disorders: depression, crying spells, alleged suicide attempts, agitation, and psychosomatic disorders. The reviewers of the child-guidance clinic suggest that Hispanics may be more tolerant of psychopathology and seek professional help at a later point of regression; or the Hispanics may find other ways of assisting the neurotic (through the help of a physician, a community ombudsman, or a folk healer) besides employing traditional psychotherapists (Stoker & Meadow, 1974). A fourth study by Trevino and Bruhn (1977) surveyed the client population of the Laredo, Texas, community-mental-health center. The results indicated that the incidence of neurotic disturbances among Hispanics was higher than expected, whereas the incidence of neurosis among Anglos was lower than expected.

There is a special neurotic syndrome experienced by some Puerto Ricans called **ataque.** An *ataque,* characterized by psychomotor seizures, is somewhat similar to a hysterical conversion reaction. The individual cries or screams, drops to the ground, and flails the extremities. The *ataque* will last from five to ten minutes (Fernandez-Marina, 1961; Grace, 1959). Garrison (1977, p. 383) describes an *ataque* as follows:

> One hot Friday afternoon in July . . . an attractive 39-year-old, married Puerto Rican woman was sitting at her bench in a handbag factory in New York's garment district, where she had worked for four years. Suddenly, to the surprise of those around her, she began to scream and tear her clothes from her chest. She ran to the window, apparently trying to throw herself through it. When restrained, she fell to the floor in an unconscious or semiconscious state, with her whole body twitching.

In the case of María, we see another example of *ataque.* María's attempts to function in both the Anglo and Hispanic cultures created maladjustment that expressed itself as *ataque.*

THE CASE OF MARÍA.[7] María was a thirteen-year-old with *sereta* or standing-out hair. Her appearance was as drab as the colors of her loose, long dresses which hung below her knees and made her good figure disappear. She was quite bright, a good student, and a good singer, and she played guitar by ear.

When the English teacher recruited her for a small drama, María had an understandably good time rehearsing her singing at home. But she seemed distressed when the teacher insisted that for her part in the play she wear lipstick, tidy her hair a bit, and wear a tighter, more revealing dress, perhaps above her knees.

Suspecting that parental disapproval lay behind María's tense reaction and having observed María being teased about her "nest" of hair, the teacher decided to reach out and visit the girl's parents. She found herself coldly treated. Her efforts to explain to the parents

[7]From "Home-School Conflict and the Puerto Rican Child," by B. Montalvo, *Social Casework*, 1974, *55*, 100–110. Copyright 1974 by the Family Service Association of America. Reprinted by permission.

the girl's wonderful talent in dramatics did not hit target, although she explained to the parents about the opportunities for María to travel with the English dramatics club to other schools. Even to this the parents were not responsive.

What was the teacher's reaction to this experience? She was, of course, on the side of the child, and she wound up by concluding that Puerto Rican parents have poor motivation for mobilizing the children's potentials, instilling them with a defeatist attitude, and that Puerto Rican parents do not see the value of education.

The next week, three days before the play, the girl suddenly felt ill. She had vomiting spells and a dramatic convulsive *ataque*, and she was rushed to a psychiatrist. He searched for any intrapersonal cues, any fears, angers, or inner conflicts that could explain a clearly nonepileptic seizure. The girl and her alarmed and concerned parents searched and searched but could find no explanation for her sudden illness.

. . . The girl could not join her teacher, the drama group, and the performance. The *ataque* had left her with a hoarse voice and so weak that all she could do was drag herself to church with her family. She had become, meanwhile, more religious and more conscious of her role as a daughter.

Without realizing it, the family members had gone to work on her, intensifying their subtle messages of disapproval immediately after the teacher's visit. The visit had catalyzed the clash, the pulling and counterpulling between school and family. This clash was resolved by the Puerto Rican subculture's reclaiming of one of its members from the school's American subculture.

Sometimes when a Hispanic expresses great anxiety and related symptomatology, a closer analysis reveals the stress to be an appropriate reaction to prejudice and discrimination. For example, if a job promotion is blocked for "intangible" reasons, the Hispanic may logically react with frustration and diffuse anger. A therapist working with Hispanic clients must be cautious not to interpret resistance to prejudice and discrimination as neurosis. As demonstrated by Martinez (1973) below, it is sometimes very difficult to ascertain if symptoms indicative of neurosis in Anglos are representative of the same pathology in Hispanics.

> A commonly encountered person in our clinic is a middle-aged Mexican-American man who breaks down into dependency, over-concern about his health, and depression following some stress. His history usually reveals a life of hard and demeaning work since childhood (and here I mean age five or six), usually in the migrant stream. There was, of course, no time for school, adolescence, young adulthood, or any of the other niceties. So now, in his early thirties or forties, he calls it quits. It is easy to discard the old stereotype of the passive Mexican with unfulfilled dependency needs and see that this man has already put in a lifetime of hard work and that his current response is, in a sense, understandable and adaptive. He has simply retired at a young age. He is now getting even, in his own way, with a society that does not provide its workers enough so that children don't have to work. But is this man "sick"? Do we prescribe chemicals or do we praise and congratulate him? I don't know the answer to these questions.[8]

Hispanics suffer from a range of neurotic symptomatology. When a therapist is confronted with neurotic disorders among Hispanic clients, he or she must sort out the economic and social factors contributing to the person's difficulties as well as the ethnic, familial, and personal factors causing psychological despair. The therapist should be alert for neuroses that are expressed in culturally specific modes, such as *ataque.*

Psychosis

Psychotic disorders constitute the primary diagnosis of Hispanic psychiatric patients. The frequency of schizophrenia among Hispanics is close to that among Anglos. For instance, in a survey of admissions to state and county mental hospitals in 1972, 29% of the Hispanics and 28% of the Anglos admitted with diagnosed as schizophrenic (Bachrach, 1975). A higher rate of schizophrenia was noted in New York City, where 50% of Puerto Ricans hospitalized for emotional problems were diagnosed as schizophrenic (Rendon, 1974).

Several factors may inflate artificially the high rate of schizophrenia among Hispanics. Hallucinations are considered a symptom of psychosis. Yet hearing voices is more culturally sanctioned and thus less pathological among Hispanics (Torrey, 1972). Nevertheless, hallucina-

---

[8]This and all other quotations from this source are from "Community Mental Health and the Chicano Movement," by C. Martinez, *American Journal of Orthopsychiatry*, 1973, *43*(4), 595–601. Copyright © 1973 by the American Orthopsychiatric Association. Reprinted by permission.

tions often are employed as a standard of maladjustment of equal import for Hispanics and individuals of other ethnicities.

Another factor that may inflate statistics for schizophrenic diagnoses is Hispanics' frequent use of dissociation (separation of mental processes so that they become split off from the main personality). Dissociation is a particularly common defense mechanism among Hispanics of Cuban and Puerto Rican extraction (Bustamante, 1968; Fernandez-Marina & Von Echardt, 1960). In most cases, the dissociation in Cubans and Puerto Ricans involves severe repression, but affect and thinking are not highly incompatible. Even though the patient may appear very distraught and unaware of underlying frustrations, it may be inappropriate to label the dissociative behavior as psychotic. The congruency of affect and behavior suggest that the clients are expressing neurotic rather than psychotic symptomatology (Rendon, 1974).

In extreme cases, *ataque,* or the "Puerto Rican Syndrome," has been considered a psychosis. Often, persons suffering from an exaggerated form of the Puerto Rican Syndrome have been raised in pathogenic environments, with weak fathers and schizophrenogenic mothers (mothers who promote disturbed behavior in their children) (Fernandez-Marina & Von Echardt, 1960). In the case that follows, we see an individual who exhibits extreme distortion in thought processes but little derangement in affect.

> *THE CASE OF LUZ.*[9] Luz, a 13-year-old Puerto Rican girl, was admitted because she had a "history of hallucinations." A diagnosis of Schizophrenia was considered upon admission. Luz had been seeing the same tall and faceless woman with long hair, a white dress to the floor, and a bouquet of flowers in her hands, repeatedly come to her for last two years. On one occasion the woman was limping and on that same night Luz's grandmother had a stroke. Lately the woman had told Luz to kill herself. Prior to admission, Luz had been found climbing the fence of a monument in a park, which was interpreted by Luz's friends as suicidal. A few hours

[9]From "Transcultural Aspects of Puerto Rican Mental Illness in New York," by M. Rendon, *International Journal of Social Psychiatry,* 1974,, *20,* 24. Copyright 1974 by Avenue Publishing Company. Reprinted by permission.

earlier Luz had been reprimanded by her mother because she had accepted a gift from a certain boy. Luz's mother had known about Luz's "visions" but they didn't concern her because Luz's grandmother and a female cousin had also seen the same woman. The father himself—the mother had said—had seen "shadows."

Luz was a good, quiet girl at home; the parents were only concerned about her lately because she seemed to be involved with a boy. This boy was said to be a member of a gang and to be related to "Junkies." The parents feared that Luz would "get married" too young (the mother had married Luz's father at the age of 14). To other adolescents in the ward, Luz stated that she was planning to sleep with five boys in order to become a leader in her gang.

Although Luz's symptoms were severe, she did not regress to a hebephrenic state as do a significant proportion of other chronic schizophrenics. Moreover, Luz was able to maintain meaningful social relationships and to respond with appropriate affect. She reacted to stress (the death of her grandmother, disagreements with her parents) with hallucinatory, suicidal thinking, but her broad adjustment remained intact.

Overall adjustment and lack of regression suggest that such cases of the Puerto Rican Syndrome may be more appropriately considered a severe neurotic disorder than a psychotic disorder. Hysterical attacks can function as a basic ego defense against psychotic breaks or as limits to extreme regression or total disorganization of the ego. The Puerto Rican Syndrome illustrates the culturally specific nature of severe emotional pathology among Hispanics. The controversy that surrounds this disorder confirms the importance of evaluating bizarre behavior in terms of the cultural milieu. The adaptive function of the behavior within the environment should be ruled out before a person is considered psychotic.

Affective disorders and psychotic depression are as common among Hispanics as among Anglos but are more common among Hispanics than among Blacks. One severe and acute depressive reaction among Puerto Ricans is called "suicidal fit." In a state of intense emotional excitement, the person attempts suicide. The suicidal fit is generally precipitated by disrupted interpersonal relationships. When female and male Puerto Ricans were interviewed about the immediate cause of their suicidal fit, 43% of the females cited a fight with a lover, 22% of the females described a fight with their parents, and 78% of the males reported a disturbance with a wife or girlfriend (Trautman, 1961). The suicide of actor/comedian Freddie Prinze fits the pattern of the Puerto Rican suicidal fit. Prinze had been depressed about the recent breakdown of his marriage and shot himself suddenly in front of his manager. Perhaps Freddie Prinze was also a victim of culture shock. He moved from New York City's Puerto Rican ghetto, a rough but culturally intact environment, to international acclaim and an amorphous cultural setting, while still in his teens. Perhaps he had not yet been able to find personal meaning in his new environment and way of life.

Personality Disorders

Personality disorders account for fewer admissions to state and county mental hospitals among Hispanics (6.2 per 100,000) than among Anglos (13.8 per 100,000) or Blacks (23.4 per 100,000). This low frequency of personality disorders is particularly interesting because such disorders are characteristic of young adults and a disproportionate number of Hispanic psychiatric clients are males between the ages of 14 and 24. A large number of commitments of Hispanic youth are for drug addiction rather than for asocial behavior (Bachrach, 1975). In fact, the data indicate that Hispanics are hospitalized less often for antisocial behavior than are Anglos. Such statistics contradict stereotypes about Hispanics that describe them as antisocial and delinquent.

Addiction

Drug addiction is the second most common reason for psychiatric hospitalization of Hispanics. About 17% of Hispanic admissions to state and county hospitals in 1972 were for drug-related disorders. Drug addiction is about three times as frequent among Hispanic as among Black and Anglo admissions (Bachrach, 1975). Addiction is a central concern to Puerto Ricans in New York City. About 23% of the persons reported to the city's narcotic register are Puerto Rican. Many Puerto Rican parents explain that they return to Puerto Rico to avoid the threat of addiction among their children (Fitzpatrick, 1971). "The literature is remarkably void of descriptions of Chicano addiction, despite the common assumption that addiction problems are widespread among American Spanish-speaking populations" (Scott, Orzen, Musillo, & Cole, 1973, p. 359). In a study conducted in housing projects in Los Angeles, Mexican-American adolescents admitted to drug use at a rate that was 9 to 13 times higher than drug-use rates obtained in a national survey (Padilla, Padilla, Ramirez, Morales, & Olmedo, 1979). These findings suggest that the problem of drug addiction has reached epidemic proportions among Hispanics; however, more studies need to be conducted on the causes of this high rate of addiction among Hispanic youth.

It is generally assumed that addicts lead lives of poverty and crime in order to support their habits. Recent evidence refutes this thesis. One group of researchers (Scott et al., 1973, p. 360) explain:

> The Chicano addict has abundant family resources available to him . . . admission data indicate that only two (3%) of the clients did not live with their families. Addiction puts strains on family relationships, and the addict may be briefly extruded from his parents' home or his marriage may dissolve, but even at these crisis points there are family members who will come to his aid . . . usually the family remained intact and put up with the tedious cycle of years of "hustling, copping, fixing, nodding out, getting sick, and hustling again." Community ties are correspondingly strong. The clients in this study are not drifters. Although many may make brief trips to Mexico or the West Coast, most return . . . The apparent incidence of psychiatric disorder is not impressive, at least in comparison to the younger middle-class Anglo youth now entering the program.

A few **tecatos** (drug addicts) began drug use through a legitimate prescription, whereas over 90% began their use of drugs from black-market purchases. Two types of addicts have been described. The "addict criminal" commits crimes to support his or her habit. The "criminal addict" has committed crimes for varied reasons, and the addiction is yet another part of the pathology. The "criminal addict" is more difficult to treat (Casavantes, 1976).

The nature of drug addiction among Hispanics differs somewhat from that of addiction among the majority culture. Addiction is a more frequent problem among Hispanics, and the role of *el tecato* in the family and community may differ from that of the Anglo addict. More research is needed to explicate the extent and causes of addiction and the precise ways in which *el tecato* functions within the community.

Alcoholism

Alcoholism ranks third among causes of admission to state and county mental hospitals for Hispanics and second for Anglos and Blacks. Whereas 20.6 per 100,000 Hispanic admissions in county and state psychiatric hospitals are for alcoholism, 50.3 per 100,000 Anglo admissions and 69.6 per 100,000 Black admissions are for alcoholism (Bachrach, 1975). Nevertheless, according to recent reviews of the literature, studies of drinking behavior indicate that the extent of problem drinking is greater among Hispanics than among the general population. These findings are supported by alcohol-associated arrest and mortality figures, which indicate that persons of Spanish surname tend to be arrested for alcohol-associated offenses and to die from alcohol-associated causes more often than the general population. Other indicators of widespread problem drinking among the Spanish-speaking population include high ratings of alcoholism as a problem in Hispanic communities and evidence that acculturation stress may cause higher rates of problem drinking (Gilbert, 1977; Hall, Chaikin, & Piland, 1977). Thus, although alcoholism appears to be a serious problem among Hispanics, they are less likely to receive treatment from public alcohol-related facilities.

Alcoholism among Hispanics may have a cultural etiology; it may, for example, develop as a defense against loss of cultural identity. According to interview data obtained from Mexican-American adults, alcoholism increased as acculturation increased (Graves, 1967). The case of Pablo, which follows, illustrates how alcoholism may ease the pain of confused ethnic and personal identity. This case also demonstrates that alcoholism as a psychological defense may be modeled by parents. Alcoholism interacts with and breeds other problems, such as Pablo's pseudosuicidal attempts and inability to hold a job.

THE CASE OF PABLO.[10] Pablo was not only a mixture of two cultures but was also a mixture of two conflicting and antagonistic races. Such a background, as will appear later, twisted his self-concept, deepened his identity and color conflicts, and almost wrecked his life . . .

Pablo sought help at the Veterans Administration Mental Hygiene Clinic for his inability to sleep, to hold a job, to stop drinking, and to stop his repeated pseudo-attempts at suicide and threats to kill his wife. He feared "falling apart." Pablo is a tall, olive-skinned, kinky-haired, 42-year-old man who can easily be taken for a Mexican. His speech evidences an excellent mastery of the English language and a superior intelligence. Pablo is the son of a Southern Negro mother and a white Puerto Rican father. Because of the Southern state laws which prohibit miscegenation, his parents were never married. Hence, Pablo bore the name of his mother.

[10]From "The Impact of Dual Cultural Membership on Identity," by V. S. Sommers, *Psychiatry*, 1964, *27*, 332–344. Copyright © 1964 by the William Alanson White Psychiatric Foundation, Inc. Reprinted by permission.

He described her as a loving but ignorant woman. He remembered his father as a shrewd, adventurous type of man, an alcoholic, who ran a sugar and rum business which took him back and forth between Puerto Rico and Florida.

As a youngster, Pablo loved and idolized his father; he shared many of his adventures and travels, and loved to hear him play the guitar and sing. He conversed with him only in Spanish. Pablo's identification and close relationship with his father came to a sudden break at the age of seven, when his father left the family. Shortly after this, Pablo and his mother moved to an all-Negro neighborhood. He hated the foreign world of the Negro ghetto. His classmates jeered at him because of his different appearance, and his inner reaction was one of terror. There was always a tug of war inside, a desire to fight, to lash out, especially when people called him a "nigger son-of-a-bitch," and when he heard his mother slandered as a "whore" . . .

Rather early in treatment the reason for Pablo's ultimate breakdown became apparent. It was the failure of his highly inadequate defense system to cope with his identity confusion and his despised self-image. He referred to himself as "being two people." Thus, he seemed to reflect the fact that he held membership in two cultures and two races, spoke two languages, carried two family names, and as he himself states: "I've lived a dual life, the one I shared with my mother as a Negro, the other I shared with my father as a white person" . . .

Pablo has been seen in individual therapy twice a week for over a year now. His superior intelligence and high motivation for therapy have been of great help in working with him, but have been counteracted by his lack of perseverance and capacity for sustained effort; success has to be immediate. He looks for magical solutions. Also, his tolerance level for frustration and anxiety is low.

Homosexuality

Controversy exists about the frequency of homosexuality in Hispanic culture. Some researchers postulate that limited economic opportunities for Hispanic males (who are often forced to accept traditionally female jobs such as cleaning hotel rooms) have spurred an increase in homosexuality among Hispanic males (Galli, 1975). Others, such as Martinez (1973), argue cogently that homosexuality has not increased in frequency but, rather, in visibility, because of changes in social attitudes toward homosexuality. Martinez (1973, p. 600) states:

> . . . Workers are in agreement that, during the past several years, the Mexican-American male homosexual has become more visible—in his overt behavior, in seeking help, and in the appearance of gay bars in the *barrio*. It is theorized that this increased visibility is just that and not necessarily an indication of more homosexuality. The larger society's change in its attitude toward homosexuals is, of course, largely responsible for this, but other forces within the Mexican-American community could also be partly responsible. One of these is the decline of the *barrio* gangs. It is theorized that the gangs served to keep male homosexuals underground by two mechanisms: by outright intimidation and harrassment, and by providing a means by which latent homosexuals in the gang would channel their sadistic and sexual impulses. The Chicano movement, with its emphasis on helping one's own people in the *barrio*, led maturing ex-gang members to return to the *barrio* to work with their old gangs by directing them into more socially acceptable activities, but thereby also weakening the gangs' authority and dominance. With dilution of the gangs' strength, their repressive and sublimative functions were also loosened, leading to the emergence of more overt homosexual behavior previously latent and to less fear of intimidation in already overt male homosexuals. No one seems to know enough about female Mexican American homosexuals even to speculate.

Martinez implies that there are many established facts about male homosexuality. In actuality, however, little is known. Carrier (1976a, 1976b, 1977), in a series of investigations, has studied family and cultural factors affecting homosexual behavior among urban Mexican males. According to Carrier, the Mexican family appears to play a far more important role with respect to the structure of homosexual behavior than does the middle-class Anglo-American family. This finding suggests that homosexual behavior may create more conflict for the Hispanic male than for his Anglo counterpart.

Some data are now available about lesbianism among Hispanics (Escarsega, Mondaca, & Torres, 1975; Hidalgo & Christensen, 1976–77). The overt increase in lesbianism seems associated with but may not be a direct product of the feminist movement. Many Hispanic women see themselves as victims of several types of exploitation: as members of the working class, as members of an ethnic-minority group, and as members of a sex relegated to an inferior position. Even within the Brown Power movement, some women experience prejudice associated with the value of *machismo*. These women feel that, according to their culture and religion, a Chicana's place is in her home and her role is to be a mother with a large family (Vidal, 1971).

Hispanic women are affected by national changes toward equality for the sexes. However, new avenues for employment and power may collide with family values if those values are built around traditional Hispanic culture. Many Cuban women experience dramatic shifts in their roles upon immigration to the United States. As members of the middle or upper class in Cuba, the women were full-time homemakers. After immigration, they begin working outside the home to provide needed income for their families. They have more power but also increased responsibility and role strain (Rogg, 1974). Among Puerto Rican immigrants, it is often easier for females to obtain work than males. Again, the women may enjoy their newfound power, but role strain often ensues.

Hispanic women may use various strategies in an effort to minimize such role strain. Some establish successful compromise in their roles and values. Others reject traditional Hispanic culture completely. For example, in May 1971, the 600 Chicanas who met in Houston for the first national conference of **la Raza** women voted on the following resolution: "We, as *mujeres de la Raza*, recognize the Catholic Church as an oppressive institution and do hereby resolve to break away and not go to it to bless our unions" (Vidal, 1971). Some Hispanic women may cope with discrimination by turning their backs to men and finding support among their Hispanic "sisters."

In the 1968 version of the *Diagnostic and Statistical Manual*, homosexuality was listed as a form of psychopathology. Since 1968, the American Psychiatric Association has removed homosexuality as a classification of pathology, asserting that it is not known whether the etiology of homosexuality is biological, psychological, and/or social. It was recognized further that a homosexual life-style is not necessarily inconsistent with overall adjustment and contentment. The exact cause and frequency of homosexuality has yet to be determined. Perhaps, as Martinez (1973) argues, we are observing an increase in visibility rather than in frequency of homosexuality. Perhaps some homosexuality is related to biological needs and some is associated with personal and social issues.

Homosexuality among Hispanics should be evaluated as it now is among Anglo homosexuals—as an alternative life-style not indicative of psychopathology (American Psychiatric Association, 1968). The therapist must be cautious in defining the clinical problems of Hispanic homosexuals. For example, the patient may want to deal with frustration about prejudice or acculturation rather than his or her homosexuality.

Our current understanding of the dynamics of psychopathology support gay patients' rights, whether Hispanic or of the majority culture, to deal with emotional problems within their chosen life-style.

In a review of the etiology and treatment of homosexuality, Acosta (1975, p. 18) cautions us by stating:

> Before initiating treatment of the homosexual, the therapist should ask these basic questions: Does the patient desire to change his sexual orientation? To what degree is he emotionally distressed? To what degree is he homosexual? What is the therapist's attitude toward homosexuality?

Obviously, the answers to these questions can greatly affect the goals, the course, and the outcome of any treatment of homosexuals. The only study that has investigated responses of Hispanic homosexuals to therapy has been that of Escarsega et al.(1975). In this study, which was limited by the small sample size, Chicana lesbians reported that they had been dissatisfied with therapy when the therapist's orientation was psychoanalytic and when there was an attempt to change the patient's sexual orientation. Clearly, much more research is needed concerning both cultural determinants of homosexuality and counseling models for working with Hispanic homosexual clients.

IMPLICATIONS FOR PLURALISTIC THERAPISTS

In this chapter we have reviewed the depth of maladjustment among Hispanics. The primary stresses that make Hispanics vulnerable to maladjustment include concern about economics, ethnic identity, and skin color. If the Hispanic is single, divorced, widowed and male, and/or over 65 years of age, vulnerability to maladjustment is even greater.

The development of preventive mental-health programs designed for target groups that are particularly prone to emotional problems is an effective way to reduce maladjustment among Hispanics. Preventive-health programs could include discussion groups for single, divorced, and widowed Hispanics. Discussion groups and social activities for the elderly population help reduce the high maladjustment rate for these Hispanics. Psychological and social programs designed to reduce poverty and unemployment tend also to reduce the frequency of maladjustment. Human-relations programs that foster positive ethnic identification can be offered in schools, churches, workshops, and private agencies. Amelioration of marginality and identity confusion can reduce stress and maladjustment. The continued research concerning stress offers productive guidelines for increasing mental health among Hispanics.

Symptomatic expression of maladjustment may be similar for majority-group and minority-group Americans. Thus schizophrenia is the most common psychiatric diagnosis for hospitalized Anglos, Blacks, and Hispanics. Yet generally one cannot compare directly the maladjustment among Hispanics to emotional disturbances of other Americans. The frequency of many syndromes varies across ethnic groups. For example, hospitalization for senile psychosis and drug addiction is more common among Hispanics than among Anglos or Blacks, whereas hospitalization for affective disorders is more frequent among Anglos and Blacks than among Hispanics (Bachrach, 1975). Furthermore, symptoms may not reveal the same degree of pathology across ethnic groups. Direct comparison of maladjustment among Hispanics and other Americans is not possible, because Hispanics experience some syndromes unique to their ethnicity; for example, no direct counterpart of *ataque*, the "Puerto Rican Syndrome," exists among Anglos.

Thorough study of maladjustment among Hispanics has just begun in the last few years. Most studies are concerned with Mexican Americans. Epidemiological studies of other Hispanics are very circumscribed. Most likely, other data concerning culturally specific syndromes and variation on frequency across ethnic groups will continue to be uncovered.

Since the pluralistic therapist cannot rely on standard Anglo nomenclature and since Hispanic nomenclature is not available, what technique can the therapist employ to ascertain the degree of maladjustments? One solution is to consider adjustment and maladjustment on a continuum of adaptation to a particular cultural mode. Rather than take a strictly psychodynamic view, the effective pluralistic therapist evaluates the client's adaptation on various sociological and psychological dimensions (DeBlassie, 1976). Specifically, the therapist looks for the interaction of sociological/environmental factors with physiological/psychological factors, some of which are included in the following lists.

Sociological/Environmental Factors	*Physiological/Psychological Factors*
Educational orientation	Basic physical needs for food and sex
Occupational orientation	Physical needs for security and safety
Financial orientation	Esthetic needs for beauty and harmony
State of health	Striving for self-esteem

Religious affiliation
Family values

Home/family
relationships

Striving for love
Striving for personal
meaning in life

Treatment and diagnosis are continuously interwoven as the therapist considers each case individually. The therapist first observes the situation and then, using existing nomenclature, organizes and assesses the observations. Purposeful intervention follows next, and, last, the therapist reobserves and reassesses to ascertain the need for future intervention or termination of treatment.

The epidemiological studies of maladjustment provide cues for determining the degree to which a client's symptoms impair adaptation. However, the results of the epidemiological studies must be weighed with the therapist's understanding of the complexity and diversity of Hispanic cultures.

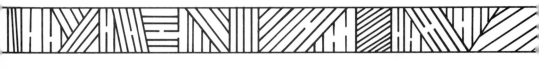

Chapter 5 Direction for Intervention

UNDERUTILIZATION OF MENTAL-HEALTH FACILITIES

It is a well-established fact that mental-health facilities cater to the needs of the majority middle-class American. Shofield (1964) explains that the most desirable patients are "young, attractive, verbal, intelligent, and successful." Using the first letters of these words, Shofield coined the term *YAVIS Syndrome* to describe the tendency of therapists to select clients who fit the American ideal of social competence. As a corollary to the YAVIS Syndrome, the poor are often incarcerated for the same behaviors for which the rich receive medical and psychiatric help (Morales, 1971a).

A number of studies corroborate the finding that poor Hispanics are overrepresented for alcohol and drug convictions and underrepresented in mental-health facilities. In 1972 about 12,300 Hispanics were admitted to the state and local mental hospitals in the United States. These mental-hospital admissions represent 3% of all admissions to such facilities, although Hispanics constitute at least 6% of the general population (Bachrach, 1975). In the San Francisco Bay area in 1972, only 4% of the Hispanic population employed the services of the main mental-health centers. In a satellite mental-health center servicing a community in which 25% of the residents were Mexican American, only 9% of the clients were Mexican American (Torrey, 1972).

Not only are Hispanics underrepresented in mental-health centers, but also they are less likely to receive extensive psychotherapy. In a community-mental-health center in Connecticut, Puerto Rican patients were 3.5 times more likely to drop out of therapy than were Blacks and Anglos (Abad et al., 1974). In an outpatient clinic in Los Angeles, the

134

records of 594 patients (65% Caucasian, 25% Black, 9% Mexican American, and 1% Oriental) were reviewed during a nine-month period. Therapy was provided by an entirely Anglo staff. The Mexican-American and Black patients, more often than the Anglos, were discharged after the first interview or seen for minimal supportive therapy. About 50% of the Caucasians, as contrasted to only 40% of the Mexican Americans and 32% of the Blacks, were placed in individual or group therapy. Of the 79 patients continuing in therapy for nine months, 78% were Caucasian, 14% were Black, 5% were Mexican American, and 3% were Oriental (Yamamoto, James, & Palley, 1968). Anglos, Mexican Americans, and Blacks requesting service from a mental-health center in East Los Angeles were matched on socioeconomic status. Anglo patients received psychotherapy over a longer time than did Blacks or Mexican Americans (Karno, 1966).

Few studies report consistently high use of mental-health facilities by Hispanics. In the state mental hospitals of Colorado, the rate of admission was higher for Mexican-American males than non-Mexican-American males and also higher for Mexican-American female alcoholics than for non-Mexican-American female alcoholics (Wignall & Koppin, 1967). In East Los Angeles 85% of the clients of a particular mental-health center were Spanish-speaking; in this instance ethnic clients were proportionate in number to the local population (Moll, Reuda, Reza, Herrera, & Vasquez, 1976). In Laredo, Texas, the utilization of community-mental-health services by Mexican Americans matched their distribution in the population (Trevino & Bruhn, 1977).

The information on utilization of public mental-health facilities by Hispanics is still not complete. What does seem clear, however, is that, when services are oriented for Hispanics, utilization increases. This point will be demonstrated throughout this chapter.

ATTITUDES ABOUT MENTAL HEALTH

Perceptions of Illness

The question has been raised whether Hispanics' low use of mental-health facilities can be explained on the basis of their attitudes about illness. If Hispanics are more tolerant of psychopathology, they are likely to consult therapists for less frequent and more severe problems (Stoker & Meadow, 1974). The fact that proportionately more Hispanics than Anglos are hospitalized for psychosis (Bachrach, 1975) has been cited as indirect evidence supporting this thesis. Direct investigation of this hypothesis is limited. However, in one extensive survey conducted in

East Los Angeles, there was no significant difference in perception of mental illness between Mexican Americans and Anglos (Karno & Edgerton, 1969).

Across ethnic groups, those expressing subjective discomfort are more apt to seek counseling than those who have not considered their problems in psychological terms. Hispanics differ in the degree to which they label their psychological discomfort, but many are well aware of their personal stress. A set of personal and social traits among *barrio* patients that was correlated with their willingness to use mental-health services included: being head of a household, in the middle adult years, divorced, and self-referred, having had a previous hospitalization as a psychiatric patient, and recognizing problems such as anxiety and depression (Kahn & Heiman, 1974). Use of military mental-health services by Hispanic servicemen was associated with their knowledge of the availability of counseling services, previous experience with counseling, and perceived feelings of social isolation (Van Vranken, 1973). In brief, Hispanics are more likely to use counseling services when they label their problems in psychological terms, such as anxiety, depression, and social isolation. The case of Mrs. C. illustrates how recognition of physical symptomatology and feelings of social isolation prompted a Hispanic woman to seek assistance from a counselor.

THE CASE OF MRS. C.[1] Mrs. C. had never seen a psychiatrist before. She came to the clinic because of "loneliness" of two months' duration, and difficulty in swallowing of one month's duration. She related the onset of her loneliness to an incident at a family gathering. Her brother accused her of insulting his second wife, and her father agreed. The patient's husband defended her, eventually knocking her father down. Although they all made up two days later, the patient began to feel lonely and worried. She became sensitive to her husband's change in job hours, which kept him away from home more than usual, and especially sensitive to her husband's usual habit of staying out "with the boys." One Sunday afternoon . . . her husband was late and the family had to rush to

[1]From "Some Factors in the Psychiatric Treatment of Spanish-Americans," by L. Y. Kline, *American Journal of Psychiatry*, 1969, *125*, 1674–1681. Copyright 1969 by the American Psychiatric Association. Reprinted by permission.

church. Her husband drove in an aggressive way, frightening her, and once there, the children were noisy. That evening the patient had the fear that she would not be able to swallow, and in fact, could not.

Before her appointment to begin outpatient treatment, on her mother's advice, the patient had gone in search of a traditional Spanish healer. For reasons that were not clear, she could not find one. When asked if she had had some reluctance to come to the clinic, she replied, "Let people think' what they will. I know not only crazy people come here."

Before her second visit, she called to say that she felt worse and asked if I would hypnotize her. By the time of the session she had recalled what preceded this exacerbation. Her husband had come home late again. She wondered if he purposefully wanted to upset her. As she said this, she fingered her crucifix. She sadly told of her loneliness as a child because of greater attention given to the older and younger siblings.

She then changed the subject and talked about an Anglo teacher who had slapped her unfairly when she was ten. There had been only two or three other Spanish children in the school, and they were also abused. The patient was "too dumb to tell" her mother of the abuse. At this point she sounded angry; however, she returned to the subject of the numerous unpleasant experiences in her own family due to "unfair" treatment at the hands of her parents and siblings. She spoke of how lonely she had been because of her husband's long hours away from home. When I asked her if she was angry about this, she gulped, drooled saliva, and said "no."

In the next hour, she spoke again about her experiences with Anglos. She described her bravery in telling one Anglo boy to shut up when she was still a girl. She said that she had "stood up" to a rude police chief on whom she had waited in a restaurant where she worked. He later apologized, and she accepted this; however, he died shortly afterward of a heart attack. She had visible difficulty swallowing at this point and attempted to change the subject. Was she afraid of her anger? She admitted that she had feared her anger might have caused his death. She then described another incident, of police brutality involving her brother, and how she had come to his assistance. The police had been so impressed by her stand that an officer was sent to apologize. He stated that his offending colleague had mistakenly "thought you were just another dumb Mexican." Soon after that, she had been involved in a traffic accident. Though she wondered if she was being punished for her anger, she was also happy since she said, "I learned to open my mouth."

She soon reported improvement in her swallowing. She made her husband change his hours and warned him: "If you go back to your old routine, I'll get worse." Her children were also better behaved. She began to speak of the possible background for her particular symptom. Eating had always presented a special problem for her. Her father used mealtimes to criticize. Her mother would hide information from him to keep him from getting angry at the table. The patient would avoid her father, she told me as she gulped.

She said she had tended to deny being angry since childhood; her mother had always held it against her father for being such a disagreeable, angry person. Her mother had suffered from trouble swallowing during the first years of her own marriage. At the suggestion of a traditional healer, she had relatives stay with her, since the healer felt she was lonely, and she was cured.

Mrs. C.'s primary complaint was physical in nature. At a previous time, Mrs. C.'s mother had sought help from a folk healer to rectify a problem she had with swallowing. Mrs. C. was able to link the physical symptoms to psychological ones—that is, her feelings of loneliness. Mrs. C.'s interpretation of her psychological problem was simplistic. She labeled her problem as simply loneliness, but it is important to note that she was facile in understanding psychological labels. Once she entered therapy, the therapist was able to help Mrs. C. elaborate on her psychological problems, labeling her anger about discrimination and her frustration toward her husband. A degree of sophistication about psychological interpretations of illness was necessary for Mrs. C. to seek counseling assistance, so that she was able to say "Let people think what they will. I know not only crazy people come here."

Some Hispanics are not experienced at labeling problems that are appropriately handled through counseling intervention. Hispanics who hold traditional values may label emotional problems as physical illnesses (Karno & Edgerton, 1969). A Puerto Rican social worker who grew up in an Eastern slum explained that his people desperately need therapy services but don't even know what is available (Delgado, 1974).

Hispanics may differ somewhat from Anglos in the degree to which they perceive family members as able to facilitate a person's recovery. In an East Los Angeles survey, more Mexican Americans than Anglos believed mental disorders began in childhood (Karno & Edgerton, 1969). These Mexican Americans might be more attuned to the ways family experiences can provoke or ameliorate maladjustment. When an extensive, stratified sample of Mexican Americans in California were asked to name their most preferred resource to assist the emotionally disturbed, 25% listed a doctor, 20% suggested a relative, 17% recommended a priest, and 14% designated a friend. When the same sample were asked about the resource they actually used the most, 36% cited relatives or *compadres*, 26% listed friends, 21% mentioned a doctor, and 16% said they confided in priests (Padilla et al., 1976). These Mexican Americans perceived family members as helpful in dealing with the emotionally disturbed.

Hispanics may further differ from Anglos in their awareness of subjective discomfort, in their perception of the roles of mental-health professionals, and in their attitude about the support inherent in the family. However, the Hispanic view of maladjustment does not preclude therapeutic intervention.

Perceptions of Therapy

It is tempting to assume that the underrepresentation of Hispanics in mental-health facilities is evidence that they hold unfavorable attitudes toward therapy. Contrary to this notion, it has been demonstrated in a number of studies that Hispanics view therapy positively. Hispanic children have expressed positive attitudes towards counseling and therapy. When Spanish-speaking and non-Spanish-speaking 5th- through 12th-graders responded to a semantic differential, the precepts of principal, teacher, father, policeman, and self were viewed similarly across the two ethnic groups. However, mother and counselor were seen as more positive, more powerful, and more active by the Spanish-speaking than by the non-Spanish-speaking subjects (Vigil, 1968). Positive attitudes toward therapy have also been expressed by Hispanic adults. On a scale devised to measure subjects' perceptions of the usefulness of psychotherapy, Mexican-American college students perceived psychotherapy as more helpful for the emotionally disturbed than did Anglo students (Acosta, 1975). An interview was conducted with Mexican-American and Anglo residents of Los Angeles. Few statistically significant differences in perception about therapy were recorded between the Anglo and the Mexican-American subjects. In both groups, 80% expressed positive attitudes about psychotherapy. More Mexican Americans than Anglos perceived that "psychiatrists really help people who go to them" (Karno & Edgerton, 1969). In an outpatient clinic in Los Angeles, Anglos were more apt to criticize their therapists than were Black, Mexican-American, and Oriental patients (Yamamoto et al., 1968). In another study, minority ethnic background was not associated with unfavorable attitudes about hospitals, although low educational aspirations were correlated with dissatisfaction about therapy, whether the patient was Anglo, Black, or Hispanic (McLemore, 1963). In an extensive survey conducted with a stratified sample of Californians, over 60% of the Mexican-American respondents indicated willingness to use the local mental-health clinic (Padilla et al., 1976).

A few studies conducted with school-age Hispanics reveal some negative attitudes about counseling. In one study, junior high school Hispanics and Anglos responded to a set of hypothetical client/counselor interactions. Ethnicity of the hypothetical counselor was not specified in the first protocol of the set, was specified as Spanish American in the second protocol, and was specified as Anglo in the third repetition. In each case, Anglos expressed more positive attitudes about counseling (Rippee, 1967). In a second study revealing negative attitudes about therapy among Hispanics, 7th- through 12th-grade Mexican Americans and Anglos ranked their attitudes about counselors on a five-point Likert scale. The Mexican Americans were significantly less willing to accept counseling than were the Anglos (Demos, 1962). In a third study, which surveyed 10th-grade Mexican-American and Anglo students in Denver, Colorado, Mexican Americans tended less often to seek the assistance of school counselors than did Anglos (Cole & Davenport, 1973). A fourth study, conducted with Anglo, Black, and Mexican-American high school graduates stratified on age, sex, and occupational aspirations, revealed dissatisfaction about counseling among all target groups. Counselors were seen as "pretty nice fellows" but as ineffectual. Satisfaction with counseling was associated with a set of factors that did not differ in a consistent manner across the ethnic groups (Mansfield, 1972).

Adverse experiences with mental-health professionals will create negative attitudes about counseling. Palomares (1971a) gives us an example of how a youth's negative attitudes about therapy are exacerbated by his feeling misperceived and unappreciated.

> . . . When you go there and they know something about you, it really makes you feel good. Like rapping to them about anything when you just see them in the hall or you are waiting for someone, and you find out that one of them does know what a Puerto Rican is, and if he does know what a Puerto Rican is, and he does know, like maybe a city or two, or he has been there, it really makes you feel good. Maybe he just has it by coincidence, but to you it feels like he is showing interest in you . . .
>
> . . . I have a lot of problems building up inside of me for a long time, now, for many years. What am I going to get out of the feeling of a person that doesn't know where I am coming from, you know . . . doesn't relate to me at all? They are strangers. I mean, how are they going to help me if they are not going to relate to me? What I hear them saying is, "Well, it is up to you. You are the one that is going to have to get yourself straightened out. You are the only one that can help with your problems." But the first thing I did to help myself with my own problems was to come talk to somebody about them.[2]

In general, Hispanics express positive attitudes about therapy. Some individuals view therapy critically, and their negative expectations limit their seeking help. Others develop negative attitudes after visiting counselors. Yet the fact remains that many who view therapy positively are not enlisting the services of public agencies. Negative attitudes about therapy do not offer a sufficient explanation for the vast underutilization of mental-health facilities.

REASONS FOR UNDERUTILIZATION

Geographical Isolation

One factor that has been correlated with underutilization of mental-health facilities is geographical isolation. Mental-health centers are often placed outside the *barrio*. The cost of transportation and the lack of child-care facilities may discourage Hispanics from traveling to these centers (Torrey, 1972).

Because mental-health facilities are often divorced from the Hispanic community, residents may not be aware of existing services. When Anglo and Mexican-American residents in East Los Angeles were

[2]From "Puerto Rican Youth Speaks Out," by U. H. Palomares, *Personnel and Guidance Journal*, 1971, *50*(2), 91–95. Copyright 1971 by the American Personnel and Guidance Association. Reprinted by permission.

interviewed concerning their attitudes about mental health, approximately 80% of both groups expressed beliefs that therapy could assist people with psychiatric disorders. Yet 80% of each group was unable to name or locate a single mental-health center (Edgerton & Karno, 1971). In an Arizona town, *barrio* residents who had employed the local mental-health services were interviewed. Use of the center was correlated with knowledge about where and how to seek help (Kahn & Heiman, 1974).

Research about the underutilization of mental-health facilities indicates that facilities should be placed within the hub of Hispanic communities. Large-scale public-relations programs are needed to educate Hispanics about the location and nature of services.

Language Barriers

Hispanic patients' concepts of emotional illness will vary according to whether English or Spanish is their primary language (Edgerton & Karno, 1971). Therapists' perceptions of their Hispanic patients differ if patients speak Spanish or English. Two therapists whose native language was English and two therapists whose native language was Spanish judged Hispanic patients as more disturbed when the patients responded to interviewers in English than when they responded in Spanish (Marcos et al., 1973).

Many mental-health facilities are staffed only by Anglos (Anderson, 1973). Few Spanish-speaking therapists are available (Torrey, 1972). Yet as many as 50% of Hispanic patients may be Spanish-speaking. The lack of Spanish-speaking therapists may prompt many Hispanics to avoid or drop out of therapy (Edgerton & Karno, 1971).

Majority-Bound Values

Programs in mental-health centers tend to be geared to the needs of majority Americans, and Hispanics may avoid these centers because they find them inappropriate or irrelevant. Many programs in mental-health centers are class-bound. Insight and nondirective therapy are offered in the structure of "the fifty-minute hour." This approach, developed for middle-class Americans, may be less effective with poor clients who need crisis intervention and who may desire more directive therapy (Torrey, 1972.)

Many services in mental-health facilities are culture-bound. Behaviors of Hispanics are misjudged; for example, some behavior may be considered crazy when, in fact, it is only different. For example, recall the Puerto Rican Syndrome, which involves repression and dissociation. This syndrome may be less indicative of pathology than originally believed by Anglo therapists. Sensory experiences, such as "hearing voices," are more acceptable in Hispanic than in Anglo or Black cultures. Anglo, Black, and Mexican-American high school students were asked to sort the following words and phrases into two categories of their choosing: *compulsive, crazy, depressed, frightened, hearing voices, neurotic, normal, religious,* and *tendency to withdraw.* Whereas 40% of the Blacks and Anglos associated hearing voices with being crazy, only 10% of the Mexican Americans made this association (Torrey, 1972). If therapists view Hispanic behavior in terms of Anglo values Hispanics may not seek out their services.

Use of Folk Medicine and Faith Healers

Many ethnic groups have evolved folk systems to explain illness. Some Mexican Americans may subscribe to folk beliefs or **curanderismo,** Puerto Ricans to **espiritismo,** and Cubans to **santería.** Folk illnesses are sets of physical and personal symptoms that are believed to be caused by natural or supernatural events (Garrison, 1977; Harwood, 1977; Rubel, 1969).

A therapist may be surprised by the wisdom of folk healers in recognizing the interaction of physical and psychological symptomatology. The system of folk illnesses is based on the belief that bodily fluids and mental processes must be in balance to maintain mental and physical health. Physical health requires a balance of the warm and cold humors. Psychological health requires a balance of warm and cold relationships, of intimacy and withdrawal (Currier, 1966). Table 5-1 schematizes beliefs about the physical or supernatural events that can upset the body's balance. For example, *susto*, which is characterized by decreased appetite, restlessness, apathy, weakness, and withdrawal, is caused by fright. The folk explanation of *susto* states that certain experiences, such as seeing a car accident or being startled by a snake, precipitate this malady. **Mal ojo,** characterized by headaches, nausea, and irritability, occurs when one is looked upon with an "evil eye" by another who has "strong vision." According to folk theory, those who have "strong vision" should only look admiringly at others when touching them. If people with "strong vision" follow this touching code, they will not be feared or avoided. **Mal puesto** is characterized by severe psychological symptoms such as hallucinations, mania, and delusions. *Mal puesto* is considered to have a supernatural cause. The victim is **embrujado**—bewitched—by a

Table 5-1. *Some of the major Hispanic folk illnesses and their folk and psychological explanations.*

Type	Symptoms	Folk Explanation	Psychological Explanation
Susto (Also referred to as *espanto*)	Decreased appetite Restlessness Fatigue Weakness Withdrawal Somatic complaints	Caused by fright or a traumatic experience; fright may be natural (an accident) or super-natural (ghost).	Failure in role expectation; corresponds to anxiety and depression.
Mal Ojo	Headaches Crying Irritability Restlessness Vomiting Diarrhea Fever	Victim looked upon by person with "strong vision" or the "evil eye".	Neurotic disorder; transient disorder; projecting the cause of illness on to others.
Mal Puesto	Hallucinations Amnesia Ideas of persecution Hysterical symptom	Witchcraft; hex placed on victim. Motives are envy, jealousy (especially sexual), and vengeance.	Severe neurosis; psychosis.
Mal Aire	Headache Chest pain Paralysis Diarrhea Stiffness	Imbalance of hot and cold elements in both the bodily functions and the environment.	Social relationships are upset.
Empacho	Constipation Pain	Intestine blocked by bolus of food.	Letting oneself be dominated.
Caida de Mollera	In infants, distress, crying, malnutrition	Fallen fontanelle.	Mother's neglect of child.
Bilis and *Envidia*	General emotional turmoil, diarrhea, vomiting	Strong anger/envy causes an overflow of yellow bile.	Emotional stress or upset.

witch. The witch is jealous of the victim's wealth or status and therefore hexes him or her by torturing effigies, using magic potions, or turning into an animal and attacking the victim. Another folk illness, **empacho,** creates symptoms of constipation and nervousness and is said to be caused by a bolus of food that is blocking the intestine (Torrey, 1972).

Psychological interpretations suggest that folk illnesses allow unconscious impulses to be expressed (see Table 5-1). The folk illnesses serve as ego defenses by suggesting that the cause of personal problems is external (Galvin & Ludwig, 1961). For example, *susto* may be interpreted as distress about failure in role expectations. Madsen (1964b) gives an excellent example of how *susto* has modulated the behavior of Memo, a young Mexican-American man in south Texas. Memo was dismissed from his job by his boss. According to Memo, there was no reason for the dismissal; yet several weeks later he admitted that he had been guilty of consistent absenteeism. On the night of his dismissal he consoled himself by drinking at a bar with his friend and coworker Alejandro and several other acquaintances. Alejandro argued that, since Memo had been fired for no apparent reason, he should confront his boss and try to regain his job. As the night progressed and more liquor was consumed, Memo began to express more and more hostility toward his ex-boss. Finally,

> . . . he announced that the following day he would see his former employer and have a showdown. Alejandro . . . said he would watch for the encounter, wished Memo luck, and urged him to be firm. Walking home from the bar, Memo fell in the street and was nearly struck by a truck. The next day he awoke with a headache, an uneasiness in his stomach, vague body pains, and a shaky hand—symptoms of the "susto" resulting from his frightening experience with the truck. A neighbor made the diagnosis, treated him, ordered him to bed for a few days. Confrontation of his ex-boss was postponed and finally forgotten. Alejandro was extremely sympathetic about his friend's illness [Madsen, 1964b, p. 432].

In *curanderismo, espiritismo,* and *santería,* illnesses may be treated without referring directly to psychological causes. *Curanderos* employ elaborate ritual, herbal tonics, massage, ventriloquism, suggestion, confession, and prayer. Healing is often complex and protracted for weeks (Edgerton, Karno, & Fernandez, 1970). *Espiritistas* emphasize a variety of admonitions and techniques for inducing catharsis (Garrison, 1977; Lubchansky, Ergi, & Stokes, 1970). In *espiritismo* the client is helped to call upon the assistance of "good spirits" to counter the efforts of "bad spirits." This training involves prayer and ritual such as special housecleaning practices. In *santería,* the practice involves prayer and sacrifices to the *orishas,* the most powerful gods and goddesses of *santería.* Some of these gods are Obatalá, the god of purity, and Eshu, the guardian of every road, whose permission must be secured before obtaining the help of other *orishas* and of Chongó, god of fire and thunder (Sandoval, 1975).

Uneasiness or conflict about therapy may indicate that a Hispanic is operating with a belief in folk illness and faith healing. A therapist should look for signs of folk belief among clients so that no misinterpretation of pathology is made. Somatically descriptive vocabulary may be characteristic of clients believing in folk medicine. For example, when a Puerto Rican accepting *espiritismo* speaks of "pain in the brain," he or she is probably referring to anxious and disordered thinking (Lubchansky et al., 1970). Somatic thinking should not be considered delusional when expressed by individuals holding folk-illness beliefs.

In some cases, therapists have successfully integrated folk concepts into modern treatment approaches. After studying *curanderismo* throughout the Southwest, one well-known transcultural psychiatrist concluded that folk treatment is particularly effective with depressive disorders, mild paranoid disorders, and ambulatory schizophrenic reactions (Kiev, 1972). In the case of a young Mexican-American woman that follows, the therapist combined *curanderismo* and modern psychotherapeutic treatment.

> *THE CASE OF A YOUNG MEXICAN-AMERICAN WOMAN.*[3] D. M., a 22-year-old unmarried Mexican-American woman, was admitted for the first time to the hospital with psychotic behavior one week after the birth of her first child. At the time of admission, she appeared grossly psychotic and suspicious, divulging little information. She was given haloperidol and improved within several days, although she retained a markedly flat affect.
>
> She was discharged after two weeks in the hospital, but was readmitted one week later with recurrence of symptoms. At the time of her readmission, she also exhibited significant signs of depression. After antidepressants were added to the haloperidol regimen, she again partially recompensated, but the flat and inappropriate affect persisted. Her family clamoured loudly for release, simultaneously expressing

[3]From "The Curandero's Apprentice: A Therapeutic Integration of Folk and Medical Healing," by J. J. Kreisman, *American Journal of Psychiatry*, 1975, *132*, 81–83. Copyright 1975 by the American Psychiatric Association. Reprinted by permission.

dissatisfaction with the hospital's treatment and the conviction that the patient was well enough to return home. The patient continued to be very resistant, and the therapy was stalled.

At this point, the patient told a Mexican-American staff member about the possibility that a hospitalized patient might actually be "hexed." At a subsequent interview, the therapist remarked that he had observed a similar case in which a patient had felt she was *embrujada*. The patient responded enthusiastically to this suggestion, acknowledging that her mother had been trying to find a *curandero* for her.

She eagerly responded to a proposal to utilize the *curandero's* herbs in the hospital and rigorously prepared herself for the ordeal with prayer and isolation. She also devised specific criteria by which she could judge when she was no longer *embrujada*. Her improvement in the hospital continued but, although acknowledging she was regaining her health, she insisted that only after receiving the *curandero's* magic would she be totally cured.

Prior to the initiation of the hospital *curanderismo*, the patient, while on a pass, was taken by her mother to a local *curandera* who administered "medicine." She returned to the hospital complaining of xerostomia, blurred vision, tremulousness, and the return of persecutory auditory hallucinations. She also exhibited nystagmus, mydriasis, and tachycardia. As her symptoms persisted over the next few days, the patient requested the hospital *curandero's* herbs, which she felt could counteract the local healer's drug. Within one day after initiation of the regimen (doxepin hydrochloride), her symptoms disappeared and she had also fulfilled her own criteria that indicated she was free of *embrujada*.

Over the next several weeks, the patient began to progress significantly in psychotherapy and a firm rapport was solidified with her as well as with her previously hostile family. However, she retained a markedly flat and often inappropriate affect, failing to regain her state of health before her encounter with the local *curandera*. A course of electroconvulsive treatment was eventually initiated, and the patient responded exceptionally well.

> She has regained her premorbid status, retaining her previous job and assuming mothering responsibility for her child.

With the aid of *curanderismo*, the therapist's medication gained an added placebo effect. Kreisman (1975) explores the ethics of integrating modern psychotherapeutic techniques in the guise of folk medicine and has concluded that, by becoming conceptually a *"curandero's* apprentice,"* he was able to experience true empathy with his client. He believes that this empathic communication is highly ethical.

If significant others are willing to consider only supernatural forces as the cause of a client's problems, it may be helpful for a therapist to accept and work with the folk beliefs. One therapist reports success with clients considered *embrujado*—bewitched—by dealing with family members as if witchcraft has indeed occurred (Leininger, 1973). This therapist provides support to the "bewitched" victim, allows the family members to express their feelings, focuses on social tensions, and assists the family in dealing with acculturation changes. By indirectly assisting the family to function as a cohesive group, symptoms of both *embrujado* and family dysfunction decrease. The method used by Leininger is described in the case of four Spanish-speaking families, below.

> *THE CASE OF FOUR SPANISH-SPEAKING FAMILIES.*[4] At the start of therapy with the four Spanish-speaking families, the author focused upon their family ties and past relationships and took their genealogies. The latter seemed to be extremely important to the families, enabling them to tell about each family member and what had happened to them in recent months, as well as to their family and friends. Furthermore, the genealogies were the key means for discovering the male and female witches, as well as the witch mediums. When the family spoke about the witches, they whispered their names and always spoke of them with intense fear because of their great power and malevolent ways.
>   . . . In a short time, they discussed the anger, fear

[4]From "Witchcraft Practices and Psychocultural Therapy with Urban U.S. Families," by M. Leininger, *Human Organization*, 1973, *32*, 73–83. Copyright 1973 by the Society for Applied Anthropology. Reprinted by permission.

and distrust which existed among them. The author listened attentively to each family member's concerns, fears, and conflicts with no attempt to modify their behavior. It was felt that this approach was important in this initial phase of the therapy so that the members could openly express their feelings to an outsider who was actively interested in them, but who was not trying to suppress their feelings. Family members made direct and hostile accusations to one another, but especially to the bewitched victim. Initially, the victim was completely overwhelmed at these accusations and occasionally cried or left the room. Gradually, the author interceded in behalf of the victim and offered her emotional and social support by protecting and defending her feelings. When this occurred, the victim's ego became stronger and more confident. She would talk in a more coherent manner and would try to handle the accusations that she felt were unfair. For example, one victim states: "You [family] 'caused' me to become ill. You have picked on me too long in this family. I did not do everything you said I did. Whenever I tried something different, I was pounced upon. I don't know why you always pick upon me."

During the course of the family "talk-out" sessions, the members discussed their past and current problems in adjusting to different "kinds of people and new ways in the city." There was evidence of conflict between their traditional cultural norms and the different sets of norms they were being exposed to in the urban community.

. . . A series of traditional cultural norms had been broken in each of the family ingroups, and the witchcraft victim was blamed for breaking them. And since the victim was perceived in each family to have violated the norm most flagrantly, she was vulnerable to most of the witchcraft accusations.

. . . As the ingroup families spoke about their angry and antagonistic feelings toward the outgroup, they were oblivious to the dynamics of their own internal problems and hostilities to the outgroup.

Early researchers of Hispanic culture believed that practice of folk medicine precluded use of medical and mental-health facilities (Weaver,

1973). The extent to which folk medicine is practiced today by Hispanics is not clearly established. Probably its popularity varies in different regions of the country. For example, in one southwestern city, 15 out of 75 Mexican-American females reported having sought help from a *curandero*. Ninety-seven percent of the sample had heard of the five main folk diseases, and 95% reported knowing someone who had suffered from each illness (Martinez & Martin, 1966). In another southwestern city, 55% of 250 families interviewed expressed a strong belief in folk illness, and only 22% stated that they held no belief in *curanderismo* (Holland, 1963). Another investigator reported *curanderismo* as a principle treatment modality throughout the Southwest (Kiev, 1968). It has been suggested that local healers, **señoras,** must be distinguished from more professional, charismatic healers. Hispanics may visit *señoras* who are neighbors and *comadres* but not seek out formal folk healers (Gonzalez, 1976). The extent to which *espiritismo* and *santería* are practiced is also undetermined. The viability of the practice is demonstrated by the uncovering of at least 20 spiritualistic temples in the Bronx, New York City, in 1963 (Lubchansky, Ergi, & Stokes, 1970). Zalamea (1978) in *Nuestro,* a national Hispanic magazine, describes a visit made to a *santera* by a prosperous Cuban businessman who was being browbeaten by his board of directors to the brink of resignation.

In contrast to these findings pointing to the viability of faith healers, an extensive survey conducted in Los Angeles revealed that treatment by a physician was clearly preferred over treatment by a *curandero* (Karno & Edgerton, 1969). In another study, Mexican Americans in Los Angeles indicated preference of a priest or a friend over a *curandero* (Derbyshire, 1968). Practice of *curanderismo* was mentioned infrequently by Mexican Americans interviewed from nine census tracts in Southern California (Padilla et al., 1976) and four Nebraska communities (Welsh, Comer, & Steinman, 1973).

Most modern-oriented, urban or middle-class Hispanics will not subscribe to folk beliefs. Yet, even if a Hispanic does hold some beliefs in *curanderismo, espiritismo,* or *santería,* there is no reason to assume that this individual will avoid therapy. Folk beliefs and faith healing are compatible with catharsis and introspection. The most traditionally oriented Hispanic may respond positively to therapy if the therapeutic process occurs in a culturally meaningful context. The conclusion can be drawn that, if Hispanics do not avail themselves of standard Anglo mental-health facilities, it is not that they are uninterested in introspection as a means of achieving personal growth. Rather, they may simply find most institutions alien or unhelpful. The therapist should look for a client's belief in folk medicine and faith healing; therapy may be facilitated by uncovering and sometimes building on these beliefs.

Finally, the underutilization of traditional mental-health services cannot be explained by the substitution of either folk beliefs or faith healing by substantial numbers of Hispanics. This conclusion seems warranted especially since usage of faith healers is largely confined to a limited number of rural and/or migrant peoples.

Discouraging Institutional Policy

In many ways institutional policies may reduce the self-esteem of Hispanic clients (Karno & Edgerton, 1969). Minority clients may be placed on waiting lists for longer periods of time than clients from the majority culture (Gordon, 1965). In one survey of child-guidance clinics, it was noted that as few as 23% of minority families received assistance, and they were forced to wait at least 28 weeks for services (Wolkon, Moriwaki, Mandel, Archuleta, Bunje, & Zimmerman, 1974). The law may be associated with institutions of health and welfare located in Hispanic enclaves. Referrals are often part of a legal sentence. Because of this alliance with the legal system, mental-health centers may be seen as aversive, punishing institutions, and Hispanics may not avail themselves of their services voluntarily (Moore, 1970). Other Hispanics may fear deportation if they seek therapeutic assistance from social institutions that are cojoined with the legal system (Edgerton & Karno, 1971).

Because of the value of **respeto,** the Hispanic client may not voice his or her dissatisfaction with an agency's services. Rather, the client may express silent discontent and not return to therapy. As Rodriguez (1973, p. 37) states:

> When cases were closed because of lack of cooperation on the part of the client, social workers did not consider that the client might wish to exercise his right to determine his own life. The rationale was that the client did not want to cooperate with the agency. This presupposed an underlying thought: The client must cooperate and accept what the agency offers, no matter how inadequate he thinks it is, or how different from his expectations, because the agency considers it is good and should not be rejected.

INTERACTION OF THERAPIST AND CLIENT ETHNICITY

How much underutilization of mental-health services is explained by the lack of Hispanic therapists? Will clients feel more comfortable and exhibit more personal gain under the guidance of a therapist who shares their ethnic background? Research on the relative effectiveness of Anglo and Hispanic therapists is rather limited, so that only tentative conclusions can be drawn.

Client Attitudes toward the Therapist

Both positive and negative attitudes about Anglo therapists have been expressed by Hispanic clients. In our earlier discussion of stereotyping, we pointed out that some Hispanics perceive Anglos as cold, unkind, and inconstant (Simmons, 1961). Hispanics typically have not described their therapist in these terms. Acosta (1975), for example, found that Hispanics express positive attitudes about Anglo therapists. In his study, Acosta had Mexican-American and Anglo college students listen to audio tapes of a dialogue between a therapist and an anxious, depressed, and angry young man. On one tape, the therapist spoke fluent English with a slight Spanish accent. To half of the students, this therapist was presented as a Mexican-American professional; to the other half, the therapist was presented as a Mexican-American nonprofessional. On the second tape, the therapist spoke fluent English with a standard "American" accent. Half of the students were told that this therapist was an Anglo professional; the other half were told that the therapist was an Anglo nonprofessional. Both the Mexican-American and the Anglo students expressed more positive attitudes toward the Anglo professional and the Mexican-American nonprofessional. The researcher theorized that the Mexican-American subjects did not find the Hispanic professional as credible because so few exist, but more research is needed to test this thesis. At present, these results indicate that in some cases Hispanics hold positive perceptions about the competency of Anglo therapists (Acosta, 1975). A second researcher questioned Black and Puerto Rican students participating in a special college program about their college counselors. In a forced-choice questionnaire administered in 1967 asking "What quality in your counselor makes you comfortable?" only 12% of the subjects selected "same racial background." In a follow-up questionnaire administered to the same group of subjects in 1968, 68% of the subjects responded that a counselor's ethnic background should be the same as that of the client. However, subjects also rated each counselor's effectiveness. Of those clients participating in therapy with the three counselors rated as most effective, only 10% reported that ethnic background should be the same. In contrast, 40% of those participating in therapy with the three therapists evaluated as least effective emphasized same ethnicity. The researcher suggested that the students responded in part to counselor effectiveness but labeled this factor ethnic similarity. When the same researcher administered a final questionnaire in 1969, 21 out of 30 students reported that it did not matter whether counselors shared their ethnic background (Beckner, 1970).

Several studies do suggest that Hispanics prefer and progress better with therapists of their own ethnicity. A randomly selected group of Mexican-American soldiers expressed a desire that counseling services be offered by ethnics and stated that they would be more apt to visit the military clinic if it were staffed by Mexican Americans (Van Vranken, 1973). Among junior high school Mexican Americans, more positive attitudes about counselors were expressed on a questionnaire when the counselor was described as Chicano rather than Anglo (Rippee, 1967). An extensive study indicated that patients from lower socioeconomic brackets engage in more self-exploration early in therapy if matched with their therapist on ethnic and class variables (Lorion, 1974). Since many Hispanic patients are members of the lower socioeconomic class, one might infer from these results that most Hispanics would disclose more personal data with therapists of their ethnicity, particularly if matched on socioeconomic class as well.

As Palomares and Haro (1971) have stated, some Hispanics believe that Anglo therapists lack knowledge about Hispanic culture and must study the history and culture of Hispanics before they can be effective therapists. Palomares and Haro (1971, p. 128) explain:

> . . . at the present time many Anglo counselors will continue to work with Chicanos in counseling relationships . . . to improve their communication with Chicanos . . . they can practice genuine dedication to all the demands of their profession. This means knowing and understanding Chicanos, their history, their culture, their expectations. This means listening to them and having compassion for their human aspirations.

In several studies, therapist ethnicity was not a significant determinant of client attitude and therapeutic gain. In a mental-health center in East Los Angeles that had a clientele that was 85% Hispanic, clients did not view the therapist's ethnicity or ability to speak Spanish as particularly helpful, whereas therapists who were bilingual and bicultural did view these attributes as helpful (Moll, et al., 1976). In a second study conducted in East Los Angeles, 30 female Mexican Americans who continued therapy for more than five visits and 30 matched clients who discontinued therapy after less than two visits were interviewed. The clients had been assisted at one of three clinics by bilingual/bicultural therapists. The less acculturated clients (as measured by three questionnaires concerning feelings of control, interpersonal behavior, and future-time perspective) were more likely to drop out of therapy, regardless of the therapist's background (Miranda, Andujo, Caballero, Guerrero, & Ramos, 1976).

The varied data about Hispanic attitudes toward therapist language and ethicity suggest that biculturalism/bilingualism may be helpful, but not necessarily sufficient, to ensure positive client attitude and therapeutic gain. Anglo therapists may be perceived positively in some cases and negatively in other cases. Much more research is needed to ascertain the particular qualities of therapists that foster confidence in their clients.

Therapist Attitudes toward the Client

Middle-class therapists may tend to reject low-income patients because they perceive these patients as hostile, suspicious, crude, and desirous of only symptomatic relief (Lorion, 1974). Since many Hispanics are poor and most therapists are middle class, many therapists may perceive their poor Hispanic patients as less desirable than middle-class patients. The therapist who perceives Hispanic clients as hostile will lack empathy and may be ineffectual or reject pertinent information. Because of a lack of information, the therapist may actually precipitate harm. As indicated in the case of the Martinez family, it is possible that in some cases harm is actually done in the name of good intentions (**es una buena joda que le dan a uno**), because non-Hispanic mental-health professionals are not familiar either with the problems of the poor or with those of Hispanics.

> *THE CASE OF THE MARTINEZ FAMILY.*[5] The case in point is the Martinez family which lives in Ormiga, a town northeast of Peñasco, Colorado. It consists of Mrs. Martinez, whose husband died of cancer in the spring of 1968, and her five children—Bob, age 20; Fred, age 16; Larry, age 14; Jake, age 13; and Fernando, age 8. At the time of the study, Bob was in the state reformatory serving an indeterminant sentence. The sentence was later changed because he escaped and was caught.
>
> Fred is a drop-out. Prior to 1967, he attended school sporadically until he was picked up by police for stealing a car. He appeared before the juvenile judge and was placed on probation. After he was released he returned to school; however, since he did not attend regularly he

[5]From "A Case in Point: An Ethnomethodological Study of a Poor Mexican American Family," by R. Ramos, *Social Science Quarterly*, 1973, *53*, 902–919. Copyright 1973 by the University of Texas Press. Reprinted by permission.

was advised by his probation officer and the school counselor to leave school. As Fred explained it, "They said since I was almost 16 and two years behind and didn't like school, I didn't have to go anymore." Fred at the time of the study had a part-time job, and when he was not working he stayed at home watching T.V. or fixing an old car parked in front of the house. In the evenings he generally went to the O.E.O. Center, "just to hang around."

Larry was in the seventh grade. Because he got in a fight with the teacher and missed the last two and a half weeks of school, he had been retained in the sixth grade, in spite of the fact that he had passing grades. He was told that he could go on to the seventh grade if he would come one week after school was out and take the tests he missed. He did not take the tests. Therefore, he was kept in the sixth grade another year.

It is important to mention two things here. One is that during the last four weeks of the spring semester Mr. Martinez was dying. He died right after school was out, and this presumably could account for Larry not taking his tests. The other is that during this semester the grades of Larry and Jake went from high average grades to straight "F's." Both boys continued to make straight "F's."

Jake was also in the seventh grade. His school record was the same as Larry's except that he did not have to repeat the sixth grade and was considered a "nicer person" by the school. The school counselor claimed that Jake was not a "hardened delinquent" like Larry and that "he is a nice boy with a lot of problems, who we are trying to help. That's if he'd only come to school."

Fernando was in the first grade. His school attendance was the same as the older boys. According to the elementary school principal, "Fernando is a smart child who does fairly well whenever he attends school. His attitude towards his teacher and the school in general is not the very best. In fact, he has referred to me as 'the punk'."

Prior to his death, Mr. Martinez was ill for about two years and for the last six months of his illness he was cared for at home by his wife. During the long and

painful illness of her husband Mrs. Martinez was not
only a nurse to her husband but mother and father to
her five boys. According to her, "Life has always
been heavy."

One point in Mrs. Martinez' account which needs
further elaboration is the problem with her employer.
Two weeks prior to the court hearing, the turkey plant
where Mrs. Martinez works was raided by the United
States Immigration Department for Mexican Nationals.
They took what constituted 50 percent of the labor force.
As a result, the foreman, concerned with getting the
work out, threatened to fire the remaining employees if
they missed a day of work. This event constitutes part
of the background knowledge Mrs. Martinez used to
make sense of the situations in which she found herself.
It needs to be taken into account if we are to
understand how Mrs. Martinez coped with other events
in her life, in particular, going to court.

I have described some general features of the family
in the case in point. Now we can proceed to the helpers
to see how they begin to get involved with the family,
to learn how they are helping, and at the same time
how they make the family's life more problematic.

The local agencies did not understand why Mrs. Martinez allowed
her children to miss school. Agency personnel provoked further schism
within the family and further threat between the family members and
the greater Anglo society.

There are four agencies connected with the family.
Each agency in its own particular way is working with
the family and the family knows each agency by the
person who either comes to the house or to whom they
have to report. These four agencies are the Department
of Welfare for the county, the Juvenile Court, the
Ormiga Public School, and the O.E.O. (Office of
Economic Opportunity) Center for Ormiga.

Each of these four agencies has one or more persons
who represent the agency to the family. The family
caseworker represented the Department of Welfare. The
Juvenile Court is represented by the probation officer.
The public school is represented by the truant officer,

the elementary school principal, Fernando's first grade teacher, the junior high principal, and the junior high counselor for Larry and Jake. The tutor-counselors represent the O.E.O. Center.

In addition to the four agencies and their representatives, I can be looked upon as a "helper." As I mentioned before, I came to know the family through the public school when the elementary school principal asked me to speak to the mother about Fernando's absenteeism. I was asked to do this primarily because I could talk with the mother in Spanish.

Each of these persons thinks of himself or herself as working either with a member or the total family. When I asked the others about their relationships with the family, all of the above people said either, "I work with the whole family" or "I work with one of the boys." Each of these people also thought of his work as helpful to the family. "We've been helping them a lot," some said. Others said, "We give them all the help we can." When asked to define the nature of the help, the only specific answers were given by the caseworker and the O.E.O. Center tutor-counselors. The caseworker said, "We help by giving them money." The tutor-counselors said, "We try to help by talking with the boys when they come into the center."

The social worker and school personnel created new problems for the Martinez family.

The caseworker was assigned by her department to the Martinez case when they were declared eligible for partial A.D.C. (Aid to Dependent Children) a year and a half before the court hearing. The caseworker used to visit the Martinez family twice a month. However, she and Mrs. Martinez had a fight over budgeting, and consequently the visits were reduced to once a month. The visits usually last anywhere from 10 to 20 minutes, if Mrs. Martinez is at home. The caseworker said, "For the last few months she hasn't been around. I've been by in the morning and in the afternoon and I haven't been able to catch her. I wonder if she has a man friend."

According to the caseworker, the relationship between herself and Mrs. Martinez is the usual client-caseworker relationship. "I'd say we have the usual client-caseworker relationship now. Unfortunately I haven't been able to relate with her. She had some unfortunate dealings with my department and she doesn't get along too well with me over this."

The caseworker did not define what the unfortunate dealings were. She also did not describe what she does when she visits the Martinez home. Mrs. Martinez, however, has described their encounters. She describes the caseworker as a dumb and snoopy woman.

"She comes in here and she sits there on the sofa. All the time she has a silly grin on her face. She smiles at me and I smile at her. This is what happens after she asks how we are getting along. I always say "OK" and she says "good." This is the way it always is now. Before, like I told you, she used to come in here and want to see everything, the kitchen, the bedroom, everything. Like I told you, I put a stop to that."

The probation officer first met the family in 1966 when Bob, the oldest son, got into trouble and was placed on probation. Since then, Fred, Larry and Jake have been assigned to him. The boys usually see him once a month at the O.E.O. Center where he has an office. According to the probation officer: "The boys always come to the center, so I usually see them more than the usual once a month. When we meet we talk about any problems that they might be having. They never report any, so I ask how they are doing in school. And they always give me the usual 'fine.' I never hear anything from the school, so I guess they are doing all right. I just keep working with them and hope that the little one (Fernando) doesn't follow in their footsteps."

Larry and Jake describe a typical meeting with the probation officer in the following way: "We go to his office and sit and he asks how we are doing and we say 'fine'. He keeps saying that if we don't behave and keep getting into trouble we are going to get into deep trouble and end up like Bob. He is OK. I guess he is trying to help us."

Another person who also entered the picture was a law student. Mrs. Martinez referred to him as "that other man from the court." The law student from the University Law School works part time at the legal aid clinic. The main function of the clinic is to provide legal aid to the poor. The law student was assigned to the Martinez case to represent Larry and Jake. It is interesting that the case was referred to the clinic by the juvenile judge.

The judge asked that a Spanish-speaking person be assigned. The assumption was that a law student with a Spanish name would be able to talk with Mrs. Martinez and be in a better position to help when she and her two boys, Larry and Jake, appeared before the juvenile judge. The judge's good intentions failed. As the law student put it: "I have a Spanish name but I don't know the language. I've been to the home twice. With my three words of Spanish used up the first minute I get there we end up grunting at each other until I leave. I doubt that she understood why I'm even there."

In the elementary school there are two people who claim to be working with the family: the principal and Fernando's first grade teacher. The principal first became acquainted with the family the year before when Larry was sent to the office by his teacher for behavioral problems. At that time the principal tried to work with Larry and Jake. Both boys were in the sixth grade. But as the principal explains it: "I don't think I ever reached Larry. I might have gotten to Jake, but not Larry. In a way I'm not too sure I blame Larry for being as bitter as he is. The principal I replaced had no right to make him repeat the sixth grade. He had done all his work, and in fact he had average grades.

"Well, I couldn't undo the harm. I found out about the situation when it was too late, the fall semester was almost over, and I couldn't send him to the junior high. But I did try to help them. I'd talk with them and I even went to the home several times. I didn't do much good. I couldn't communicate with the mother. What bothers me now is that Fernando is following in Larry's footsteps. Fernando is just as bitter."

Fernando's teacher first met him in September, 1969, when school started and Fernando arrived a week late. Due to his antischool behavior and high absenteeism his teacher felt she needed to learn more about the family. She explained: "I feel sorry for him but he must learn to behave while in school. I try to help him as much as possible but he doesn't come very often and when he does he is very rude to me. I wish his mother would come and visit with me so we could talk. I don't know how she expects us to help them if she never comes or calls us."

In the junior high, the people who have contact with the family are the principal, the counselor, and the truant officer. The contact that the principal and the counselor have with the family is through the truant officer. His job has been, and still is, to go to the home and find out why Larry and Jake are not in school and to reprimand the mother for not sending them to school regularly. On his return from his home visits he reports to the principal and if the principal considers it important, he calls the counselor in to discuss alternative solutions to the problem.

The relationship between the home and the junior high is a poor one. The family, especially the mother, hates the truant officer. It was on the recommendation of both the junior high principal and counselor that the truant officer referred the family to the juvenile authorities. The principal felt that by taking the mother to court they would be able to help the boys. He said: "By dragging them to court, we felt that the truant officer and the judge could talk some sense into her head. If that does not help we'll see that they [the children] are taken out of the home and placed where they can be helped. It is our duty as school people to help those boys."

At the O.E.O. Center the two people who help the boys are the counselor-tutors. They have known the boys for one year. One counselor-tutor described the help they give to the boys as follows: "We generally just talk with Fernando and the older boys (Fred, Larry and Jake) and give them something to do, like draw. Drawing usually keeps them occupied, although it hasn't been working

lately. The older boys have found such worthwhile
entertainment as making holes in the wall to see the
girls in the restroom. We didn't know what to do with
them. We can't run them away. That's what we're here
for—to work with them, to tutor them. We've been
meaning to visit the mother, especially now that the
boys are getting wild, but since we've been here we
haven't had a chance. We understand they've had a hard
life. We wish we could do more to help them.

More trouble was created because the agencies did not unify their
efforts.

On October 22, 1966, the family had to go to
juvenile court. Larry and Jake, because of their
absenteeism, were referred by the school to the juvenile
authorities for violating the attendance law of the state
of Colorado. A week and a half before the court date I
became acquainted with the family. At this time I
learned that the mother and the boys did not know why
they had to go to court or who had "turned them in."
The family had gotten a letter from the Penasco Juvenile
Court requesting that they appear on the above date.
The letter did not give any reason why they were being
summoned to court. The boys assumed that it was due
to their absenteeism and that is what they told their
mother when they read the letter to her. Their
assumption was correct.

The family was very vague about whether they
would attend the hearing or not. When asked about the
court hearing the boys would only say, "The letter said
we have to be there on the 22nd at eleven o'clock." The
mother, when asked about the hearing, would turn to
the boys and say: "I don't know how you are going to
get there. I have to work. I'm tired. I send you to
school and if you don't want to go and if that's what you
want [to be taken to court] that's what you'll get. I tell
you I'm tired. I suffered so much with your father, and
now with you. I have to work. I can't miss my job.
Even if I could go, how would we get there? We
have no car." The mother, at least, was not planning
to attend.

In fact she thought her solution (that is, not to attend) was a reasonable one. Whenever she yelled at the boys about getting themselves to court and about her having to work, she ended the shouting by looking at me and saying, "No?" At first I did not know what to make of the "no?" Since the "no?" followed the yelling at the boys and since the situation was a tense one for me, I took the "no?" to be part of the yelling at the boys and I did not attribute any importance to it. I took it to be the emphasis we use in Spanish when we stress a point, until after witnessing her shouting four or five times, it occurred to me not to smile when she turned to me and said "No?"

When she did not get my usual response, the smile, she repeated her "no?". To me the intonation of her voice and her facial expression when she said "no?" the second time conveyed the meaning "what's wrong?". The "no?" no longer was what I first thought: her simply emphasizing her statements. By giving or at least conveying to me with her second "no?" the meaning "What's wrong?", she conveyed to me that she gave her original "no?" a different definition than I had. Therefore, with this new knowledge, I proceeded to learn what definition she gave her original "no?".

I asked, "I don't understand. What does 'no?' mean?" [*"No entiendo. ¿Qué quiere decir 'no?'"*]

She answered with: "It's reasonable, no? I have to work, how can I go?" [*"Es justo, ¿no? Tengo que trabajar, ¿cómo voy ir?"*] "I am not sitting down, I work. Everybody knows that." [*"No estoy sentada, trabajo. Todo el mundo lo sabe."*]

In essence, then, she defined her "no?" to mean, "I work and everybody knows that. Therefore, they'll know why I'm not there." She gave me the impression she assumed that others would see her decision not to attend as a reasonable one.

At this time, a week and a half prior to the court date, I began to inquire why the family had to appear in court. The elementary school principal did not know. The truant officer and the junior high principal had not informed him that they had referred the family to the juvenile authorities. Since the elementary school principal did not know that the junior high had referred the family, I assumed the boys had to go to court for some other reason such as stealing. They had been doing some car stripping.

The caseworker, when asked about the court hearing, said she did not know anything about it. In fact, she said: "I didn't know they had to go to court. I wonder if I should go. I've been to one of these hearings and I don't know what goes on in them. Maybe I should go. Do you think I should go? Look, Wednesdays are my days off in the office, so if you think I should go give a call and I'll pop right over."

Because of her lack of interest in the family, I assumed she might be a hindrance to the family if she went. Therefore, I advised her not to go.

The counselor-tutors at the O.E.O. Center did not know about the hearing. One of the counselor-tutors did express a concern about the situation and on my advice she began to inquire about the court hearing. She discovered that a truant officer, on the recommendation of the junior high principal and the counselor, had referred the family to the juvenile authorities. He was also working with the probation officer in preparing a case.

The case that the truant and probation officers were to prepare, according to the junior high principal, was to "show that Mrs. Martinez was an irresponsible mother." The counselor said to me, "Once we get her before the judge and the truant officer they'll shape her up. That's the only way we can get her to realize she is doing a poor job. We'll help those boys in one way or another."

After learning that the family, due to their ignorance of the gravity of the situation, was not making an effort to attend the court hearing, I decided to intervene. I talked the mother into going. I did this by volunteering to take the family in my car and by pointing out that the judge, not knowing that she had to work, would think she did not love her children if she were not present. I also pointed out to her that she and the boys ultimately would have to appear before the judge and that if she did not attend the hearing on the 22nd, the judge would be very angry with her whenever she did appear before him. In essence, I advised her on the advantages of going to the hearing.

People were surprised to see the family in court. When the counselor-tutor and I arrived with the mother, Larry and Jake, the student lawyer from the legal aid clinic, whom I had never met, came out of the court building saying in a very surprised voice, "Oh? You're here?" When the truant and probation officers walked into the court room and found the family there, they said, "Oh? You made it?" Before the start of the hearing the judge stuck his head out from his chambers and said, "They're here?" Everyone was amazed that the family appeared.

There is another interesting feature of the hearing. The student lawyer did not know what advice to give the judge. After hearing from the truant officer all the negative things about the family, the judge asked the student lawyer if the mother understood English. He said no. The judge then asked the lawyer what he would recommend be done. The student lawyer told the judge he did not know what to recommend. The lawyer then asked if I would speak to the court, since I was working with the family. I gave a brief account of the family's history and their many problems. I also pointed out to the court that at the present time several people in the community besides myself were trying to help the mother solve her problems. After my presentation the judge turned to the boys and told them that if they would promise to attend school regularly, he would put them on probation. Of course they promised to attend school.

The case of the Martinez family is deliberately long in order to illustrate a number of important points. The first point has to do with the intricacy of the case and the large number of individuals and helping agencies involved. The poor frequently have multiple problems that bring them into contact with multiple social-service agencies whose services are fragmented and not coordinated. This is clearly shown in the case of the Martinez family. Also illustrated in the case is the problem of language. Mrs. Martinez could not speak English, and none of the individuals involved in the case was bilingual. There was no one, for example, who could explain to her that her children were having difficulty in school or how the welfare department intended to assist her. Further, as is true in many families, the Martinez children depended entirely on their mother for economic support. She was the sole wage earner and, because of economic need, had to work even though it prevented her being involved in the school-related problems of her children. The morning in court, which she did not understand at first, probably cost her a day of work, a fact often overlooked by middle-class workers, who can usually take a day off from work without losing pay by using vacation or sick leave. Finally, the painful loss of the father seemed to be an overlooked consideration in the problems that the children were experiencing. There was no male figure in the family that the children could turn to. The father had been ill for several years before his death, creating a stress situation for the entire family. How were the children to react when there was no one who understood their predicament and with whom they could counsel for solace and guidance?

In some cases, non-Hispanic helping professionals may not hold negative attitudes about Hispanic clients; yet their guilt about discrimination against Hispanics may prevent their effective functioning, as in the case of Mr. M. that follows.

> *THE CASE OF MR. M.*[6] Mr. M. was a 40-year old Spanish American from the San Luis Valley. When he was 35 his somewhat dominating mother had died, and he had moved with his wife and six children to Denver. He soon discovered that his wife could obtain work more easily than he. He began to miss his home and to resent his wife's increasing independence when he was 40. He began to think his wife was having an affair with one of his friends. He beat her up, and she obtained an order for his hospitalization. He was subsequently rehospitalized on three occasions and, in the process, his wife obtained a legal separation. As his illness progressed he also became more obviously depressed. His last admission, when I began to treat him, was precipitated by his hearing voices urging him to kill himself.
>
> He had always arrived at the hospital mute and agitated. Though he would eventually respond to

[6]From "Some Factors in the Psychiatric Treatment of Spanish-Americans," by L. Y. Kline, *American Journal of Psychiatry*, 1969, *125*, 1674–1681. Copyright 1969 by the American Psychiatric Association. Reprinted by permission.

medication, he would never talk about his problems, and upon discharge he would stop his medication and refuse follow-up care. Once, however, he did join the other Spanish-American patients to complain that a Spanish patient had been secluded because of Anglo prejudice.

Initially, all he would say to me was, "I just want to be a normal American." I acknowledged his right to desire this, but asked if he felt this had been denied him. He eventually expressed considerable hostility toward Anglos. After this, he began to express his anger at his wife for "bossing" him around, vowed to divorce her, and seemed very well. Following his discharge, he took his medication and came to see me regularly. One day he cautiously revealed to me that he had also been seeing a *curandera* (female folk healer) for "stomach troubles." She had sworn him to secrecy, but he promised to tell me more at the next session.

The next time he seemed upset and reported having had persecutory dreams. Eventually he said that the *curandera* had not merely given him an olive oil tonic but had also expressed an interest in his life and had commented that he seemed lonely. He thought she was offering to be his mistress, became frightened, and said he would never see her again. Instead, he returned to his wife. This went well until she refused to have intercourse. I wondered if his return to his wife was wise. I never saw him again. Three months later his wife called in to inquire about the bill. She incidentally mentioned that he had killed himself. She had found my telephone number in his pocket.

In this case, the therapist was once again able to empathize with the patient's anger over social and economic inequalities but did not go further. The patient was lonely and, in suggesting that he leave his family, I had overlooked this. The therapist could only have aroused a sense of frustration stemming from this lack of empathy for the most personal aspect of the patient's problems. The patient could not trust the therapist to help him cope with the problems in returning to the family.

Why had this happened? This minority patient had the ability to arouse guilt in his Anglo therapist, and the therapist found it easier to deal with this guilt by declaring his innocence and joining with the patient to denounce Anglo society and his quisling wife for causing the patient's problems.

One study suggests that Anglo therapists may be more accepting than the general population of minority groups. A researcher interviewed practicing psychotherapists concerning their attitudes about Mexican Americans, Blacks, Japanese Americans, Chinese Americans, and Jews. About 23% of the therapists had stereotypical views of these groups. Mexican Americans were the most common targets of stereotypes about changeability and suspiciousness, followed by Blacks, Jews, Chinese Americans, and Japanese Americans. These same therapists were asked to respond to a social-distance scale; they demonstrated social distance from various minority groups in the same order and relative position as had the previously tested general population. However, across the categories of social distance, therapists were, overall, more tolerant of each ethnic group than was the general population (Bloombaum, Yamamoto, & James, 1968).

A tolerant Anglo therapist may offer certain advantages for the Hispanic client. If the client is angry about discrimination, the Anglo therapist can be extremely helpful in assisting the client to work through these fears and frustrations. In the case of Mr. O. below, an Anglo therapist helps the client express his frustration about Anglo/Hispanic relations. The client establishes a meaningful relationship with the therapist that generalizes to Anglo coclients in his therapy group.

THE CASE OF MR. O.[7] Mr. O. is a 28-year-old Spanish-American teacher who wished to join a therapy group "to find out how the Anglo mind works." Mr. O. had been divorced six years before. Thereafter, he had become depressed, had begun to drink heavily, and had earned for himself a reputation as a "tough little guy." At the suggestion of the authorities, he had undergone treatment for alcoholism. He had started individual treatment a few months before joining the group because of an Anglo girl friend. He explained: "I got too close to

[7]From "Some Factors in the Psychiatric Treatment of Spanish-Americans," by L. Y. Kline, *American Journal of Psychiatry*, 1969, *125*, 1674–1681. Copyright 1969 by the American Psychiatric Association. Reprinted by permission.

her, and she dropped me, and I was afraid I'd get depressed again."

At first, the all-Anglo ongoing group did not overtly acknowledge that Mr. O. was Spanish. Yet that hour there was much talk of ancestry. "My relatives have had master's degrees for at least three generations," said one seductive female patient. "My second husband is descended from President X," said a second. "I'm so glad O. is in the group. He's the first member that's been able to help me," said a third, trying another tactic. When I asked what this was all about, the group became angry with me. "Maybe you have a problem with your ancestry, Dr. Kline," our male Jewish patient challenged me.

The following week Mr. O. said he had felt uncomfortable because his background had not been openly recognized. He wondered if he had really been accepted. He then told of experiences with discrimination and received much support. At the next week's group session I had to announce the unexpected necessity of terminating the group. Weeks passed, and Mr. O. became more involved in the group's dynamics, but whereas once it was through his experiences as a Chicano, as he had called himself, now he also spoke of an old feeling that he had been rejected by his wife and mother. However, as he did this, and the group talked increasingly of the forthcoming termination, he also began coming late.

Finally he made an extremely hostile remark to our heavily cathected "borderline" female patient. She predictably fell apart and eventually ran from the room. "Why don't you kick me out? You see, I'm a rat," said Mr. O. The next week, as the group discussed the incident, Mr. O. admitted he had wanted to be thrown out: "The group's ending. Sure, I felt rejected. I'm scared. I want to leave first." He became hostile to everyone, and when this was pointed out, he replied, "I guess you don't like Mexicans." "We know you've been treated unfairly because you're a Mexican," said the "borderline" lady, "but that's not why we're mad at you." Mr. O. missed the next meeting (second to last), but sought me out a few days later. He explained, "I

wanted to prove I could get along without the group. I
can, but I'll be back. It's my group, too."

Mr. O. identified the group as "Anglo," did not
expect to be helped, but came in order to joust with his
enemies . . . he stayed when he was helped to recognize
his own stake in the group—that it could help him to
face uncomfortable feelings.

In general, therapists with respect for their Hispanic clients can be
effective facilitators of personal growth. The therapist will be accepting
of different attitudes and behaviors that are associated with the clients'
culture and values, life of poverty, and personal/social history. Therapists
who lack appreciation for, and insight about, Hispanic culture may be
critical of Hispanic clients. Their negative sets are counterproductive to
broad therapeutic goals.

IMPLICATIONS FOR PLURALISTIC THERAPISTS

Hispanics' underutilization of mental-health services cannot be
explained in terms of their attitudes about illness or counseling. Although Hispanics differ somewhat from Anglos in their interpretation
of psychopathology, Hispanics express positive attitudes about therapy
and therapists. Utilization of mental-health facilities should increase
when the following policies are instituted:

(1) Centers are located in Hispanic communities.
(2) Therapists and receptionists speak Spanish.
(3) Hispanic culture and values are respected by staff.
(4) Waiting lists, if they are necessary, do not discriminate against
ethnic-minority people.
(5) Association with the judiciary is limited.

To a large extent, the medical model must be replaced by a social-action
paradigm.

Research presents contradictory findings about Hispanic clients'
attitudes toward Anglo, bilingual, and bicultural therapists. There is an
absence of research on the critical question of the relative effectiveness of
Anglo versus Hispanic therapists with Hispanic clients. Research on this
issue is riddled by massive methodological questions, such as how to
measure client gain and how to control therapist variables other than
ethnicity. A primary block to research on this issue is the limited number

of Hispanic therapists. A review of rosters of professional organizations in 1971 revealed that less than 2% of the members of the American Psychological Association were Spanish surnamed (Ruiz, 1971). The proportion of Hispanic mental-health professionals is dramatically less than the proportion of Hispanics in the United States (Olmedo & Lopez, 1977).

Recently, Ruiz and Padilla (1977) and Ruiz, Padilla, and Alvarez (1978) have proposed a model to predict the relative effectiveness of Anglo and Hispanic therapists with Hispanic clients. The model is well illustrated in Figure 5-1. Quadrants 1 through 4 represent possible combinations of commitment to the Hispanic and Anglo cultures. According to this model, we can predict that an Anglo therapist would understand and thus be effective with clients from quadrants 1 and 3 (the bicultural and acculturated clients); and these clients could be expected to be comfortable with an Anglo therapist. A bilingual/bicultural therapist will be attuned to and effective with bicultural clients. Most likely these therapists will also understand the dilemma of the marginal client; however, the bilingual/bicultural therapist may lack empathy for unacculturated clients. Research suggests that the unacculturated client is least likely to seek assistance from a mental-health center. Bilingualism and biculturalism may not be sufficient qualities to satisfy the needs of unacculturated clients. These clients require therapists highly familiar with pluralistic therapy. The therapist must help these clients adapt to their traditionally oriented environment. Perhaps effective therapy with unacculturated clients cannot be achieved within the typical mental-health setting.

It is hoped that the number of Hispanic therapists will increase and that systematic research will be conducted regarding the effectiveness of Anglo and Hispanic professionals with Hispanic clients. Palomares (1971c, p. 135) recalls an encounter with a group of Mexican-American and Mexican children that well summarizes the complexity of the ethnicity issue as it relates to therapist effectiveness and client gain.

> After the interview had terminated, an angry debate erupted among the children. While we were finishing the discussion, an older boy from Tijuana, Mexico, newly arrived in the United States, had entered the room. He asked me who I was and I told him my name was Valo. (I often use only my first name in informal situations). . . . He asked me where I was from, and I told him Coachella, a town near San Diego. I added that I had grown up under the same conditions as most of the children in the discussion, and that probably my situation had been like his also. He then said in a degrading tone, "Oh, you're just a **pocho** then." He meant to imply that I

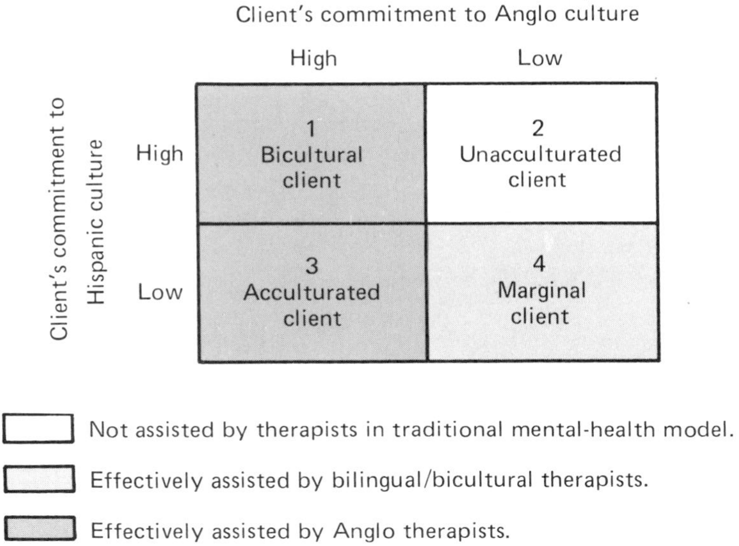

Client's commitment to Anglo culture

		High	Low
Client's commitment to Hispanic culture	High	1 Bicultural client	2 Unacculturated client
	Low	3 Acculturated client	4 Marginal client

☐ Not assisted by therapists in traditional mental-health model.

▨ Effectively assisted by bilingual/bicultural therapists.

▧ Effectively assisted by Anglo therapists.

Figure 5-1. A model to show the interaction of Hispanic clients' ethnic orientation and therapist ethnicity (see text for explanation).

was less than a genuine Mexican, because I was not from Mexico, but from the United States.

Immediately several of the boys in the group bristled and came quickly to my defense. They said things like, "Well, what are you? Just a Chicano from T.J. [Tijuana]."

This hurried, five-minute encounter exhibited the kind of hostility that can erupt when one youngster insults the unique status of another youngster or another person by using denigrating terms.

From the older boy's viewpoint, a real doctor, such as he understood from his experience in Mexico, was never just a person, and certainly spoke Spanish differently. His comments and attitudes revealed a degrading stereotype concerning the mixed position of Chicanos in this country, as well as a rigid understanding of professional behavior and performance.

From my own immediate reaction—one of anger and hurt at such a quick and harsh putdown—and that of the children who rallied to confront the challenger, it became apparent how differently we have been conditioned to perceive and relate to the counselor as a professional and as a person.[8]

[8]From "Nuestro Sentimientos son Iguales la Differencia es en la Experiencia," by U. H. Palomares, *Personnel and Guidance Journal*, 1971, *50*(2), 137–144. Copyright 1971 by the American Personnel and Guidance Association. Reprinted by permission.

Chapter 6
Implementation
of Pluralistic Therapy

In this chapter we will review a number of recommendations for increasing Hispanics' awareness of, and positive expectations about, mental-health counseling services. These suggestions for implementation of the pluralistic approach have appeared in various sources, and our goal here is to integrate and expand on them.

PUBLIC RELATIONS

A number of suggestions have been made in the past to increase Hispanic awareness of mental-health services. The most efficient way is probably the use of television and radio. Communication experts have advocated the use of the mass media for public information and education. Radio and television have been effective in reaching the Hispanic population. For example, radio announcements on Spanish-speaking stations in Tucson, Arizona, that explained the nature and location of mental-health services were effective in increasing the number of Mexican-American clients at La Frontera Mental Health Clinic (Heiman, Burruel, & Chavez, 1975). Similarly, programs shown on Spanish-speaking television stations about emotional disturbance and ways of handling stress have increased referrals to local mental-health centers (Boulette, 1974).

The limited existing literature concerning utilization by Hispanics of Spanish-language television contains some interesting information. For example, although two-thirds of all "foreign-language" programming on 40 radio and 9 television stations is in Spanish, very little is really known about the users of these media (Lopez & Enos, 1973). The Lopez and Enos (1973) analysis of 750 Hispanic media users in Los Angeles County constitutes a major contribution to our understanding of the importance of mass media to Hispanics. Their study clearly indicates that consistent viewing of Spanish-language television by Hispanics is a class-linked phenomenon. The primary users of Spanish television were found to be poor (75% had less than $10,000 annual family income); minimally educated (88.3% had a high school education or less); older (75.2% were age 30 or more); foreign born (75.5% were from Mexico); and monolingual (100% Spanish-speaking only). Only 1% of the respondents had no television set, and 50% had two or more sets. Thus, Spanish television programming seems to be well utilized, especially among low-income, monolingual, older, and foreign-born Hispanics.

In a survey conducted in three Southern California communities, Mexican Americans stated that they had learned about the availability of mental-health services from friends and relatives *or* from local public-service announcements on the radio or television (Padilla et al., 1976). The striking thing about this finding was that the respondents themselves were not users of mental-health services in these communities but were informed about the availability of services should they have need for them. This fact attests to the value of public-service announcements, since effective communication was achieved with Hispanics. It is important to note that these radio and television announcements were prepared and delivered by Hispanic mental-health professionals, familiar with the cultural nuances of the people they were attempting to communicate with (Boulette, 1974).

Although Spanish-language television seems to be well utilized, minimal efforts have been made to use this medium for advertising counseling services. The few educational mental-health programs that have been translated into Spanish are practically useless because these translations cannot be understood by low-income Hispanics, who are often poorly educated both in English and in Spanish. On this point Boulette (personal communication, 1976), who has conceived, written, and produced over 40 Spanish-language educational mental-health television programs, states that care must be taken to identify the potential viewer and to design programs with this viewer in mind. Boulette elaborates that, after her material had been researched, written, and organized, it was rewritten in a restricted Spanish linguistic code. Simple words and short sentences with concrete, idiomatic, and down-to-earth expressions were used. An informal delivery, repetition of key words and ideas, and concrete examples of abstract concepts were also utilized. Thus, these educational programs considered the viewer's

Spanish preference and need for a particular kind of Spanish. A subtle Mexican motif, soft Latin music, and traditional sayings and humor provided ethnic identification and cultural reinforcement. Additionally, bilingualism, traditions, and cultural pride were discussed, reinforced, and interwoven into the program's educational content.

Boulette related how her TV programs were easily and economically converted into audio cassettes that could be used by radio stations. The cassettes have been used in a variety of other settings, such as prenatal and well-baby clinics, Planned Parenthood, community centers, private homes, Head Start programs, bilingual school programs, parenthood-preparation classes, migrant-health projects, and in the waiting rooms of hospitals, and welfare, mental-health, and other agencies.

In sum, a review of the scant literature indicates that Hispanics can be effectively reached via the mass media. More importantly, research indicates that public-service announcements bearing on mental-health issues are needed.

Another important facet of public relations involves removing or limiting the stigma associated with mental-health counseling (Giordano, 1973). Community advocates, such as former patients or community leaders, should be encouraged to speak publicly about the counseling services available in the community. Publicity on radio and television can be helpful in this regard. Some agencies have eliminated the word "mental" from their name; names such as *La Frontera* (the frontier), *El Centro* (the center), or *La Casa del Communidad* (the community house) may be more acceptable to the Hispanic population.

Good public relations means improving access to mental-health agencies by decentralizing them (Giordano, 1973). If it is possible financially, waiting lists should be eliminated (Padilla et al., 1975; Torrey, 1972). As we mentioned earlier, many child-guidance clinics have six-month waiting lists, and many Hispanic families may never receive services (Wolkon et al., 1974). Such practices are counterproductive to the goal of increasing Hispanics' use of mental-health facilities. At the least, clients should be informed of the length of time they will be required to wait for services, and these commitments should be honored. Mental-health facilities should be located in Hispanic communities or transportation to them and babysitting should be provided (Padilla et al., 1975). Since many Hispanics work regular 40-hour weeks, effective facilities should offer evening and Saturday hours (Padilla et al., 1975; Torrey, 1972).

Of course, respect for Hispanic values and design of services with those values in mind is a most powerful public-relations tool. A "personalized institutional welcome" encourages Hispanics to continue their involvement with a mental-health organization (Recio-Andrados, 1975). In accordance with *personalismo*, a warm living-room appearance is therapeutic, and a comfortable drop-in room should be provided (Padilla et al., 1975; Phillipus, 1971). The presence of religious symbols (Torrey, 1972) or an attached chapel is supportive for religious clientele. Home visits by mental-health workers can foster feelings of *personalismo* (Torrey, 1972). In a random survey of the Mexican-American population in Lubbock, Texas, 76% of the people surveyed indicated that they would like a helping professional to talk with them in their homes. Staff at the local agency underestimated significantly the clients' desire for home visits (Mack, James, Ramirez, & Bailey, 1974). Hospitalization should be avoided as it disrupts vital support of the family, *compadrazgo*, and friends (Torrey, 1972).

In accordance with traditional values held by many Hispanics, opportunities should be provided for dealing simultaneously with physical and emotional symptomatology. Mental-health centers should work effectively with local medical services (Phillipus, 1971). Important referrals are obtained from hospital emergency rooms, and physical treatments, such as drugs, diets, massage, and heat treatments, can provide psychotherapeutic as well as physical relief (Torrey, 1972).

SELECTING AND TRAINING PROFESSIONAL STAFF

Bilingual/Bicultural Staff

In previous chapters, we have specified a number of reasons for selecting bilingual staff members for mental-health facilities serving Hispanics. Therapists may interpret clients' statements differently if they speak in English or in Spanish (Marcos, 1976), and clients may find it impossible to express adequately their deep feelings in a second language (Padilla et al., 1975).

Use of a third-party interpreter is not a viable alternative. One researcher suggests that the presence of interpreters may distress Hispanic clients. The traditional emphasis on *dignidad* leads to embarrassment if personal matters are discussed when a third party is present (Garcia, 1971). In addition, untrained interpreters may change the meaning of information being communicated, and important nuances of expression are lost in the translation process. Even when the interpreter is a family member, confusion may arise in the counseling session. For example, a parent may be reluctant to discuss sensitive material when a family member is serving as the interpreter. In other cases, the family member who serves as the interpreter may actually answer the question without giving the client the opportunity to answer for himself or herself. One of the authors knows of a case in which a man was brought to a mental-health center because of his depression. During the interview the therapist asked the non-English-speaking client if he had ever felt like committing suicide. The man's daughter, who was serving as the interpreter, without waiting for the father to answer, replied "No, my father has *never* thought about killing himself."

Many mental-health professionals have emphasized the need for Spanish-speaking and bilingual staff to serve Hispanic clients (for example, Padilla et al., 1975; Phillipus, 1971). Moreover, bilingual support staff, such as bilingual receptionists, can help set a familiar mood and reinforce *personalismo* for the client who is coming to the counseling center for the first time (Phillipus, 1971).

Elsewhere we have discussed the limited research about the relative effectiveness of Anglo and Hispanic therapists. The studies do not indicate consistently that Hispanics hold more positive attitudes about therapy when their therapist is of their ethnicity (Acosta, 1975; Beckner, 1970; Lorion, 1974; Rippee, 1967). In addition to the limited research about clients' attitudes toward Hispanic and Anglo therapists, research about therapists' effectiveness according to their ethnicity is also incomplete. Some studies indicate that clients prefer bicultural therapists (Rippee, 1967; Van Vranken, 1973). What little research there is does lead us, however, to propose that bicultural therapists may be particularly helpful with clients of bicultural and marginal life-styles.

In the case below, Karno and Morales (1971) outline an effective procedure employed to hire bilingual/bicultural staff for a mental-health center serving the large East Los Angeles Mexican-American *barrio*. As we can see from the case, it took two and a half years to attain a bilingual/bicultural staff, but the effort and time paid off in the ultimate zeal of the staff.

THE CASE OF A COMMUNITY MENTAL HEALTH SERVICE FOR MEXICAN AMERICANS IN A METROPOLIS.[1] A key decision was to recruit, to the greatest extent possible, Spanish-speaking personnel for all positions. Another decision was to recruit persons who

[1]From "A Community Mental Health Service for Mexican Americans in a Metropolis," by M. Karno and A. Morales, *Comprehensive Psychiatry*, 1971, *12*, 116–121. Copyright 1971 by the American Psychopathological Association.

had lived in, worked in, or otherwise "knew," identified with, and had strong commitment to the community to be served. These recruitment criteria were, of course, secondary to qualities of personal and professional competence and integrity.

The entire initial full-time staff of twenty-one was recruited over 2½ years time. Two of the first and most important positions to be filled were those of community mental health psychologist and supervising psychiatric social worker. Both positions were filled by persons of Mexican descent who had grown up in, been educated in, and were well known in the East Los Angeles community. They provided much of the critical leadership and design of the program and embodied a rare combination of sociocultural awareness, concern and clinical competence. Fifteen of the staff were completely fluent in Spanish, four were conversant (with varying degrees of limitation) in Spanish, and three persons had a rudimentary knowledge of Spanish but enthusiastically and rapidly learned more. Ten of the 22 had been born in and had grown up in East Los Angeles. Twelve of the staff were Mexican American, and two were of other Latin American (Cuban and Peruvian) descent. There was a remarkably high degree of social, personal and professional involvement on the part of the staff in the community itself, and with but a few exceptions, a very cohesive esprit de corps, somewhat in the nature of a shared, secular, missionary role. The characteristics of the professional staff obviated the use of translators in the diagnostic and therapeutic process, an awkward device which has been utilized experimentally in a New York City mental health program serving Puerto Ricans.

Some studies suggest that Anglo therapists with a sensitivity to Hispanic culture can be effective in pluralistic therapy (Acosta, 1975b; Beckner, 1970). We propose that Anglo therapists may be particularly effective with acculturated and bicultural clients. Because of theoretical controversy and the limited number of experimental investigations, recommendations will not be made about the proportion of Hispanic therapists necessary for the effective functioning of a mental-health counseling center.

Awareness Training for Non-Hispanics

Although the relative effectiveness of Hispanic and Anglo therapists has not been determined, it is well known that Anglo professionals must be cognizant of all facets of Hispanic culture. Continuous in-service training and workshops for staff members concerning Hispanic culture are vital (Garcia, 1971; Padilla et al., 1975).

One social-work researcher has recommended that professionals be required to obtain special licenses in order to work with Hispanics. Certification would require passing a test on Hispanic culture (Garcia, 1971). Another researcher (Leon, 1973) theorized that therapists in training who plan to work in Hispanic communities should be involved in special experiential course work within the *barrios*. To test this theory, Leon compared the therapeutic effectiveness (as measured by client gain on a self-concept scale) of Chicano counselors with and without special training in the *barrios*. No significant results were reported, but the null results may reflect limits in experimental design. Change in clients' self-concepts may not have been sufficiently sensitive for reflecting short-term counseling gain. Better-designed studies incorporating Anglo counselors should be conducted.

It is obvious that an Anglo therapist must not only be familiar with Hispanic culture but must also be respectful of it. Anglo therapists need to scrutinize their behavior for signs of prejudice. Therapists can analyze their openness to Hispanic clients by reviewing videotapes of their therapy sessions. Observation through one-way mirrors by fellow Hispanic professionals can be helpful in uncovering verbal and nonverbal discriminatory messages. Concomitant with respect for the client and recognition of the effects of discrimination on Hispanics, Anglo therapists must not allow guilt about prejudice to interfere with their ability to advise or confront clients when necessary (Kline, 1969).

The therapist who is motivated by guilt to work with Hispanics will probably be ineffective for several reasons. First, he or she may be fearful of an encounter and become too ingratiating. Further, the therapist may communicate feelings of anxiety to the client, which may cause the client to become defensive, thus creating an impasse between therapist and client. Second, a therapist motivated by guilt may "try too hard"—and, if the client does not respond, the therapist may communicate frustration and lessen the effectiveness of counseling. Finally, a therapist may not understand the client's feelings of anger over societal pressures and may discourage expressions of anger that could be cathartic. Some therapists may, in fact, spend time trying to convince their clients that they are no different from non-Hispanics, thereby jeopardizing the trust that the therapist hopes to establish.

In general, the therapist must be comfortable with Hispanics, so that he or she does not withdraw from or overreact to them. A broad in-service training program to achieve this goal might include frequent workshops, ongoing group discussion, observation sessions by peers, and experience in the community.

ROLE OF THE PARAPROFESSIONAL

The use of paraprofessionals offers several advantages. First, there is an acute shortage of doctoral-level Hispanics in the helping professions (Olmedo & Lopez, 1977; Ruiz, 1971). The use of Hispanic paraprofessionals gives clients the opportunity to work with personnel of their own ethnicity. Second, because of their knowledge of the community and its resources, paraprofessionals can act as advocates for clients in many situations in which the professional would be far less effective. Finally, paraprofessionals can be employed to follow up on clients' progress after the termination of therapy.

In New York City's juvenile courts, Puerto Rican paraprofessionals have served as case workers in cases involving Puerto Rican defendants. The paraprofessionals interpret case findings from a cross-cultural perspective. After the court ruling, these paraprofessionals go on to serve as liaisons between the Puerto Rican defendant and social-service agencies (Dohen, 1971). Mexican-American former drug addicts work as agents for preventive mental health. These paraprofessionals enter schools as **Los Veteranos** (Veterans of Life) and are strong models for the school children of how to live fulfilling lives without using drugs (Aron, Alzar, & Gonzales, 1974). Ex-addicts have also been used as street workers to help addicts break their drug habit (Munns, Geis, & Bullington, 1970).

To illustrate how the paraprofessional can facilitate the work of the mental-health professional and at the same time assist people in trouble, let us look at the case of Miss Martinez (Hallowitz & Riessman, 1967). Miss Martinez has come for help to a neighborhood service center in New York.

THE CASE OF MISS MARTINEZ.[2] Miss Martinez came to the Center reporting that she was eight months

[2]From "The Role of the Indigenous Nonprofessional in a Community Mental Health Neighborhood Service Center Program," by E. Hallowitz and F. Riessman, *American Journal of Orthopsychiatry*, 1967, *37*, 766–778. Copyright 1967 by the American Orthopsychiatric Association, Inc. Reprinted by permission.

pregnant and that her common-law husband had deserted her last month. She worked until two weeks ago, but had been forced to stop working and move into a basement apartment with a brother and his family. The few dollars she had accumulated were now gone and she had applied to the Welfare Department for assistance. They had rejected her at intake because they contended that she must know the whereabouts of her common-law husband; they couldn't believe that she could live with a man for two years and not know more about him.

The aide, who spoke Spanish, explained to Miss Martinez why Welfare had to make an investigation and encouraged her to tell whatever she could about her husband. All she knew was that he worked for a cab company, but didn't know which company or where he had lived prior to their getting together. The aide suggested to her that they go together to the police station to see if it were possible to locate her husband. (The aides have had excellent relations with the Police Department—they have visited the police station on a number of occasions, and various policemen have dropped in at the Center to chat and keep warm). The captain of the station, upon hearing the details of the case, dispatched a member of his staff to the central taxicab bureau. There it was discovered that the woman's husband was in fact a cab driver, that he was wanted on charges, but could not be located and had disappeared. These facts were then reported to the Department of Welfare Intake Unit, who felt that they were sufficient to warrant opening the case for further investigation.

When the aide checked with the investigator assigned to the case shortly afterward, he was told that the field supervisor would not fully accept the evidence that was presented and still could not believe that the woman didn't know where her husband was.

Uncertain of what his role should be at this stage, the aide turned to his professional supervisor. The latter, in the presence of the aide, phoned the investigator and subsequently the Department of Welfare supervisor. The aide was able to observe his supervisor moving from the stage of reasonable discussion to the point of righteous indignation, pointing up that the record was clear, that the woman had worked and was self-maintaining during eight months of pregnancy, that our aide had visited the home and had observed the living conditions and found they were as the woman had reported them, that it was not atypical for a woman in these circumstances not to know more about the husband than she did and the very fact that the Police Department couldn't locate the husband should be proof enough of her cooperativeness, her dependability and reliability.

That afternoon the investigator stopped by the Neighborhood Service Center to talk further with our aide. The aide indicated that we wanted to work cooperatively with Welfare, that we didn't want to serve as a pressure group and pointed up all of the things which the aide had done prior to raising this issue. The investigator agreed that the woman could receive Welfare assistance, arranged for an emergency allocation back payment for carfares; the grant also included money for a layette and for future carfare which would enable her to take advantage of the prenatal service at Lincoln Hospital.

The aide then helped Miss Martinez find more adequate living quarters. On the day she moved, which happened to be a Saturday, the aide assisted her with the moving, helped her to wash down the walls, hang curtains, etc. (This is highly significant as the nonprofessional is now providing a model to the helpee, the client—a model which seems to say that helping people even outside the line of duty, not on a work day, is a good thing. The nonprofessional was functioning as one neighbor helping another and was implicitly suggesting a model whereby the helpee in the future might help another neighbor. He was persuading by example in line with our goal of transforming clients into helpers and citizens.)

Shortly after delivery of the baby, the woman stopped by the Center to see the mental health aide. She was relaxed and friendly and obviously enjoying the baby. She indicated to the aide that in a couple of months she would like to return to work. There was a neighbor who could care for the baby during the day at a modest stipend. She complained to the aide that her

problem is that she has no marketable skills. She had
taken some commercial course work when she was in
high school, but these skills were very rusty. The aide
was able to arrange a modified training program for her
while she was at home with the baby. This was worked
out in cooperation with the Department of Welfare.
When she is ready to return to work, both the aide and
the social investigator will attempt to find suitable
employment for her.

The case of Miss Martinez illustrates nicely how a knowledgeable
paraprofessional aide can serve as an advocate for a client with social-
service agencies that are not sensitive to the particular socioeconomic
dilemmas of some Hispanics. Aides can perform other important functions that professionals might not be able to do. In a second example,
Hallowitz and Riessman (1967) describe the case of Mrs. Garcia, in which
an aide saved the professional valuable time, was able to enter a situation not open to the professional, and restored some balance to the client's
life. In this case, the ability of the aide to establish rapport with Mrs.
Garcia's husband by discussing what life was like in Puerto Rico and
now in New York helped the aide to begin resolving some of the problems between Mr. and Mrs. Garcia. The slow, resolute way in which the
aide went about solving the crisis, the note on which the case ends, is
interesting.

THE CASE OF MRS. GARCIA.[3] When Mrs. Garcia
swallowed a large number of aspirins and appeared as an
emergency patient at Lincoln Hospital, the staff
psychiatrist ascertained that she was not a psychotic
woman. Apparently, she was reacting to a problem with
her husband, and her suicide attempt was the classic
"cry for help," a way of getting attention and assistance
from "the system." After talking with her at some length
and after deciding that Mrs. Garcia was not likely to
repeat her suicide attempt, the psychiatrist made an
appointment for her to return to the hospital the
following week. Since she was so distraught, he called

[3]From "The Role of the Indigenous Nonprofessional in a Community Mental Health
Neighborhood Service Center Program," by E. Hallowitz and F. Riessman, *American
Journal of Orthopsychiatry,* 1967, *37,* 766–778. Copyright 1967 by the American
Orthopsychiatric Association, Inc. Reprinted by permission.

the Neighborhood Service Center and asked to have one of the aides come over and pick up the lady, to work with her and obtain further information about her family problems.

This was arranged. An aide escorted Mrs. Garcia to the storefront, picking up her sister on the way, and all three sat down together. Mrs. Garcia's husband had been beating her for some time, she reported. When he went out and came home at 3 A.M. and she complained, he beat her. If she didn't complain, he accused her of not caring, and beat her.

Recently the situation become worse; her husband had thrown her out of the house, put a new lock on the door, and told his wife that he wouldn't allow her to see the children anymore. In desperation she fled to her sister's apartment. But next day a neighbor told her that her children had cried all night, and this sent her into the hysterical fit which culminated in her taking the pills.

The aide listened attentively. He then asked his supervisor, the center director, to join the conference. After talking for about half an hour—the aide, Mrs. Garcia, her sister and the supervisor made a plan together. The aide would visit Mrs. Garcia's husband at home and have a long, informal talk with him.

As the plan was discussed, the supervisor grew a little anxious and said to the aide, "How do you feel about going there?" The aide, a short, stout man, responded, "What do you mean?" The supervisor was a little embarrassed, but said, "Well, Mr. Garcia sounds fairly tough." Whereupon, the aide said rather simply, "Well, I can protect myself, can't I?" and the supervisor responded, "Oh yes, of course."

It was clear the next morning that the supervisor's alarm was misplaced. The two men had sat until late in the night, talking about the old days in Puerto Rico where both of them had been born, the problems they shared in New York, their views about women and the neighborhood. In the course of it all, the aide explained to Mr. Garcia that unless something was worked out amicably with his wife, the situation would grow more difficult. Now that the hospital had been involved in a suicide attempt, the police and the courts could easily step in and the aide was sure that Mr. Garcia didn't really want all that trouble. Mr. Garcia firmly agreed that the children could be given over at least temporarily to Mrs. Garcia, provided she returned to Puerto Rico.

"But she doesn't want to go back to Puerto Rico," the supervisor interjected upon hearing the story.

At this point the aide, with a very calm expression, said, "One thing at a time."

A few days later, he was able to persuade Mr. Garcia to let his wife have their apartment and the children, at least for the time being, and he helped Mr. Garcia to find a room.

From these two cases, it is clear that the provision of psychosocial first aid is not the sole aim of paraprofessionals. Paraprofessionals, in facilitating services from a variety of agencies and institutions, come into intimate contact with deliverers of service and particularly with low-echelon management. They have a dual purpose in working with these personnel: (1) to ensure that the individual receives adequate service and (2) to enlarge the perspective of the social-service institutions and increase their understanding of the unique needs, attitudes, and values of the Hispanic population. Further, while the paraprofessional aides are problem solving for clients, the professionals are free to deal with more severely disturbed clients and to work with higher-echelon staff of the social-service agencies for the purpose of improving their policies and practices. Whether these functions of paraprofessionals and professionals are carried out successfully depends largely on the type of individual selected to be an aide and the type of training provided. Let's consider these two points further.

Selecting the Paraprofessional

There are no set criteria for selecting paraprofessionals. What is clear, however, is that potential paraprofessionals must be long-standing community residents, familiar with the problems of people living within the community to be served, knowledgeable about existing community resources, and known and trusted by people of the community. How are all these essential qualities to be found in a single individual? To say that it is not easy would be an understatement. In a review of the literature on the selection of paraprofessionals, a model described by Hallowitz and Riessman (1967) appears to be one of the more satisfactory approaches to paraprofessional selection. In this model, the first step was to convene a meeting of the applicants for the position. In this group meeting, the nature of the position, salary, personnel practices, and selection procedures were discussed. Questions from the applicants were answered, and all those who continued to be interested in the position were invited to the next phase of the selection process.

In the second phase, applicants were divided into small groups and interviewed by several members of the staff. The interviews were observed through a one-way mirror by four raters: a psychologist, a social worker, a psychiatrist, and a nurse.

> The interview . . . was directed at ascertaining the candidates' attitudes toward the neighborhood—whether or not they rejected the people who lived in the area; attitudes toward people on welfare; feelings about discrimination, minority groups, disturbed people, etc. We used such open-ended questions as: "What kinds of troubles do you think children have in this neighborhood"; "What do you think about welfare"; "What kind of troubles do you think parents have"; "What are the things you like or don't like about this neighborhood"; "What do you think about the police? the schools? etc." [Hallowitz & Riessman, 1967, p. 773].

The raters judged each applicant on a series of characteristics that included empathy, attitude toward authority, comfort in the group, ability to communicate ideas and feelings, trainability and flexibility, capacity for self-awareness, reaction to stress, pathology, and relevant work and life experiences. Other important considerations were the ability to communicate and potential for serving as a "bridge" between the community to be served and the professional staff.

In their assessment of this model of selection, Hallowitz and Riessman state that the group-interview method proved so successful that individual interviews were not necessary for final selection of applicants for training as paraprofessional aides. This model appears more satisfactory than other methods of selecting paraprofessionals because it is structured, it uses the ratings of independent judges, applicants are well informed of the selection process, and important information concerning the applicant's knowledge of the community and its problems can be obtained. One drawback to the model is that the selection process does not ensure that the individuals selected are trusted members of the community where they are to work. Accordingly, an extension of the model described here would be to include community leaders among the interviewers and raters. Their community input, if properly used, should ensure that the individuals selected to be paraprofessional aides are in fact able to bridge the gap between the community and the helping professionals and agencies serving the community.

Other descriptions of the selection of paraprofessionals have not been specific about the procedures used to select aides. One report (Munns et al., 1970) states only that ex-addicts were employed as street workers; Serrano and Gibson (1973) argue for the importance of aides on the staff of a community-mental-health center, without mentioning how the New Careers case aides were selected. Abad, Ramos, and Boyce (1974) similarly state only that their paraprofessionals were "indigenous to the Puerto Rican community" and that "they represented some of the more acculturated members of the community, and it was a natural role for them to serve as 'bridges' between other Puerto Ricans and the Anglo agencies and institutions." They go on to say "Our staff included two individuals related to Puerto Rican clergymen, and a third person who, besides being a recognized community leader, was also an *espiritista*" (p. 592).

This description raises the question of using faith healers— *espiritistas, curanderos,* and *santeras*—as paraprofessionals. The argument for recruiting faith healers as paraprofessionals or as auxiliary professionals (some individuals contend that faith healers are professionals; see Torrey (1972) for example) is that they are recognized by the community and their particular skills are a natural part of the helping professions. This is a legitimate argument, but there is as yet no good evidence that faith healers desire to be associated with mental-health centers or that they make good "bridges" between the Hispanic community and traditional mental-health institutions. Since most acknowledged faith healers have their own clientele whom they usually charge for their services, it is entirely possible that they would be content to continue serving the community independently. This is a subject about which much has been said but concerning which little empirical study has been done. The one thing that is definite is that faith healers are a part of the Hispanic culture and that some Hispanics do utilize their services. This alone should be reason enough to look to faith healers as a potential reserve when considering the most effective ways for providing help to Hispanics.

Training of Paraprofessionals

As with selection, there are few agreed-upon models for the training of paraprofessionals. Again, the most useful guideline for training is found in Hallowitz and Riessman (1967). In their model, training occurs in three phases. In the first phase, the trainees are instructed in the client-intake interview process, conduct door-to-door community surveys, and escort selected clients to clinic appointments and visits to social agencies such as the Department of Welfare, the police department, schools, and the like. Further, job simulation and role playing are emphasized, and didactic presentations are kept to a minimum. In the second phase, the aides devote several weeks to specific client services. This phase of training is divided into half-day periods. In the first period, clients are assisted; in the second period, training continues based on the aides' on-the-job experiences. The third phase of training consists of continuous on-the-job training through regularly scheduled seminars with the professional staff on such topics as interviewing techniques, therapeutic modalities, and community organization.

Although the Hallowitz and Riessman training model is not innovative, it does demonstrate how training for paraprofessionals should be organized. A critical factor in the training of paraprofessionals that Hallowitz and Riessman do not mention is the need for reciprocal exchange of ideas between aides and professional staff; that is, the aides are, in principle, experts in their community and should be given the opportunity to share their expertise with the professional staff. The aides can instruct the professionals on how their services are perceived by the community and on whether community needs are being met. There are usually occasional conflicts between the aides and the professional staff (Peck, Kaplan, & Roman, 1966). However, if paraprofessionals are used in a mental-health center for the real purpose of extending services, then their opinions must be respected. With this in mind, it is critical that every effort be made during training to establish a trusting relationship between the soon-to-be paraprofessionals and the existing professional staff.

A final point on training must be made. In all probability prospective paraprofessionals will not have attained the same educational level as the professional staff, and will not be of the same social class, and may differ from them racially and culturally. For these reasons, some aides will have difficulty keeping records, meeting deadlines, following traditional channels of communication and lines of authority, and responding to supervision. These considerations do not negate the fact that paraprofessionals play an important role in providing services, but these problems must be dealt with realistically in training. For example, if a prospective aide does have difficulty in record keeping but demonstrates other skills, then decisions must be made that determine what will be required of the aide once he or she becomes a member of the staff. In the case of poor record keeping, it is possible to assign duties so that records are kept by either another aide or some member of the professional staff. This kind of flexibility is critical if paraprofessionals are to be successfully employed and if pluralistic models of helping are to be implemented.

THERAPEUTIC SERVICE MODELS

Another important factor in working with Hispanics concerns the organization of the service-delivery system itself—that is, the actual way in which therapeutic services are offered to a community. Padilla and his fellow researchers (1975) suggest three models for service delivery. We will discuss each of these models separately.

The Barrio Service-Center Model

This model is based on the assumption that the majority of the stress experienced by Hispanics is economic in origin. This model seems to fit particularly well with the "health-service catchment area" concept, in which a community center is staffed with personnel who can effectively intervene on behalf of the surrounding population to get jobs, bank loans, and many other basic economic services. Four examples of the *barrio* service-center model will be described briefly.

First, Lehmann (1970) described the operation over a two-year period of three store-front neighborhood service centers in New York City as follows:

> [The] typical client [is] a Puerto Rican woman in her mid-30's with two or three children and there is no father present. She is usually an unemployed housewife . . . on welfare with income less than $3,000 a year. She is almost certainly born in Puerto Rico . . . and there is only about one chance in three she speaks English well [p. 1446].

Lehmann admitted that "their [that is, the centers'] record for problem solving was less than brilliant" (p. 1454) but attributed their limited success to their accessibility and informality, their open-door policy with respect to problems and people, and their use of community residents as staff.

A second example of the *barrio* service-center model was described by Abad et al. (1974) in an article identifying demographic and subcultural characteristics of a sample of Puerto Rican residents of New Haven, Connecticut. The "Spanish clinic," or *la clinica hispana* as it is called by the Spanish-speaking community, provides walk-in services five days a week and includes psychiatric evaluation and follow-up treatment, individual counseling, couple and family therapy, referral services, home visits, and transportation. The staff is bilingual/bicultural and includes a Spanish psychiatrist, a part-time Puerto Rican social worker, and a paraprofessional indigenous staff that includes community leaders with public visibility. The clinic is prepared to intervene in a variety of problem situations, even if the situations are not of a "clinical" nature.

For example, one of the "most frequent roles within the Spanish community is that of intermediary between Spanish speaking clients and other agencies" (p. 592). The researchers state that the clinic benefits everyone: the clientele receive help with problems, which allows them to function more effectively within their environment, the *barrio* agency gains the reputation of being a "helpful" institution, and community support of the clinic is enhanced.

A third example of the *barrio* service-center model was reported by Burruel (1972), who described the creation of *La Frontera*, a mental-health outpatient clinic situated in south Tucson, Arizona, designed specifically to provide care for the Chicano community. Burruel described the ongoing services of the clinic, including "diagnosis and treatment for adults and children with emotional or personality problems and general problems of living" (p. 27). Treatment modalities include "individual therapy, conjoint, family and group therapy" (p. 27). Community representation was originally excluded from planning and administration of the center until "pressure was applied" (p. 29). Currently the administrative board is a "policy-making board which incorporates representatives from the community" (p. 29). Under the leadership of a Chicano full-time director, deliberate effort was expended "to make the services relevant to the Chicano community . . . by searching for bilingual and bicultural mental health professionals" (p. 29). A deliberate effort to attract patients from the catchment area was implemented by announcing services on the Mexican radio stations and by eliminating the waiting list that is typical of traditional mental-health clinics. It is stated that patients may be seen "immediately, hours later, or at the latest, the next day" (p. 32). The response to this innovative program is described as follows: "Underutilization of mental health services by Mexican Americans has not been the case at *La Frontera*; 61.5% of the total patient population consists of Mexican Americans" (p. 28).

The fourth and final example of the *barrio* service-center model was described by Schensul (1974), who brought the insights of an applied anthropologist to the creation of a new mental-health center specifically for a Hispanic population. Schensul described how a group of young Chicanos working in Chicago's West Side developed the idea in the summer of 1971 to create a community-controlled youth facility to be called *El Centro de la Causa* (Center for the Cause). The original operating budget of $1800 was raised by a community fiesta. According to Schensul, within months the activist group had convinced a church organization to provide $40,000 for staff and seed money. Within three years, the operating budget was over $400,000. This funding was used to train community residents as paraprofessionals in mental health and to support mental-health training and reading-improvement programs, English classes, recreation and youth activities, and programs to prevent drug use. Schensul concluded that whatever success was achieved by *El Centro de la Causa* was primarily because of the youthful Chicano activists and their consistent efforts to maintain community involvement.

Mental-health personnel in schools, such as counselors and social workers, can employ the *barrio* service-center model. Emphasis is placed on helping students find part-time employment while continuing school. Government grants can be obtained for furthering such goals with students. There have been a number of federally funded programs to assist minority youths, such as the "School Opportunity Center" program, providing special grants to provide extensive tutoring; "Project Incentive," involving extensive vocational and career counseling, plus field trips that broaden students' horizons; the "School Achievement Center" and related organizations providing special instruction for students with academic promise; and the "Economic and Youth Opportunity Agency" (EYOA), offering support for potential dropouts (Dworkin, 1968). Very often, poor Hispanics are uninformed about scholarships and financial aid for college. The *barrio* service-center model applied to schools emphasizes financial and academic support for students, as well as individual counseling.

In sum, this model recognizes that many problems of Hispanics are grounded more in poverty than in culture. Hispanics are taught new ways to manipulate and change their environment (Padilla et al., 1975) while increasing their overall adjustment.

Family-Adaptation Model

Based on the concept that the family is an important cultural feature in providing emotional support against stress, a variant of group psychotherapy is evolving that we call the family-adaptation model.

Maldonado-Sierra and Trent (1960) described a "culturally relevant" group-psychotherapy program for chronic, regressed, schizophrenic Puerto Rican males, founded on assumptions about the Puerto Rican family structure. The father is typically described as a dominant authoritarian figure and the mother as submissive, nurturant, and loving. The oldest male sibling is perceived as a figure whom the other siblings respect, admire, and confide in. In this article and in a second (Maldonado-Sierra et al., 1960), the authors describe how these assumptions become the basis for a therapeutic program.

In brief, the patients spent several weeks together in a variety of activities under the supervision of an individual who represented the oldest male sibling. A few days before group sessions began, the group was introduced to an older male therapist who represented the father figure. He maintained dignity, remained aloof, and restricted his social interactions to brief exchanges. A third therapist, an older woman, fulfilled traditional mother-figure expectations; she distributed food and chatted informally with the patients.

The complexities of this type of group-psychotherapy process are too great to describe in detail here. The important point, however, is that this analogy of the Puerto Rican family allowed patients to work on their problems from the point of view of family structure, social roles, and cultural themes that are particular to Hispanics.

The family-adaptation model deserves further exploration with less severely disturbed Hispanic clients as well. The use of cultural themes, such as *machismo, respeto, comadrazgo/compadrazgo*, the role of women, and *personalismo*, in therapy, especially family therapy, could prove extremely valuable in developing more adequate therapeutic models. Limitations of space preclude a refined definition of these terms, but the basic concept is that sex roles of Hispanic men and women are very rigidly defined: males value highly the virtues of courage and fearlessness (*machismo*); respect is given elders, and there is an adherence to traditional cultural norms and values (*respeto*); extended-family relations, especially between godparents and godchildren, are ritualized and have a religious connotation (*comadrazgo/compadrazgo*); and interpersonal relations are based on trust for people mingled with a distaste for formal, impersonal institutions or organizations (*personalismo*).

As we noted earlier, there has been little exploration of family roles as a therapeutic approach with Hispanic clients. Such an approach would appear to have merit especially in those situations in which several family members must be counseled. Therapists who are familiar with family dynamics could, for example, use family therapy to better understand how family members conform to their culturally ascribed roles in times of stress. Moreover, this technique could be used to analyze how the entire kinship network responds as a support system during periods of extreme mental stress. Weaknesses in the kinship support system could be detected and remedied. Concomitant with this, the knowledgeable therapist might have the client act out situations that demand elaboration of cultural traits such as *machismo* or *personalismo*; the client would have a better understanding of the conflict between his or her cultural values and those of the dominant majority culture. To illustrate this point, Abad et al. (1974) noted that conflict about the *respeto* concept is particularly common in parent/child relationships among Puerto Ricans on the mainland. They state:

> Influenced by their Anglo peers, children, especially adolescents, strive to be more independent and rebel against restrictions that they might well accept if living on the island. An unknowing therapist in such a situation may too quickly conclude that the adolescent is acting appropriately against rigid expectations, and in so doing, the therapist may alienate himself from the parents, make them defensive, and ruin any chance for further family intervention [p. 588].

In addition, the family-adaptation model can be applied to the architectural design of community-mental-health centers. There is evidence suggesting that centers with "living room" reception areas appear to be the most attractive to Hispanic clientele (see, for example, Phillipus, 1971). This homelike informality becomes even more attractive, of course, when the client is greeted by someone who can speak Spanish, who can evaluate the problem rapidly, and who can implement immediate disposition.

The Professional-Adaptation Model

The major characteristic of this model is that the professional and paraprofessional staff of the community-mental-health center receive some form of specialized nonstandard training or in some way "adapt" themselves to the specific requirements of serving the Hispanic population. Two examples of the professional-adaptation model follow.

First, as we noted earlier, Karno and Morales (1971) described the effort in East Los Angeles to design a community-mental-health service that would attract local Mexican Americans. Major innovations were implemented in staffing, service quarters, and treatment programs. At the end of a two-and-a-half-year recruitment program, the medical director had attracted 22 full-time professional, paraprofessional, and clerical personnel, the majority of whom were bilingual. Service quarters were "in the heart of the . . . community, convenient for . . . transportation, and comfortable . . . and inviting" (p. 118). The treatment program was based on prevention; its major thrust was mental-health consultation to a wide variety of community-service agencies. As a backup, the center offers short-term crisis-oriented treatment using individual, family, group, and chemical therapy. The center seems to be fulfilling its objective of providing appropriate treatment for Mexican Americans; the first 200 patients matched the local population figures.

A second and somewhat similar example of the professional-adaptation model has been created for the Hispanic population of Denver (Phillipus, 1971). Three of the eight team members are Spanish speaking, and the center is located in the neighborhood of the target population. Prospective patients enter a reception area furnished to resemble a living room. The initial contact person is usually a secretary-receptionist and is always a Spanish-speaking person. The patient is referred immediately to a team member to assess the problem and begin whatever action is appropriate. The rationale for this procedure is that treatment is directed toward crisis resolution, which by definition is incompatible with rigid adherence to the traditional 50-minute-hour schedule. The staff began to refer to one another and to the clients by their first names when it became apparent that the use of more formal address was alienating some members of the Hispanic group. Unequivocal data bearing the appropriateness of the program are difficult to obtain. Nevertheless, new referrals increased to the point where proportional representation of the target population relative to the general population was soon reached.

In sum, the physical structure of the counseling center is oriented to Hispanics' needs. The center is located in the hub of the community. Schools and churches may house the mental-health center, since these structures are often the most accessible to the public. In the Bronx, New York, a mobile crisis-intervention and suicide-prevention unit was staffed by a psychiatric nurse, two mental-health workers, and a driver who was a resident of the area. The mobile unit stopped many crises before great harm had been done. In its first six months of operation, it responded to 160 calls and dealt with problems ranging from suicide and homicide to alcoholism, drug addiction, depression, and other psychological and social problems. By traveling around the community, the unit solved crises that might not have been brought to the traditional clinic (Ruiz, Vasquez, & Vasquez, 1973).

The professional-adaptation model proposes that mental-health facilities be used for a variety of functions, such as dances and other social gatherings, in order to be integrated into the community. Their services will become familiar to, and accepted by, residents (Padilla et al., 1975). In Connecticut, bilingual staff at a mental-health center worked with Puerto Rican spiritualists to provide crisis intervention and education about child rearing, nutrition, alcohol, and drugs (Abad et al., 1974).

The professional-adaptation model stresses consultation with related agencies. In a mental-health center in East Los Angeles, consultation with a number of public and private health agencies, various professionals, and law-enforcement agencies was continuous. Consultation was client-centered; that is, client rather than agency needs were emphasized. In-service training was provided for the staff to teach them how to consult with various agencies (Karno & Morales, 1971). In New York City, a mental-health agency consulted with 22 local organizations, including churches, youth services, storefronts, recreation centers, and neighborhood centers. Workshops were organized for the agencies' staff members, and technical assistance was offered for program planning (Scheidlinger & Sarcka, 1969). Personnel at the various agencies reported that the consultation aided them in designing effective programs for their Hispanic clients but did not affect their individual attitudes about Hispanics (Scheidlinger, Struening, & Rabkin, 1970).

RESEARCH AND EVALUATION

In this chapter we have discussed ways to increase the availability of mental-health-counseling services for Hispanics. This chapter, however, would not be complete if we did not address the question of research and evaluation. We are aware that many therapists, either because of time limitations or because of differences in orientation, do not conduct research. Our comments here are not intended to imply that every therapist should become involved in the research process. It is our intent, rather, to show that research can direct program implementation and that evaluation studies are essential to determine if programs or therapies are effective.

Information on the prevalence and incidence of mental-health-related problems among Hispanics is particularly critical because of the underutilization of health services, and such information is necessary if relevant programs are to be designed. Studies are also needed on the ability to recognize overt signs and symptoms of illness in oneself or others and to seek and accept diagnosis and treatment when necessary. Such perceptions affect the rate at which people seek mental-health services. Differences in the rates of mental-health-facility utilization between Hispanics and the general population may be due as much to differences in the degree of recognition of illness and in modes of dealing with it as to variation in the extent of disability in the population or in availability of treatment resources. It has been suggested, for instance, that tolerance of psychotic behavior among Mexican Americans may affect the severity of symptoms and the requirements for hospitalization (Fabrega, Swartz, & Wallace, 1968). On the other hand, it may well be that Hispanics recognize the irrelevance of most available counseling services and choose to keep their family members at home rather than seek institutionalized forms of help. Similarly, many Hispanics have spoken about the important role of folk healing but have not provided documentation to substantiate the claim of high utilization of folk healers by Hispanics.

Direct-attitude studies of the population could help determine why some Hispanics seek mental-health counseling and others do not. This type of research is very difficult to validate because it involves assessing motivation. Also, a person's attitudes and perceptions do not always match his or her behavior. Nevertheless, a fundamental question is: "How do sociocultural modes of defining and dealing with maladjusted behavior influence the course and consequences of that behavior?" Thus, the goal of research in this field must be to determine exactly how the Hispanic community responds to psychological problems and mental illness and to tailor service programs to meet these culturally specific needs.

Research is needed also to ascertain the relative effectiveness of bilingual/bicultural staff and paraprofessionals with particular Hispanic populations. A mental-health facility or counseling center should plan methods of evaluation to identify and strengthen effective techniques and models. Researchers must be trained in the workings of service agencies, practitioners and administrators must be knowledgeable in research procedures, and both groups must work together to use research findings and outcome studies for the overall improvement of therapeutic techniques and service-organizational models.

The type of research outlined here is difficult to conduct, yet it is essential. Both researchers and practitioners are necessary in effective program development. If researchers do not communicate with practitioners, their findings will not affect social systems. If practitioners do not rely on researchers, their services will not become more systematic. Unfortunately, different theoretical assumptions may limit the interaction of these professionals. The researcher's belief in objectivity may block communication with practitioners who operate on a belief in the efficacy of their therapeutic approaches. In pluralistic counseling ways must be found to overcome these barriers.

IMPLICATIONS FOR PLURALISTIC THERAPISTS

It is important to recognize that much of the discussion in this chapter has focused on ways of changing the current mental-health delivery system. Many of the suggested changes are beyond the control of the individual therapist. Nonetheless, the pluralistically oriented therapist should understand the reasons for these system changes and be supportive of them. It is also important to state that these recommended changes are not specific only to the needs of the Hispanic. As a matter of fact, in the *Report to the President from the President's Commission on Mental Health* (1978), we find many of the same recommendations. What seems critical is that the individual therapist advocate for change when it is apparent that services will be improved.

In an earlier chapter, we documented the limited use of state and county mental-health centers by Hispanics. Equally limited is the representation of Hispanic clients in school counseling centers. Hispanics' limited use of these social services cannot be explained on the basis of their attitudes or cultural practices. Hispanics perceive illness much the same way as Anglos do and express generally positive attitudes about therapy. The practice of *curanderismo* and *espiritismo* is not extensive enough to explain underutilization of mental-health agencies. Moreover, folk beliefs and the practices of faith healers can be compatible with more conventional therapies.

In actuality, the low utilization reflects the irrelevancy and inappropriateness for Hispanics of many available services. Research reveals consistently that the following recommendations will increase use of services:

- The mass media should be used to publicize services.
- Mental-health facilities need to be established within Hispanic communities.
- Services must be offered at reasonable rates.
- Emphasis should be placed on crisis intervention.
- The traditional "50-minute-hour" model must be discarded when it is not appropriate.
- Waiting lists should be eliminated when possible and waiting time kept short.
- The services of members of the community should be enlisted for paraprofessional work.
- Research and evaluation should be an integral part of the planning and conduct of programs for Hispanics.

Despite these helpful recommendations, many questions remain. In what situations are Anglo therapists effective? When are bilingual/ bicultural therapists essential? How can pluralistic therapists be effectively trained? What system is best for delivery of mental-health services to a specific Hispanic subpopulation? Given Hispanic staff availability, what mental-health system would be best for an urban community or for a rural community?

Although research is incomplete and sometimes inconsistent, a critical factor is emerging. In all cases, mental-health programs must be based on respect for Hispanic culture. Family unity, *personalismo*, and other cultural values need to be integrated into the structure of institutions that serve Hispanics (Pollack & Menacker, 1971). Values such as brotherhood and affiliation should be emphasized rather than the Anglo values of professionalism and self-determination (Atencio, 1971). Programs should be built on the interconnectedness of Hispanic family, community, and culture. A comfortable, home-like environment is provided. The aid of trusted paraprofessionals is enlisted. The traditional businesslike atmosphere of the community-mental-health center is replaced by more culturally relevant models. In sum, the mental-health center, school counseling center, or whatever other facility is designed for helping people should be organized in such a way that potential users recognize that promotion of their well-being is the central concern of the facility.

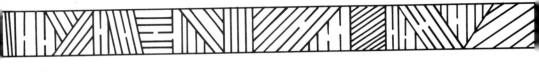

Chapter 7 Responsible Goal Setting

The therapist and the client must decide together what the goals of therapy are. The therapist must help the client achieve independence and growth in order to cope with current and future problems in a more integrated fashion. This task entails an understanding of the client's problems and coping style. When defining goals with Hispanics, the therapist must employ information about Hispanic culture and culturally appropriate ways of confronting personal life problems.

TARGETING POINTS OF STRESS

In goal setting, it is important to differentiate between stresses due to personal factors and stresses due primarily to societal factors. Problems of a personal or individual nature can arise that are independent of ethnic-minority-group membership. When Hispanics are experiencing stress of a personal nature, their response will be similar to that of non-Hispanics experiencing the same stress. For example, if a young person graduating from high school is uncertain about whether to attend college or which major to pursue, the stress of that decision probably has very little to do with whether the student is Hispanic or not. Regardless of ethnicity, a young person in such a dilemma would probably complain of feelings of uncertainty, indecision, insecurity, personal inadequacy, and general apprehension concerning his or her own expectations and those of his or her family. Finally, ethnicity would probably have relatively little influence on the type of counseling approach designed to help such a client formulate and achieve life goals with a minimum of personal discomfort.

There is also stress that originates outside the person and that is basically societal or environmental. Our interest, of course, is societal stress associated with ethnic-minority-group membership. Thus we focus on prejudice against Hispanics and the effect of discriminatory practices on character formation, personality function, and coping ability. We have already documented, for example, that Hispanics are victims of the "poverty cycle"—depressed personal and family incomes, minimal education, overrepresentation in menial occupations, and elevated rates of unemployment. This cycle is self-perpetuating: the victims are less able to subsidize their own education and that of their children and thus are less likely to qualify for better, higher-paying employment. Furthermore, compared to other ethnic groups, Hispanic youth have fewer role models who have achieved success through continued education or training. Other stressful consequences of poverty include decreased social status, inadequate health care and nutrition, and a generally reduced quality of life.

As this discussion suggests, the therapist can identify three "types" of Hispanic client, according to the source of the stress that motivates self-referral for counseling. Some clients will complain of personal stress and present problems similar to those of non-Hispanic clients. Others will be experiencing stress due to societal factors; their problems will resemble those of all people who are victims of prejudice and discrimination. But most Hispanic clients will probably seek counseling for stress stemming from both sources.

When counseling Hispanics, the therapist may have to evaluate whether the individual is presenting problems that emanate from personal or societal stresses. The treatment plan and the goals may differ as a function of this judgment. A brief example may help to clarify this point. Assume that a Hispanic male in his late 20s is referred for counseling by the court because of trouble with the police. The client, whom we will call Antonio, claims that the problem is police harassment and has nothing to do with his behavior.

The first step in formulating a counseling program for Antonio is to evaluate the accuracy of his reporting and the quality of his judgment. The counselor must deal immediately with the question of whether or not Antonio is distorting reality. One needs to know, to use Antonio's words, whether he is a hapless victim of "police oppression" as he claims or whether his relationship to figures of authority is essentially "paranoid."

The answer to this question is important because it tells us whether stress is mainly internal or external. This information can be used to create treatment programs of maximum relevance and efficacy. If it turns out that Antonio is psychotic and is imagining or exaggerating his treatment by the police, then the counselor may respond with immediate support, determine whether medication is necessary, and begin preparing for whatever intervention model is most likely to bring about change in the direction of less inappropriate behavior. If, on the other hand, Antonio is not psychotic and is reporting accurately, then a much different approach is called for. Before describing a counseling program for Antonio based on the opinion that he is neither psychotic nor paranoid but is reporting discrimination accurately, let's discuss how such an opinion might be reached.

The therapist working with Antonio must examine his or her own biases concerning relations between ethnic-minority-group members and organized power structures such as social-service agencies, governmental bureaucracies, and the police. This self-examination is important. Our first point concerning this issue is that preconceptions and prejudices are dangerous because they obscure critical judgment. The skilled and responsible counselor responds to the needs of the client, not to idiosyncratic prejudgments. Regardless of whether the counselor's introspection revealed a "conservative" or a "liberal" perception of relations between police and Hispanics, it is a fact that some police, in some locales, on some occasions, do harass Hispanics. It is equally true that some Hispanics, especially males, develop paranoid reactions of psychotic proportions and that imaginary police harassment is sometimes incorporated into a delusional system. Thus, when clients report harassment, it is crucial that counselors avoid prejudgment and evaluate each report on its own merits.

In cases such as Antonio's, the accuracy of reporting can be evaluated in several ways. If Antonio presents additional material for discussion that is unbelievable—for example, religious delusions—then it is more likely (but still not absolutely certain) that his description of interactions with the police are equally distorted. His credibility can also be evaluated through the use of informants—for example, family members, friends, fellow employees, and so on. It goes without saying that evidence of previous delusional periods—whether reported by informants or documented by official records—tends to discredit current reporting. Psychological-assessment devices, including tests and interviews, can help determine current personality functioning, but they may be of questionable validity when used by professionals with only superficial understanding of the client's culture (Padilla & Ruiz, 1975). We will elaborate on this point later in this chapter.

In sum, it is essential that the therapist first be clear about the source of the problem. How a therapist reacts to the client should be based on the source of the problem, rather than on some preconceived notion of what is good for the client.

The Hispanic client's attitude about family is also important in goal setting. The import of this factor varies from family to family. The individual's desire to change his or her role in a family must be considered within the framework of the family's overall functioning. For example, a wife's desire to assert herself may severely strain the system of interaction within a traditionally oriented family. The same behavior may be the source of relatively little stress within a well acculturated family (Murillo, 1971). In the case of the traditionally oriented family, the development of assertive behavior will require changes in the family's system of interacting. Development of assertive behavior within the acculturated family may require less intervention within the family system and more supportive therapy for the identified client.

Even a highly acculturated Hispanic may express personal concerns that are flavored by feelings of closeness and responsibility to family, as in the case of Miss L. (Knoll, 1971).

THE CASE OF MISS L.[1] Miss L., in her late thirties, was unmarried and lived alone in the barrio. She had been referred to the agency by a Spanish-speaking community organization worker after she had been injured at work and could no longer receive unemployment compensation benefits. Miss L. had emigrated from Mexico with her parents when she was a young girl, and she eventually settled in Detroit. Both parents had been dead several years. Her siblings manifested serious psychiatric problems, and one sister, diagnosed as schizophrenic, had long been hospitalized.

Miss L. had devoted her early years to providing a livelihood for her younger siblings; now that they were all married or living away from home, she found herself alone. Her only outlet was a few church activities. She was frequently depressed and suffered from several psychosomatic illnesses. Underlying the depression was an unresolved oedipal conflict and rage toward her parents and siblings for responsibilities placed on her. Even when she recognized some of these feelings, Miss L. continued symbolically to express rage against relatives and siblings who were still making emotional demands on her—demands that she provoked. She found

[1]From "Casework Services for Mexican Americans," by F. R. Knoll, *Social Casework*, 1971, *52*, 279–284. Copyright 1971 by the Family Service Association of America. Reprinted by permission.

herself responding through psychosomatic symptoms that tended to undermine her well-being.

The short-range goal was to establish a casework relationship and to attempt to diagnose her problems. Miss L. accepted referral only because the referral came from a Spanish-speaking community organization worker whom she respected and who, in essence, depended on her for carrying out church-related social projects.

Miss L. demonstrated a curious mixture of cultural traits. Although she identified with the Mexican culture, she also denied this connection by speaking only English, by seeking experiences beyond the Mexican community, and by desiring to be Anglicized and to participate in the "American way of life."

Miss L. was acculturated in language and general behavior. Yet, establishment of therapeutic goals required recognition of the importance of her family. According to Anglo standards her attachment to her siblings might be considered "too strong." According to Hispanic values, her response was admirable. Because of the naturalness of this attachment, the therapist did not attempt to diminish it. Rather, therapy focused on helping Miss L. resolve conflicts preventing her from enjoying that attachment.

Eventually she obtained some insight regarding the origin of this conflict, which resulted from her unresolved oedipal conflict. She even began to refer some family members to the agency for marital counseling and another to a psychiatric clinic, believing that they too could find relief from their problems.

Miss L. was fairly well-motivated, sophisticated, and a verbal client with middle-class values who was able to use the services of a family agency through the referral of the community organization worker. She went through a process of establishing a trusting relationship with a community organization worker that she was able to transfer to a caseworker who was working closely with the community. As a relationship developed, she began to commute to the main office (enabling the caseworker to spend time in the community with other clients who could not travel to the main office) and continued to make steady progress.

A host of other cultural factors may be significant in establishing therapy goals: the relationship of siblings to each parent; attitudes about skin color; degree of attachment to ethnic power movements; defense mechanisms used, such as dissociation; common modes of handling stress, such as employing projection or rationalization; adoption of *personalismo*; belief in *dignidad*; degree of acceptance of traditional life-style; and adherence to folk medicine and faith healing.

Because of the possible frustrations associated with poverty, the therapist must consider a Hispanic client's socioeconomic status when setting therapy goals. Research indicates that poor clients profit as much from therapy as do middle- and upper-class clients if their particular concerns are recognized (Lorion, 1973). Unfortunately, difficulty defining low socioeconomic status and explaining the therapeutic process often retards determination of the most effective therapeutic approach for poor clients (Cobbs, 1972). Thus, the most effective therapy procedures for poor clients have not been established. Nevertheless, research about therapy with poor clients leads to one specific recommendation when counseling the Hispanic poor: it is advisable to consider economic difficulty as a top priority when setting goals. Personal problems are handled as concomitants or following resolution of economic crises (Galarza et al., 1970).

In the case of Mrs. M. below, we see how one client brought a range of problems to the therapeutic situation (Knoll, 1971). The therapist first focused on her economic plight and then explored her personal problems.

THE CASE OF MRS. M.[2] Mrs. M., a thirty-year-old Mexican American, was referred by a local Spanish-speaking priest for help with placement of a one-year-old child. She had three children and was separated from her husband whose whereabouts were unknown. Mrs. M.'s current problem resulted from her father's leaving for Mexico for an undetermined period of time and her having to move from the chicken farm that provided both housing and a small income. Her father had helped care for the children while Mrs. M. worked. When he left for Mexico, Mrs. M. found a job that paid fifty dollars weekly and a prospective

[2]From "Casework Services for Mexican Americans," by F. R. Knoll, *Social Casework*, 1971, *52*, 279–284. Copyright 1971 by the Family Service Association of America. Reprinted by permission.

apartment renting for approximately sixty-five dollars a month. She had no relatives in the city and few friends who were in a position to help.

Casework interviews focused on foster and institutional care facilities, the possibility of obtaining Aid to Families with Dependent Children, and possible aid from relatives, friends, *comadres* (*comadres* or *compadres* are counterparts to extended family makeup). Services were offered also in an area that involved the older children. Helped to examine realistic alternatives and clarify her goals, Mrs. M. decided not to place her child. She requested no further agency service until she again perceived a need for concrete help.

Two years later, Mrs. M. called the agency and asked for help in obtaining furniture. She had found a better paying job in an automobile factory, had saved her money, and was in the process of buying a home. The family was faced with an immediate need to move. Mrs. M.'s father, who had returned from Mexico, had been working as a caretaker in a building in which a basement apartment was provided. When he asked for an increase in salary, he was dismissed. The family then moved into a high-crime area, close to the children's school, where the grandfather was assaulted. In panic, Mrs. M. agreed to use her savings to buy a house in a suburban working-class neighborhood—closer to her work but where there was little likelihood of her father's finding work. Therefore, full financial responsibility for the family rested on Mrs. M. After discussion of her plans, the worker contacted a neighborhood agency that specialized in providing clients with various articles of furniture.

In conclusion, we are suggesting that the therapist integrate information about the source of the client's distress, economic and social needs, and cultural variation into therapeutic goal setting. The therapist should not simply assume that the Hispanic family functions as a patriarchy; he or she should not rely on a single concept such as *machismo* or low self-esteem to explain all behavior of Hispanic clients; and he or she should not assume that the individual client manifests all the personality traits that have been enumerated as characteristic of Hispanics as a group. A culturally aware therapist will focus on a complex interaction of factors such as the effects of poverty, the interaction of physical and psychological symptomatology, extended family and *compadrazgo* relationships, approaches to *respeto* and *dignidad*, authority shown to elders, changing roles associated with moving from rural to urban life, and changing roles created by increasing mobility.

While the therapist is considering the complexity of cultural factors, he or she must view objectively the individual personality traits contributing to emotional problems. "Pseudocultural" effects (in which clients describe their problems as cultural conflict while masking psychological distress) should be identified (Seward, 1958). It is helpful to distinguish intrapsychic conflict, disturbance associated with personal anxiety and poor coping skills, from extrapsychic conflict, distress caused by social factors such as poverty and discrimination (Ruiz, 1977; Ruiz & Padilla, 1977). In the case of intrapsychic conflict, problems can be explained through interpretations exclusive of culture and social factors. If the primary distress is due to personal factors, therapy goals and procedures for the Hispanic client may be similar to those procedures employed with clients of other ethnicities. Determination of the type of disturbance requires sophistication but is essential if pluralistic counseling is to be effective.

INTERPRETING TESTS

Results of psychological and educational inventories have long been employed for verifying therapy goals, advising clients about realistic options, and measuring client gain. Prediction is limited by the reliability and validity of each instrument, the ability of the testee to perform under testing circumstances, and the competency of the test interpreter.

Obtaining accurate results is more difficult when testing Hispanics, because normative characteristics of most standardized tests are usually based on non-Hispanic populations and therefore may not be reliable for the poor and for minorities. Moreover, these tests may lack validity in measuring competency in terms of the Hispanic environment. Hispanics may differ from clients of other ethnicities in response style. On the whole, they are more terse, and this terseness is sometimes interpreted as a lack of intelligence or fluency or as defensiveness (Padilla & Ruiz, 1973). Test results may differ depending on whether instructions are given in Spanish or in English and whether the examiner is Anglo or Hispanic (Padilla & Ruiz, 1973; Sattler, 1970). As a consequence of these many factors, it is difficult to determine if a score reflects individual personality, cultural-group membership, personal experience, examiner effect, or an interaction of these variables (Padilla & Ruiz, 1975).

APTITUDE AND INTELLIGENCE TESTS

Attempts have been made to restandardize aptitude and intelligence tests so that they are appropriate for bilingual and Spanish-speaking Hispanics. The translation of English tests into Spanish is a complex process. For example, translation of the Peabody Picture Vocabulary Test (PPVT) required several steps. A Spanish-language version was developed. Then some items were reordered or replaced because their connotations were changed after translation. These tests were administered to an experimental group, and item difficulty was ascertained. Items that were effective discriminators of student competency were retained in the revised edition. The revised test was administered to a cross-validating sample to check reliability (Simmons, 1974), and, as a result, a highly reliable instrument was developed.

However, it cannot be assumed that the traits measured in Hispanic children by the Spanish version of the PPVT are the same as those measured in Anglo children by the English version. Translated items may differ subtly in connotation and import from the original items. A test designed for Anglo students, even if translated into Spanish, may not effectively measure skills such as insight, cognition, and coping that are most appropriate within the Hispanic culture. A culture-free test is not possible. Hispanics may do relatively poorly on a test designed for Anglos, but the reverse is also true. Anglos will experience difficulty answering items selected to measure mastery of the Hispanic culture. In addition to standardization of language, a number of other factors must be considered: Are items equally relevant to each ethnic group? What kind of Spanish is used—standard Spanish or some regional variant of Spanish (*pochismo*)? How are the Spanish skills of bilingual students measured? What is the examiner's ethnicity? A composite of these variables could prevent a test from assessing accurately the skills of Hispanic clients.

It is not surprising that Hispanics very often score below Anglos on intelligence and aptitude tests, particularly if the tests emphasize English-language usage. For example, when Hispanic and Anglo children were administered the PPVT and a test of spatial relations, Anglos scored better on the PPVT and Hispanics better on the spatial-ability test (Kershner, 1972). Frequently, aptitude and intelligence tests normed to Anglo subjects are inefficient predictors of scholastic achievement for Hispanics. Thus, when Anglo and Mexican-American subjects from the University of California at Riverside were administered the Scholastic Aptitude Test (SAT), language and math scores did not predict college grades for Hispanic students (Goldman & Richards, 1974). Similarly, Hispanics achieved lower scores than Anglos on the Miller Analogy Tests (MAT) (Hountras, 1956). Although the MAT scores were strong predictors of academic achievement for the Anglo students, they did not correlate with graduate-school grade-point averages for the Hispanics (Duling, 1974).

In the case of Pedro (McGehearty & Womble, 1970), a counselor wisely interpreted a Hispanic child's score on the Wechsler Intelligence Scale for Children and prevented the child from being mislabeled as mentally retarded. The counselor recognized that Pedro's scores fell within the normal range for Hispanic children and that the fact that Pedro's overall performance was higher than his verbal score was typical for bilinguals.

THE CASE OF PEDRO.[3] Pedro's teacher asked the counselor to investigate the possibility of placing him in a class for mentally retarded children. She had a class of fifth grade students who were lively and aggressive. She had noticed that Pedro, rather than joining in the hubbub, was very quiet and withdrawn. He seldom did any work, usually just sitting quietly at his seat, looking at her with a blank stare when she asked him about unfinished assignments. She expressed the thought that he was unable to comprehend what was going on in the class. She felt that he understood the English language well enough so that this could not account for his failure in school. Several of his teachers had written comments in his cumulative folder confirming that he appeared to be a slow learner, shy, and unresponsive.

The counselor administered the Wechsler Intelligence Scale for Children to Pedro and found that his scores were in the low normal range compared with the general population, except for the Performance Scale which was in the normal range. Compared with other children in

[3]From "Case Analysis: Consultation and Counseling," by L. McGehearty and M. Womble, *Elementary School Guidance and Counseling*, 1970, *5*, 141–147. Copyright 1970 by the American Personnel and Guidance Association. Reprinted by permission.

the same school who are handicapped on currently used intelligence tests because of cultural and language differences, Pedro should have been working in the upper half of his class. Clearly, Pedro was not functioning in a way conducive to learning in the classroom setting. The counselor pondered the best strategy, considering her own limited time.

Because of her sophistication in test interpretation the counselor recognized that Pedro's primary need was personal, not academic. Counseling rather than remediation was provided.

There were three other boys in Pedro's room who were having difficulty in one way or another in getting along with their classmates. The counselor arranged to meet with them twice each week for 30-minute sessions. The atmosphere was very relaxed, unstructured and permissive, with only one ground rule—the boys were not allowed to hit each other. They were free to use any manner of speech that came readily to them, including Spanish, and to indulge in mild horseplay.

1st Session. The topic of discussion was family fights. Brother and sister fights, mother and father fights were all discussed. During this session, Pedro giggled at frequent intervals, often at inappropriate moments. He seemed quite embarrassed.

2nd Session. The topic was pimples and other physical problems of growing boys. While they were in the fifth grade, they were all at least one year behind for the grade because of their language handicap. Pedro did not respond to this topic in any particular way.

3rd Session. The problems of stealing and involvement with the law were discussed, along with placement away from one's own home. Pedro opened up for the first time and talked freely about the fact that he had been placed in Boy's City (home for neglected or homeless children) by his mother and father when he was six years old. He engaged in some acrobatics with his chair as he talked about this. He expressed strong feelings of having been thoroughly rejected by his parents. He thought they had placed him there because they did not want him.

As the sessions continued he evidenced other patterns of behavior. The fourth session, immediately after having revealed so much about himself in the third session, he was much quieter; when he did talk he spoke in Spanish mostly to the other boys. The counselor had established the pattern of letting the boys know that she understood enough Spanish to follow the general trend of their talk, but did not attempt to stop them, or force them to speak in English. This contributed to the sense of acceptance, or nonthreatening person that she was fostering. Pedro tried other kinds of "testing" of her from time to time to be sure that he could trust her and that she would neither reject him nor allow him to manipulate her.

As he continued in the group he developed more self-confidence. He used one of the other members, a boy with some neurological impairment and a rather naive outlook on life as a tool to deliver fantasies to the group. He would tell his friend, Carlos, all kinds of fantastic tales, the type one would expect from a five year old. Carlos would repeat the tales to the group, obviously believing them. Pedro would be watching the counselor to see if she was being taken in by these creations. She would listen attentively and comfortably and point out the impossibility of the tale, but she would display a grin of admiration for the creativity of the author. Later on the group discussed stealing at greater length. This seemed a good vehicle to help Carlos learn to take responsibility for his own behavior. Positive and negative possible consequences were discussed, with the counselor avoiding expressing values of her own as much as possible. She was attempting to help him develop a responsible attitude toward his own behavior, rather than projecting responsibility on someone else. They talked of how no one else "makes" you be anything, that each person has choices along the way, and really makes of himself the person he becomes. Rather than feeling sorry for himself because of what he perceived to be parental rejection, he was encouraged to be self-directing.

Challenges to the use of standardized intelligence and aptitude tests with Hispanic children are not new (see Padilla & Ruiz, 1973). However, several recent criticisms of testing have presented new arguments that must be considered when such tests are used with Hispanics. Mercer (1973, 1977) has argued cogently that most tests are Anglocentric and that the proper use of testing instruments must incorporate sociocultural information about the Hispanic being tested, in order to determine how closely the Hispanic matches the Anglo normative group on which the instrument was standardized. Toward this goal Mercer (1977) has designed the System of Multicultural Pluralistic Assessment (SOMPA), which assesseš the current level of functioning and the potential of children from Anglo, Chicano, and Black cultural backgrounds. The SOMPA has four sociocultural scales: (a) urban acculturation; (b) socioeconomic status; (c) family structure; and (d) family size. When these scales are used with the Wechsler Intelligence Scale for Children (WISC), it is possible to determine the Chicano child's relative rank among children from similar sociocultural backgrounds. This allows the tester to more accurately assess the child's true intellectual potential. The SOMPA is beginning to be used by school personnel in the Southwest with greater frequency. It is hoped that eventually such a model will replace the more traditional means of testing Hispanic children. Of her approach to testing, Mercer (1977, p. 171) states:

> Using a *pluralistic model*, the psychologist evaluates the child's performance relative to others from the same sociocultural background on the WISC-R measure of school functioning and makes inferences about the child's estimated learning potential. Through this process, we hope that it will be possible to identify the gifted Chicano child whose potential may be masked by the inability of present assessment procedures to take into account the cultural specificity of the test and the distance between the child's location in sociocultural space and the culture of the school.

In another examination of testing practices, Olmedo (1977) reviews several culture-fair selection models that have been proposed in the past few years by psychometricians. In his review, Olmedo concludes that the major problem of testing is with the predictiveness of the tests and suggests that "experts would do well to devote more of their energies to investigating just what it is that we are trying to predict and to what extent these criteria are biased against Chicanos and other minority groups" (p. 191). Garcia (1977) takes this argument one step further by suggesting that "testing as a predictive device is limited by the social context in which it operates" (p. 210). Garcia thus argues that tests will have predictive value only when mainstream society is ready to admit minority groups (including women) into mainstream enterprises, such as higher education and the professions.

The pluralistic counselor must, obviously, weigh all these considerations before employing a standardized aptitude or intelligence test with a Hispanic client. The model proposed by Mercer (1977) has definite value with Mexican-American children, but no similar device is available for use with other Hispanic children. Similarly, testing of Hispanic adolescents or adults presents problems for which solutions have not been proposed. Finally, the pluralistic counselor must determine whether Garcia's (1977) pessimistic view of the entire testing enterprise is justified. There are a few sure guidelines to offer the counselor, but the astute counselor will weigh the alternatives before deciding whether or not to test.

PERSONALITY INVENTORIES
Projective Tests

A survey of clinical psychologists' use of psychological tests (Wade & Baker, 1977) revealed that both projective and objective tests are used by clinical psychologists of all major therapeutic orientations with substantial percentages of clients. We have no reason to doubt that such tests are not also used extensively with Hispanic clients. A search of the literature, however, uncovered few published articles pertaining to the use of personality instruments with Hispanics. A review of these scant articles follows below.

The earliest two articles report work on the Rorschach (Kaplan, 1955; Kaplan, Rickers-Ovsiankina, & Joseph, 1956). Both studies compared Rorschach performance of two subcultural groups rated as being high in "cultural integrity" (Navaho and Zuni) with that of two other groups who were more acculturated to the larger society (Mormons and Mexican Americans). On the assumption that military veterans have had greater exposure to the majority-group culture than nonveterans (that is, are more acculturated), these four groups were also subdivided on the basis of military experience.

Several reservations concerning the first study must be pointed out before citing conclusions. Many users of the Rorschach have assumed that the instrument is "culture-free," in the sense that it could presumably provide insight into an individual's personality structure that is "uncontaminated" by culture or ethnic-group membership. Kaplan (1955) rightly rejects this assumption and uses the instrument in an effort to detect precisely these kinds of differences. The problem comes in interpretation. If and when differences appear, there may be some difficulty in determining whether they are due to individual personality, culture-group membership, personal experiences with the majority group, some other extraneous variable, or the interaction of all these factors.

Despite these reservations, Kaplan's data suggest that more acculturation through military experience influences Rorschach performance. Specifically, veterans perceived "human movement" with greater frequency and relied more often on "color" to explain their percepts. It is suggested, with appropriate caution, that these differences may reflect more creativity and extroversion among veterans from these culture groups.

The second study (Kaplan et al., 1956) is more relevant. From the pool of multicultural Rorschach protocols decribed above, these researchers selected records of six veterans from each of the four cultural groups. Two judges performed a series of sorting tasks with the 24 records. One judge, who knew which cultures were represented and who had personal experience with all four, achieved considerable success in sorting Rorschach records into the correct cultural groups. The second judge, who was informed only that the Rorschach protocols could be sorted into distinct categories and had no knowledge of the groups involved, was unable to sort the records into meaningful groups. On the basis of this finding, the researchers conclude that they have provided modest support for the idea that cultures manifest "modal-personality" patterns, since Rorschach responses from the Mexican-American group were "unique" and "homogeneous" enough to be discriminated from one Anglo-American and two Indian groups.

The reader should be cautioned against unequivocally accepting these findings. In their discussion of the research results, Kaplan and his fellow researchers state:

> The only systematic difference that is striking to us is the apparent lack of involvement and motivation for outstanding performance on the part of many [Mexican] Americans . . . the [Mexican] American subjects appeared not to be more than superficially involved, and were not attempting to give more than a minimum number of responses to the tests [p. 179].

This "lack of involvement and motivation" raises additional problems of interpretation. To what extent was the Mexican-American culture correctly identified on the basis of decreased frequency of percepts? Why were these Mexican-American subjects motivated to respond in this fashion? One possibility is decreased verbal fluency; another is lack of interest in the task, and there are doubtless other possible explanations. The problem is that we cannot evaluate whether fewer Rorschach responses in this case reflect a common cultural trait, individual personality differences, or simply indifference toward an examination procedure perceived as meaningless.

Let's consider a subsequent study of Rorschach and Thematic Apperception Test (TAT) responses from Black, Mexican-American, and Anglo psychiatric patients. Johnson and Sikes (1965) compared the responses of 25 subjects from each ethnic racial group. Subjects were matched for age, educational background, and occupational level.

Numerous statistically significant differences appeared from group to group. The most distinct differences on the Rorschach appeared on the measures of hostility. The Mexican-American group was high on "potential hostility," and the Black subjects were high on "victim hostility." Interesting group differences were those related to family unity. Mexican Americans consistently viewed the family as unified. Further, the Mexican-American group clearly differed from the other groups in mother/son and father/son relationships. Mexican Americans consistently described the mother as noble and self-sacrificing and the father as authoritarian and dominant.

The major point, for our purposes, from the Johnson and Sikes investigation is the finding that Mexican-American patients manifest a unique pattern of responses to both the Rorschach and the TAT.

As part of a larger investigation of ethnic differences in psycho-pathology, Fabrega, Swartz, and Wallace (1968) administered the short version of the Holtzman Inkblot Test to 19 Anglo-American, Mexican-American, and Black hospitalized schizophrenic patients. The results indicated that the projective data did not differ appreciably among the three matched patient groups. Nonetheless, ratings of psychopathology made independently by resident psychiatrists and nurses suggested that the Mexican-American schizophrenics were more clinically disorganized and regressed than patients in the other two groups. Although the researchers do not explain this apparent discrepancy, they do suggest that the Mexican-American subjects in their study may have been "sufficiently acculturated to Anglo patterns and values to no longer show the projective responses typical of Mexicans" (p. 232).

The only study to use a projective test with children was conducted by Holtzman, Diaz-Guerrero, and Swartz (1975). In this study Mexican children and Anglo-American children were administered the Holtzman Inkblot Test. In general, the Anglo children had faster reaction times, used larger portions of the inkblots in their responses, gave more definite form to their responses, and integrated more parts of the inkblot into their responses. These children also used more color and ascribed more movement to their percepts than did the Mexican children. The active fantasy life of the Anglo children also produced a higher amount of deviant thinking and anxious and hostile thought content. Although several interpretations can be given to these differences on the inkblot test, it would be premature to make much of the differences until more studies of this nature are conducted with children.

In general, the varied responses of Anglos, Blacks, Mexican Americans, and Mexicans to the Rorschach and Holtzman inkblot tests suggest that these tests tap personality factors as they vary with cultural and social milieu. More research is needed to explain the precise sociocultural factors leading to different responses. Once the characteristics of the populations that lead to different responses have been determined, the direction of differences can be operationalized. Until that time, the results of projective tests administered to Hispanics should be interpreted with caution.

Objective Tests

A unique response pattern among Mexican Americans was found by Mason (1967) in a study employing the California Psychological Inventory (CPI), an objective personality inventory. Subjects were 13- and 14-year-old American Indian, Anglo, and Mexican-American disadvantaged junior high students participating in a summer educational-enrichment program. Mexican-American males and females manifested response patterns that were different from each other, as well as from the responses of the other two groups. Of perhaps even greater relevance here is the observation that

> the limited verbal facility of the present population necessitated modification of the usual administration . . . and . . . the test was administered in six separate sessions, allowing time for completion and opportunity for assistance with unfamiliar vocabulary [p. 146].

As you evaluate the validity of this type of test for the Mexican American, consider Mason's statement that "one Mexican girl initially responded to the item, 'I think Lincoln was greater than Washington,' by stating that she could not answer because she had never been there!" (p. 153).

In a study of social adjustment required by certain specified life-change events, Komaroff, Masuda, and Holmes (1968) compared the responses of Blacks, Mexican Americans, and White Americans on the Social Readjustment Rating Scale. Subjects were instructed to rate a total of 43 "life-change events" (such as death of spouse, divorce, and marital separation) according to how stressful they were. Despite some significant sampling errors, such as overrepresentation of Black and Mexican-American females, several highly relevant findings emerge. Although all three groups ranked the items similarly, the Blacks and the Mexican Americans had more in common with each other than the Whites did with either of the other two groups. Examination of content indicates that both Blacks and Mexican Americans rated items relating to labor and income (such as "mortgage greater than $10,000" or "major change in work responsibilities") as much more stressful (requiring greater readjustment) than did the White majority group. The researchers suggest that these differences occur because of impoverished conditions that American ethnic-minority-group members experience. The authors related this to the "culture of poverty" wherein the minority group members live in poverty while being surrounded by highly visible affluence. Another finding is that Mexican Americans rate events such as "death of a close family member," "death of a spouse," or "major personal injury or illness" as *less* stressful than do Anglos or Blacks. The interpretation is that the Hispanic extended-family structure provides support during these types of crises and that Anglos and Blacks cannot rely on such a structure.

The final—and in some ways most telling—comment about this study involves language fluency. Clearly referring to ethnic-minority-group subjects, Komaroff, Masuda, and Holmes (1968) state that their questionnaire

> as originally worded contained some language that, in trial runs, was not understood by many of those asked to read and complete it. For this reason, the wording was simplified on certain items [p. 122].

Furthermore, subjects were

> given a verbal synopsis of the instructions . . . rather than the written instructions such as had been given to the white American group . . . because many subjects balked at having to read detailed instructions [p. 123].

These points lead us to question the validity of a paper-and-pencil questionnaire for Mexican Americans. Since some Mexican Americans are monolingual in Spanish or only partially bilingual, the translation of tests or the substitution of oral instructions for written ones may be necessary. However, such practices are hardly advisable in the absence of normative data on translated tests or on tests with unstandardized procedures.

In another study, Reilley and Knight (1970) used the Minnesota Multiphasic Personality Inventory (MMPI) to investigate personality differences between college freshmen with Spanish surnames and those without, at a university in the Southwest. Of 36 comparisons, several showed significant differences between the two groups. The Mexican-American group scored higher on the *L* (lie) scale of the MMPI, which was interpreted as suggestive of more strict moral principles or overly conventional attitudes. Similarly, the non-Spanish-surnamed group scored higher on the *Pa* (paranoia) scale, which was taken to indicate that they were more subjective, sensitive, and self-concerned and less trusting.

It was also found that Mexican-American males and Anglo-American females scored higher than their counterparts on: *Pt* (psychasthenia), indicating worry and anxiety; *Sc* (schizophrenia), reflecting social alienation, sensitivity, worry, and the tendency to avoid reality by use of fantasy; and *Si* (social introversion), indicating the tendency toward introversion, modesty, and shyness.

Again, caution must be exercised in the acceptance of these personality differences, since Reilley and Knight themselves conclude that

> a sophisticated interpretation of individual profiles should include consideration of the total pattern of scales within the context of other pertinent information about the individual . . . particularly . . . college students [p. 422].

Two other studies comparing MMPI scores of Anglos and Mexican Americans have recently appeared. In the first of these studies, McCreary and Padilla (1977) compared the MMPI scores of Black, Mexican-American, and Anglo male misdemeanor offenders referred to a legal-psychiatry clinic for presentencing psychiatric evaluation. Comparisons were made of unmatched and matched (on education and occupation) groups. Cultural factors seemed to be related to differences between Mexican Americans and Anglos on the *L*, *K*, and overcontrolled-hostility scales, and socioeconomic factors appeared to explain differences on the *Hs* scale. It was also found that the Mexican-American males were classified more often as psychopathic, whereas the Anglo and Black males scored well into the sociopathic range.

In the second study, Plemons (1977) administered the MMPI to 40 bilingual Mexican-American and 109 Anglo-American psychiatric patients in a community-mental-health center. There were controls for the major variables of age, sex, ethnicity, socioeconomic status, and presenting problem. In addition, in the analysis of the MMPI scores between groups, Plemons used a correction factor for the *K* scale, which measures defensiveness and guardedness. Significant differences between the two groups were found on the validity scales (*L* and *K*), with the Mexican Americans scoring higher. Further, no significant differences were found on the clinical scales with the usual correction for *K*. However, without *K* corrections, significant differences were found on *Pd*, *Pt*, and *Ma* with the Mexican Americans scoring lower. These findings support the notion that Mexican-American psychiatric patients respond differently than Anglo Americans on the MMPI, implying cultural differences. The differences on the *L* and *K* scales suggest that the Mexican-American patients answer MMPI questions in a way that is self-enhancing and denying of psychological problems. Another way to say this is that the Mexican Americans try to "look good" on the test. Plemons states that

> the lower *Pd*, *Pt*, and *Ma* scores without the *K* corrections may support this idea by indicating attitudes of conventionality, concern with social status, unwillingness to admit to anxiety and psychological distress, and a less overt way of dealing with life problems. The findings of this study would lend support to the idea that Mexican Americans may not experience less distress than Anglo Americans, but they may be less apt to report distress [p. 149].

In conclusion, the few studies employing the MMPI with Hispanics indicate that norms for this instrument as well as other standardized personality tests must be developed for this population. Until ethnic-specific norms are available for the MMPI, test results of Hispanic clients should be interpreted with caution. It has been established that the average elevation of scores for Hispanics will differ from that for clients of other ethnicities. Whether the pattern of scales also differs in meaning (for example, is a pattern of lower scores on *Pd*, *Pt*, and *Ma* to be interpreted in the same way for Hispanics as it would be for Anglos?) has not been investigated. The difficulties of using the MMPI cross-nationally are clearly discussed by Butcher and Garcia (1978). Problems of translation equivalence and interpretation of results still must be resolved before the MMPI and other standardized personality instruments can be used with some degree of validity.

Semantic Differential

Although it is not technically a personality inventory in the same category as the MMPI or the TAT, the semantic differential has been used by investigators to measure personality and attitude factors. With Hispanics the use of the semantic differential is best seen in the work of Martinez (1977) and Olmedo, Martinez, and Martinez (1978). In this work, subjects are instructed to rate four concepts—"mother," "father," "male," and "female,"—along 15 pairs of bipolar adjectives, such as "hard/soft," "weak/strong," and "simple/complex." In a review of several studies using the semantic differential with high school and college students, Martinez (1977) reports a number of important differences between Anglo and Chicano students as well as between males and females of both ethnicities. For example, results indicate that Mexican-American males perceive "male" as more potent and "father" as more inactive, whereas Anglo males see "male" as less potent and "father" as more potent. Male Anglo subjects also attribute more potency to "father" and less potency to "male" than do females of both ethnicities. Further, females of both ethnicities attribute less potency and more activity to "father"; however, female Anglo subjects rate "father" as less potent than do female Mexican-American subjects. Martinez states that some of these differences are congruent with the concept of *machismo* among Hispanics.

Olmedo, Martinez, and Martinez (1978), also using the semantic differential, demonstrated that a combination of semantic and sociocultural variables could be used to assess the acculturation level of Hispanic adolescents. In a follow-up study, Olmedo and Padilla (1978) showed that a similar technique could be used to classify Hispanic adults along an acculturation dimension. Taken together, these data support the notion that, in addition to sociocultural factors, Hispanics differ from majority-group members along a series of psychological dimensions, which can be assessed easily by means of a semantic-differential questionnaire.

In sum, these results emphasize the need for further investigations concerning Hispanics' responses to verbal personality questionnaires. Cultural ideology and acculturation level may affect choice on objective personality instruments such as the MMPI or the semantic differential.

Other Tests

Response patterns of Mexican-American and Anglo children have been compared on the Bender-Gestalt (F. U. Rivera, 1974) and Human Figure Drawing (Laosa, Swartz, & Diaz-Guerrero, 1974) tests. In each case, significant differences were reported. However, further testing on both these instruments, as well as on other tests not reviewed, is necessary before the nature of the differences between Hispanics and non-Hispanics can be completely understood.

Recommendations

Having discussed projective techniques and objective inventories, we shall focus on the use of paper-and-pencil instruments. The absence of normative data on paper-and-pencil tests for Hispanics is particularly critical since such instruments are frequently used as rapid and economic means of evaluating potential clients to a psychiatric clinic.

In many psychiatric and community-mental-health clinics, the initial test evaluation of a new client begins with the administration of some type of "basic battery" of psychological tests. In settings dealing with functional disorders, these batteries typically include some type of printed form eliciting biographical information, a "quick form" of some paper-and-pencil test of intelligence, an objective personality inventory (usually the MMPI), and a semi-projective measure of personality (such as one of the many available Incomplete Sentence tests or, less often, some type of human-figure drawing). A client's performance on batteries such as these is extremely important since it is used to determine whether treatment will be offered and, if so, what type. For example, clients who obtain low IQ scores and who manifest limited verbal fluency would probably not be recommended for the type of intensive insight psychotherapy that provides skill in human problem solving. And yet such a performance typifies what one would predict from a psychiatric patient who is Hispanic. Thus, while there is already some doubt about the adequacy of mental-health treatment for the Hispanic population (Karno, 1966; Kline, 1969; Phillipus, 1971), there are also no data correlating performance on "basic batteries" with response to treatment.

Rather than issue a general recommendation for more research, we will attempt to specify more precise goals. Research is needed that compares test performance as a function of English and/or Spanish instructions. Careful attention must be paid to the wording of items, not only in terms of difficulty of reading level but also with regard to ease of translation. In addition, there is increasing reliance on computer technology in the administration, scoring, and interpretation of psychological test protocols. A number of computer programs are available, for example, that print out psychological reports based on client responses. Some of these programs, but not all, utilize actuarial approaches such as "code-type" interpretation of the MMPI. Yet none of these computer programs has norms specific to the Hispanic population. The thrust of all these observations is to emphasize the need for normative studies of personality-assessment instruments for Hispanics.

Finally, research is also needed to determine the influence of examiner characteristics on psychological-test performance among Hispanics. It is extremely difficult to formulate hypotheses with precision, however, because of the paucity of relevant research. A recent review of the literature (Padilla & Ruiz, 1973) failed to reveal any studies that dealt specifically with examiner effects on test performance among Hispanics.

We would suggest that ethnicity, age, sex, and socioeconomic status ("class") of examiner are variables with potential influence on the personality-test performance of these clients.

In sum, these are a few problem areas requiring extensive research to ensure the validity of personality assessment among Hispanic clients.

THE INTERVIEW

Proper interviewing is an important ingredient in the therapeutic process. Only when vital information is obtained in the first few interviews can the therapist and the client arrive at some obtainable goals in therapy. In earlier chapters, we stressed a number of factors important in counseling Hispanics. These factors will again be considered here. When interviewing Hispanic clients, it is important to focus on cultural and socioeconomic conditions before setting therapeutic goals. The lives of people in need of counseling are filled with unmet goals and aspirations, unrealistic goals and aspirations, or unformulated goals and aspirations. This may be even more true of people who occupy the lower socioeconomic strata of society, who are culturally different, and who experience prejudice and discrimination daily. Hispanics are among these people. Accordingly, the pluralistically oriented therapist must attempt to unlock the client's personal life goals, understand how these may have been thwarted, and help the client set new and realistic goals in therapy. To do this the interview can be divided into five areas of inquiry. We will discuss each in turn.

Cultural Domain

The interviewer must understand something about the cultural background of the client. Was the client born in the United States? If the client immigrated, from where and from what type of economy (rural or urban)? What is the client's preferred language and ethnic identification? Regardless of whether the client immigrated or is a second-, third-, or even a later-generation citizen, what is the client's tie to the culture of origin? What does the client know and think of the culture and institutions of the United States? Finally, what are the client's goals and expectations with regard to culture? Is the person acculturated? Does the individual feel culturally marginal? Is the client bicultural? All of these are questions that we have discussed in other chapters and that are important in therapeutic goal setting.

Family Domain

The family plays an important role in the life of the Hispanic. Accordingly, the therapist should inquire about the client's family— nuclear, extended, and fictive (that is, godparents or *compadres*)—and the extent of familial interaction and exchange. Does the individual have a network of family members that can be looked to for emotional support and assistance? Can the therapist call in and work with a family member in designing a therapeutic plan for the client? Similarly, how are specific family members associated with the client's problems? Would the client be better or worse off with more or less familial interaction?

Resource Domain

In addition to family members, the Hispanic may or may not have other community resources to turn to in times of crisis. Has the client sought help, for instance, from a trusted physician, clergyman, faith healer, or friend? Padilla, Carlos, and Keefe (1976) have shown that these community-resource persons are often turned to first, before professional helpers. Has the client exhausted these community resources without obtaining relief prior to consulting a professional? Was the client referred to a professional and/or community-mental-health center by one of these community-resource persons? Is there a trusted community individual who can be called on to assist the professional helper? Ofter a clergyman or some other individual from the community would be more than willing to assist if called on by the therapist. Is this true in the case of this client?

Economic Domain

We have repeatedly shown how an individual's problems are often linked directly to socioeconomic stresses. Is the individual employed? By whom? And under what working conditions? Where does the client live? And under what living conditions? How many of the client's symptoms would disappear if his or her economic pressures were relieved? Is the client knowledgeable about social-service agencies in the community? If the client is familiar with these social-service agencies, has the client sought help and with what success? What skills does the individual possess for employment? Are the client's problems causing economic stresses (for example, loss of employment) and further hardships? These are just some of the questions that the therapist must ask before setting a course of action. We have seen in numerous illustrative case histories that clients gain insight into other dimensions of their problems once economic stresses have been relieved.

Symptom Domain

Individuals from the lower socioeconomic classes often experience more physical symptoms than do other individuals. It is these physical symptoms that often lead them to first seek relief from a physician. Is this the case with the client being interviewed? What is the client's interpretation of these symptoms? Was relief from physical symptoms sought from a physician? A faith healer? If the symptoms are other than physical, what are they? And again, how does the client or the client's family interpret these symptoms? Is a folk explanation offered (such as *susto* or bewitchment)? A supernatural explanation such as "punishment from god"? Finally, does the client hold an expectation that the therapist can assist in the relief of these symptoms?

We have posed many questions here for the therapist to explore when interviewing a client. In addition to the questions grouped above by domain, it is also important to explore the client's attitude toward and perception of the client/therapist relationship. What does the Hispanic client expect of the therapist? Of therapy? Further, how does the client perceive his or her role in therapy? Some writers have maintained that lower-class clients expect the therapist to be directive. Is this the case with the client being interviewed? Can the client articulate his or her goals for therapy? How willing is the client to enter into a partnership in goal setting? Finally, how realistic are the goals that are being planned for the client? Does the client believe that the goals are achievable? Are there barriers to achieving the goals that the therapist should know about?

Counseling with the poor and culturally different client is not easy. The pluralistic therapist will have to be sophisticated in probing the client during the interview for information about the client and realistic goal setting. We have tried to show by numerous examples that the pluralistic counselor may first have to attend to economic or culturally related problems in goal setting prior to working with the client on other equally important emotional problems. In conclusion, the content of what is said between the client and therapist in the interview is extremely important. For this reason, the therapist who assists Hispanic clients must know what to ask during the interview.

IMPLICATIONS FOR PLURALISTIC THERAPISTS

Goal setting in therapy is essential. In this chapter we have discussed a variety of issues surrounding therapeutic goal setting with Hispanic clients. We have shown that it is important to pinpoint the locus of stress. Is the emotional stress due to personal or societal factors? Very often emotional problems experienced by Hispanics are due to personal factors and can be dealt with by a therapist as would the problems of any other client, irrespective of ethnicity. Likewise, it is true that some ethnic-minority clients experience stress that is directly attributable to societal factors. Goals may be very different depending on the source of stress, even when the behavioral manifestations of the disturbance are the same for both types of stress.

Psychological-assessment instruments are frequently used to measure behavioral and psychological functioning. They are used with Hispanic clients despite the fact that there is little literature on testing with Hispanics. What literature exists suggests that there are differences in patterns of responses on personality-assessment instruments such as the MMPI or the TAT. Further, assessment of intelligence with Hispanics has become a controversial issue. Recent developments indicate that sociocultural considerations must be taken into account when computing the IQ of a Hispanic client. These data lead to a number of points to remember when evaluating these clients psychometrically.

- Do not assume that a test is valid for Hispanics unless they are represented in the standardization population.
- Since test results may be influenced by examiner ethnicity, this factor should be considered when evaluating results. Whenever possible, Hispanic examiners should be employed. This is especially true if the test must be administered in Spanish.
- Whenever possible, employ criterion-referenced tests—that is, tests normed to skills needed for particular tasks. In this way, measurement of needed competencies leads to specific instructional programs. This is especially true of aptitude or vocational tests. Criterion-referenced instruments are effective retests as an index of change toward educational goals.
- Do not relegate Hispanic children to special educational and similar classroom programs on the basis of Anglocentric standardized tests alone.
- Do not relegate Hispanic clients to a therapeutic program on the basis of personality instruments alone, especially if it is known that Hispanics may deviate from majority-group norms in their pattern of responses on a particular personality inventory.

Proper interviewing is an especially important aspect of the goal-setting process. We have indicated throughout that the pluralistic therapist must be attentive to the cultural background of Hispanic clients. We have also indicated that life stresses such as poverty, unemployment, incomplete schooling, and poor facility in English are all important pieces of information that the therapist must know about if realistic goals are to be set. This is information that must be obtained in the initial interviews. Finally, goal setting is a joint partnership between client and therapist, and therefore the client's perceptions and expectations of the therapist and therapy must be known if realistic goals are to be agreed on and achieved.

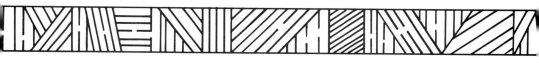

Chapter 8 Culture and Therapy in Process

FOCUSING ON COMMUNICATION STYLES

Nonverbal Communication

Therapists should be aware of styles of nonverbal communication that are characteristic of Hispanics. It would, of course, be impossible to make a complete list of Hispanic nonverbal-communication styles; in any case, such a list would deny individual differences that are probably at least as great as differences across ethnic groups. Moreover, much of the meaning of nonverbal messages is determined by the context in which they occur. Despite these difficulties with interpretation, we can make several generalizations concerning nonverbal communication.

In the field of *proxemics*, the study of personal space, relatively consistent differences in distancing have been noted between Hispanic speakers and speakers of other ethnicities. In one study, parents of first- and second-grade lower-class Puerto Ricans and Blacks and middle-class Whites were observed unobtrusively. The middle-class Whites stood farther away from the listener while talking than either the Blacks or the Puerto Ricans (Aiello & Jones, 1971). In another study, pairs of Anglo, Black, and Mexican-American adults, adolescents, and children were observed without their knowing it. The Mexican Americans of all ages clustered more closely together than the Anglos or Blacks, and the Mexican Americans stood more closely together indoors than outdoors. Distancing varied with environment among the Mexican Americans but not among the Anglo and Black subjects (Baxter, 1970). Differences in distancing are consistent between the sexes across ethnic groups. When lower-class Blacks, Puerto Ricans, and Whites were observed in pairs and in social groups, females of all ethnicities stood closer together than males (Jones, 1971).

In the field of *kinesics*, the study of body movements, several differences have been noted between Hispanics and subjects of other ethnicities. Puerto Ricans tend to avert their eyes from a speaker as a sign of respect (Lewis, 1966). In contrast, Anglo culture calls for eye contact to indicate attention and respect for the individual with whom one is communicating. Among some Hispanics, particularly Puerto Ricans, bowing one's head is a sign of respect (Pollack & Menacker, 1971). Anglo Americans might interpret ·this nonverbal message to indicate disinterest, disrespect or shyness.

Touching is common among Hispanics. When pairs of Anglos, Blacks, and Mexican Americans were observed unawares, it was noted that Mexican Americans touched one another significantly more often than Anglos or Blacks (Baxter, 1970). In contrast to this broad study with general populations of Anglos, Blacks, and Mexican Americans, some data indicate less touching between Hispanic fathers and their adolescent sons than between fathers and sons of other ethnicities (Pollack & Menacker, 1971).

Although the precise meaning of each gesture cannot be provided, awareness that styles of nonverbal communication vary across ethnicities can enhance understanding. The following extract gives an example of how failure to recognize the cultural relativity of nonverbal communication can result in misunderstanding and personal suffering (Negron, 1971, p. 112).

> A student complained to me about the fact that she had been suspended from school because she had been accused by one of her teachers of being disrespectful. I asked her what had ensued in the classroom. She indicated that when the teacher spoke to her she bowed her head, because in Puerto Rico when a teacher speaks to you, you do not look at the teacher directly. You bow your head. That's how you show the respect you have for the educator. The teacher, on the other hand, not understanding the culture and the mores and customs of the islanders of Puerto Rico, resented this. She felt that this was a sign of disrespect, and without speaking to the girl about it, suspended her from the classroom. We immediately contacted the teacher and explained that this was a sign of respect, not of disrespect. This is a small example of what I mean about a lack of sensitivity and understanding.

In therapy, as in the classroom, an awareness of possible differences in nonverbal communication may prevent misunderstanding and inappropriate confrontation. In addition, a study of personal space and body movements among Hispanics leads to several specific recommendations:

1. Shaking hands and placing an arm on the shoulder of a Hispanic client may increase the client's comfort and facilitate openness. In some cases an embrace between the client and therapist is appropriate.

2. Chairs should be placed close together, probably closer than the Anglo therapist would be inclined naturally to place them. A distance of less than two feet is preferred by many Hispanics (Hall, 1959).
3. The therapist should not attempt to maintain eye contact with a Hispanic who constantly avoids it. If eye contact is demanded, the client may assume that the therapist does not respect him or her or that the therapist cannot command respect.

Self-Disclosure

The style and pace of self-disclosure may differ between Hispanic clients and those of other ethnic backgrounds. During the standardization of his self-disclosure scale, Jourard (1971) observed that Black and Puerto Rican college students disclosed less about themselves to significant others, such as parents and friends, than did Anglo students. When a modified version of Jourard's self-disclosure questionnaire was administered to White, Puerto Rican, and Mexican-American ninth graders residing in Louisiana, Mexican Americans were significantly less willing to disclose information about themselves than were Anglos and Blacks; and Mexican-American males disclosed less than Mexican-American females (Littlefield, 1969).

In these two self-disclosure studies, no mention is made of examiner ethnicity. In a third study, a Mexican-American examiner solicited Mexican-American and Anglo college students' attitudes about disclosing personal information to a model Anglo therapist and a model Hispanic therapist, presented on audio tapes. Although self-disclosure was high for all subjects, the Mexican-American students indicated significantly less willingness to disclose to either therapist than did the Anglo students (Acosta, 1975(b); Acosta & Sheehan, 1976).

These studies consistently reveal less self-disclosure among Hispanics than among Anglos of various ages. It follows that, if a Hispanic client discloses personal data very slowly, the therapist should view this behavior as a culturally normal response. Limited self-disclosure should not be used as the single criterion for evaluating client resistance. Moreover, the therapist should press for self-disclosure only after determining that the client's normal ego-protective functioning is not being broken down. Clients uncover deep thoughts and feelings more readily after a trusting relationship is established with a therapist. Total and immediate transparency is uncommon among clients of any ethnicity, and the client's right to withhold painful material until he or she feels ready to handle it must be respected in an effective and trusting therapy relationship. The therapist must distinguish limited self-disclosure as a cultural style from limited self-disclosure as an indicator of psychological defense or resistance.

Directive and Nondirective Styles of Therapy

It is common knowledge that clients differ in the degree to which they seek advice and direction from others. Some clients are comfortable accepting advice from their therapists, and others resent it. If the client's attitude about direction and advice is ignored, a power struggle between client and therapist may ensue, and communication will be hampered (Haley, 1963).

Several researchers suggest that Hispanics, particularly the poor, prefer therapists to communicate in a directive style (Abad et al., 1974; Torrey, 1972). It has been observed that Puerto Ricans expect their physician to take an active part in the doctor/patient relationship, to offer advice, and to prescribe medication (Abad et al., 1974). Attitudes about therapy were elicited from a random sample of Mexican Americans in Lubbock, Texas. Subjects were interviewed in either Spanish or English, according to their preference, by a Mexican-American examiner. The vast majority of English- and Spanish-speaking subjects preferred that a mental-health professional offer direct advice, define problems for the client, and attempt to cheer up the client (Mack, James, Ramirez, & Bailey, 1974).

Behavior modification can be viewed as a directive approach in therapy and has been rated as effective with Hispanics in several studies. Question-asking behavior of Mexican-American pupils was increased by use of modeling and praise (Zimmerman & Ghozeil, 1972). Reading behavior was increased among Mexican-American and Anglo fourth- , fifth- , and sixth-grade students by employing a menu-choice technique. In the menu-choice approach, subjects were allowed to select their own reinforcement from pictured choices (thus assuring the desirability, or positive valence, of the reinforcers). The menu for Mexican Americans was developed by talking to teachers and students, surveying literature, and watching the children select objects during play. The researchers selected 17 items, listed in Table 8-1, as particularly attractive to Hispanics. Interestingly, items on the ethnic menu were picked as frequently by Anglo as by Mexican-American children. The authors point out that the increase in target behavior—more reading—came at a later point in the experimental period for the Mexican-American subjects than for the Anglos. They suggested that the Mexican Americans might be less aware of the process of behavior modification and unfamiliar with the use of reinforcers. Once familiar with the process of menu reinforcers, however, the Hispanics were good subjects. It would seem likely that the therapist could modify a number of client behaviors by using menu-choice reinforcement. Of course, more research is needed to test the extent of

Table 8-1. *A Reinforcement Menu.*

Certificate: The certificate has elaborate printing and states: "(student's name) has worked hard in reading this week." It has four spaces where star seals are placed when earned. On the day the student selects this item, his name is printed in the blank space, and he receives one star. The certificate is kept at school until he has earned four stars. It is then "official" and may be taken home.

Sit quietly at your desk and do nothing. From earlier observations of student activities during free time, sitting and doing nothing was the most frequently recorded behavior and appeared to be a desirable reinforcer.

Talk with a friend. Students selecting this option had to converse in a manner which would not disturb others in the room. This reinforcer was identified as "most probable" prior to the initiation of the study.

Play games—checkers, chess, Password, Scrabble, football game, etc. (For a game requiring two persons, each one must earn the right to select that item.) A wide variety of games were stocked in each experimental classroom. Because these games could be played at times other than when earned by demonstration of particular reading behaviors, the potency of this particular reinforcer may have been somewhat attenuated.

Beads for making wampum and necklaces (six beads each day). This reinforcer allowed the student to engage in an activity over a period of time, thus providing for immediate reinforcement as well as delayed reinforcement when the wampum or necklace was completed.

Color or draw with crayons, chalk, or pencil.

Work on mosaics.

Pencil to keep.

Eraser to keep. Teachers had reported that it was difficult to keep students supplied with pencils and erasers. In addition, students frequently argued over the ownership of a pencil or eraser.

Marbles to keep. Many boys and girls in the school district played marbles during recess periods.

Tape recording—Stories and history of the people of Old Spanish California and Mexico (listen to earphones). These recordings included readings taken from *The First Book of Mexico* by Sam and Beryl Epstein (New York: Franklin Watts, 1955).

Tape recording—Stories and history of the people of pioneer America (listen on earphones). These readings were from *To California by Covered Wagon* by George R. Stewart (New York: Random House, 1954) and *Lore of Our Land* by Hector M. Lee and Donald Robinson (Eds.) (New York: Harper and Row, 1963).

Tape recording—Music of Mexico (Listen on earphones).

Tape recording—Popular music (Listen on earphones). Three tape recorders with listening post, each accommodating 12 sets of earphones, were made available for the project. If a student chose to listen to a tape as a reinforcer but was unable to hear the entire tape before the end of the reading period, he was asked to earn the reinforcer the next day to hear the remainder.

Comic books written in Spanish (e.g., Historietas de Walt Disney, Tawa, Kaliman el Hombre Increíble).

Comic books (e.g., Archie, Batman, Superman). A student could win the opportunity to read one comic book per day. If he were unable to finish reading it in the time allotted, he was asked to earn the reinforcer the next day in order to complete it. The use of Spanish-language comic books was another attempt to generate an ethnically valued reinforcer for Spanish-surname students.

If you don't care for any of the items listed so, write below another item that you would rather have. If the student wished to select an activity other than those listed in the reinforcement menu, he was asked to describe it in the available space beneath the last item. This concluding free choice item in the reinforcement menu was necessary to allow the maximum range of reinforcement choice, and it also offered a method of generating new valued reinforcers based on student input.

applicability of this approach (Hosford & Bowles, 1974). In a third study, positive reinforcement and extinction were reported to be successful for modifying overall adjustment of drug addicts in an inpatient setting (Aron et al., 1974). Thus, three studies suggest that directive therapy in the form of behavior modification may be effective with Hispanic clients. Whether this directive approach is more effective with Hispanic than with Anglo clients has not been thoroughly investigated.

Data are, however, also accruing that are not congruent with the thesis that Hispanics prefer directive therapists. The client gain in directive group counseling, noninterventionist group counseling based on Rogers (1970), and no-counseling control settings was compared using a sample of ninth- and tenth-grade Puerto Rican boys. Client gain was measured by increase in occupational aspiration, positive teacher ratings, gain in grade average, increased attendance at school, and decreased number of referrals to school administrators because of discipline problems. No significant difference in gain was noted across the three groups. The experimental subjects responded to a questionnaire concerning their attitude about the group therapies. No significant difference in attitude about counseling was recorded for subjects in nonintervention and directive group counseling (Naun, 1971).

Several researchers point out, however, that directive therapy in the form of confrontation, sarcasm, or teasing can be inappropriate for Hispanics. Teasing to stimulate a person toward action (labeled confrontation or paradoxical intention by psychotherapists) is so uncommon to Hispanics that a word does not exist to express it. In working with Puerto Ricans, the therapist wants to avoid inducing **vergüenza** (shame). Confrontation must be limited and slow in order to avoid feelings of attack (Montijo, 1975). Thus, directive therapy based on confrontation may be inappropriate for Hispanics because it conflicts or contradicts the value of *dignidad*.

Another study (Moll et al., 1976) presents indirect evidence supporting nondirective therapy with Hispanics. These researchers obtained most information from their Hispanic interviewees when they adopted **la plática,** an informal interview. In *la plática,* subjects were allowed to discuss tangential issues, and the interviewers let the subjects set the pace of the conversation.

Recall Shofield's (1964) research about the YAVIS Syndrome that indicated that therapists prefer to work with young, attractive, verbal, basically middle-class clients. One can question whether Hispanics really want more directive therapy or whether directive therapy is imposed on them by therapists. Directive therapy is fast and allows the therapist more time to work with preferred, middle-class patients who are perceived as more amenable to insight therapy (Padilla, 1971).

Reviewing the preference for directive versus nondirective therapy among various cultural groups, Wallace (1970) explains that disillusioned groups favor control procedures such as confession, penance, and indoctrination. Secure groups prefer catharsis. Using Wallace's (1970) model, one can postulate that Hispanic clients prefer directive therapy when they are disillusioned about the possibility of changing the external forces that precipitate stress. On the other hand, perhaps therapists are the "disillusioned," insecure group. Reliance on directive therapy by therapists working with Hispanic clients may reveal fear among these therapists about the behavior of Hispanics if they do not control them. At this point, it would seem premature to limit the mode of therapy with Hispanics to the directive style. In many cases, intervention, advice, and reinforcement are appropriate, but research does not rule out Hispanics as good candidates for insight and nondirective approaches.

INITIATING THERAPY

The initial meeting is very important in establishing the client's trust in the therapist and in the therapeutic process (Hall & Lindzey, 1970). The therapist working with Hispanics must be aware of several culturally specific factors to be successful in building a trusting relationship during the initial contact hours.

The therapist must be certain to pronounce the client's name correctly, making especially sure that both parts of a hyphenated name are included. For many Hispanics, especially Puerto Ricans, both the mother's and the father's lineage constitute the family name (Christensen, 1975). For instance, in the case of Hernandez-Rodriguez, Hernandez is the last name of the father and Rodriguez is the last name of the mother and is retained in respect for her and her family.

In some cases, it may be necessary for the therapist to contact the client rather than waiting for the client to initiate the contact, as in the case of Family X.

> *THE CASE OF FAMILY X.*[1] Family X is made up of the parents and three children: a girl 6 years old and two boys, aged 7 and 16. Mr. and Mrs. X were legally married at one time, but because of serious marital problems and pressures from Mrs. X's family, were divorced three years ago. However, they managed to resolve their problems and came together again; the church never considered them divorced. The family lives in a small house in the back of a large empty lot that has not been taken care of properly. Weeds have taken over the majority of the land so that they conceal the house.
>
> The probation department referred Family X to the community center because neither the father nor the mother were able to communicate in English. The probation officer explained that this family needed counseling and also "someone who could speak their language." The parents were unable to control their 16-year-old son, Freddy, who had been placed on probation for running away from home regularly.
>
> Mrs. X had been told to call the center for an appointment. This might have been sufficient to start the helping process for an Anglo-Saxon Protestant family; for a Mexican-American family it was not. Not only was it difficult for the family to overcome the shame of having to deal with the law, but Mr. X—who made all the decisions—had been disregarded by the probation officer. It was decided that establishing contact was up to the center, on the assumption that this would be difficult or impossible for Mrs. X.

The importance of the family in Hispanic culture leads to the recommendation that the initial therapy contact should be open to all family members involved directly and indirectly with the identified patient.

[1]From "Initial Contacts with Mexican-American Families," by I. Aguilar, *Social Work*, May 1972, *17*(3), 66–70. Copyright © 1972 by the National Association of Social Workers, Inc. Reprinted by permission.

The director of the community center called Mrs. X, identifying himself in Spanish as a social worker who knew that her son had been in some trouble, and explained that the center was a voluntary not a governmental agency. It was suggested that Mrs. X. ask her husband if he could come with her to the center. She agreed to do so and to call back later in the evening when her husband came home from work, adding, "It is good to talk to someone who can speak Spanish." The fact that Mrs. X had been asked to consult her husband about a conference for the two of them put her in a situation in which she did not have to decide on her own. Her husband was now involved in the decision-making.

Mr. X. was included in the helping process from the beginning. Had he been left out, it would have meant that Mrs. X. was assuming an improper role and that Mr. X. was being put down by her.

It is appropriate for the therapist to shake hands with the client and, after a warm relationship has been established, to embrace the client (Padilla et al., 1975). Because of Hispanic emphasis on *personalismo*, a leisurely opening to therapy facilitates client comfort, as we see in the continuation of the story of Family X.

A few days later, Mr. and Mrs. X came to the center for the interview. True to Latino custom, the first hour was leisurely, the talk mainly about familiar things that they could comfortably share with the worker. Conversation centered about Mexico, where they had lived until about two years before. They shared information about their respective families and mentioned how difficult it was for them to get used to the American way of life. Here they had no close relatives nearby to whom they could turn when problems arose. It was disconcerting for them to have to bother people outside the family.

It was no wonder that Mr. and Mrs. X were having a hard time, not only with their son, but with the society surrounding them, which was completely alien to them and highly threatening to their way of life. In their own little house at the end of the big lot, hidden by the growing weeds, they had found an island isolated from the outside world—up to the time that their son had gotten into trouble. But then they had to face the world, and it was difficult to understand and more difficult to be understood.

They were not pressed to talk about their son's situation in detail. They decided to come back the following day to talk about this problem after the probation officer had come to see them.

The purposes in mind for this first interview were accomplished: to meet Mr. and Mrs. X personally and to establish a comfortable relationship that would lead to a partnership once they were able to share their problems with the social worker. The next step would be to share a common purpose, in this case, helping Freddy.

If a Hispanic is referred by a government agency, such as the court, the therapist may need to clarify to the client that the mental-health facility is distinct from the referring agency. The therapist may need also to explain the role of the agency to the client or intercede between the referring agency and the client, as is seen below.

The following day Mr. and Mrs. X came a little late to the meeting and were reluctant to talk about their conference with the probation officer. Mr. X just kept silent, looking down. Mrs. X, red-eyed, finally said, "I am very ashamed. You should have heard what the probation officer said about us. He blamed us for all the troubles with Freddy and said that if we were not able to speak English, we should go back to Mexico. Perhaps worst of all, our daughter heard all of this because she had to translate for us."

It was suggested that they arrange to meet the probation officer the next time at the center; there the social worker could translate for them and make the necessary interpretations. Thus, the harmful effect of the probation officer's prejudices against them would be minimized. Mr. and Mrs. X were assured that they had certain legal and moral rights that had to be respected —among them the right to be treated as human beings. Major differences between the systems of law in the United States and Mexico were explained, as were the functions of the probation department and the role of its officers.

Mr. and Mrs. X then seemed somewhat relieved and looked less tense and fearful. Mrs. X thanked the social worker and, looking at her husband, said: "We are not ignorant and dumb. We just did not understand anything about what was happening."

A warm, easy opening to therapy allowed the social worker to best assist Family X. Despite the pressing need for therapeutic intervention, the social worker may have jeopardized the relationship if disclosure had been pushed more rapidly. Because of the social worker's sensitivity to Hispanic norms, the family was able to communicate with the probation officer to work toward control and final amelioration of Freddy's problem.

The therapist should employ *dignidad*; he or she should allow the father and elders to speak first and listen respectfully to them. If children are present, the therapist should bring them gradually into the conversation by encouraging them to comment on their parents' statements (Ruiz et al., 1978).

The therapist must be alert to subtle signs of dissatisfaction with the therapy process. Remember that a Hispanic may not express discontent openly because of the importance of *respeto*. Karno (1966, p. 518) demonstrates that, if a Hispanic client is discouraged with the therapeutic relationship, he or she may drop out of therapy rather than criticize the therapist:

> Richard Lopez was punctual, polite, and deferential for nine consecutive weeks. It is suggested, however, by his sudden, unanticipated, and permanent withdrawal from the therapeutic encounter, that the relationship between him and his therapist was of a kind considered by many observers as common for Mexican Anglo relationships in institutional settings, viz—external compliance masking internal and hostile rejection . . . The therapist, in this instance, failed to record a single fact, thought, or feeling concerning this patient's ethnicity, in regard to appearance, language, family relationships, or life experiences, despite an otherwise detailed evaluation in the tradition of the medical-psychiatric history. In his notes on the therapeutic sessions, the therapist, despite his general high level of competence and sensitivity, failed to make a single reference to the patient's ethnic identity, an insensitivity which I believe, may have been an important factor in the failure of therapy.

THERAPEUTIC MODALITIES

Group Counseling

Group counseling has assisted Hispanic clients in ameliorating personal problems and expanding personal awareness (Maes & Rinaldi, 1974). Descriptive studies report success in group counseling with

Hispanics of various ages, socioeconomic classes, and ethnohistories. For example, in a hospital in East Harlem in New York City, group psychotherapy with Blacks and Puerto Ricans was conducted by a bilingual social worker. Review of individual case studies revealed many successes. Moreover, 75% of the group members followed through on referrals to other hospital units. Success with group counseling has also been reported among elementary school Hispanics. School counselors perceived group counseling as particularly effective for furthering children's skill at expressing their feelings in English, stimulating self-respect and pride in Hispanic culture, and clarifying personal values (Maes & Rinaldi, 1974). Successful group counseling with college students was reported by two Anglo student-personnel deans who conducted a 15-hour encounter weekend with six Blacks, four Chicanos, and four Anglos (Walker & Hamilton, 1973). Counseling techniques included teaching listening skills, focusing on feelings, and reinforcing participants' interaction. The leaders cite as evidence for the success of the group the increased frequency of self-revealing statements and the stages passed through by the group that were congruent with healthy group process as posited by Rogers (1970). Some successful groups have been based on behavioral principles. Members are asked to define behavioral goals, **metas.** They are taught relaxation and contracting techniques. Group discussions assist clients in applying behavioral principles to their *metas* (Herrera & Sanchez, 1976).

The effectiveness of group counseling has been analyzed in several experimental studies with young adults. In one study, ten Blacks and Puerto Ricans ranging from 15 to 31 years of age who had been labeled destructive and aggressive and who had been truant from school participated in a group-counseling session that was characterized by free expression of negative feelings and bombardment with positive feedback. The clients' self-reports about the group experience were quite positive, and truancy and aggressiveness decreased (Rueveni, 1971). In a second study of group counseling with young Hispanics, three groups made up of Mexican Americans, Blacks and Anglos joined encounter groups modeled after the National Training Laboratory (NTL) design. After ten weeks, significant changes in attitude toward self and others were reported on a semantic differential, a Q-sort, and an index of social distance (Hamilton, 1969).

Group-therapy processes designed particularly for Hispanic clients are emerging. A number of group activities appropriate for the general Hispanic population (Ruiz, 1975) and for Hispanic drug addicts (Aron, Alger, & Gonzalez, 1971) are described in Table 8-2. The relative

Table 8-2. *Group-counseling activities oriented toward*
Hispanics.

Una palabra	Each member states a Spanish word and expresses his feelings associated with it. Other group members offer feedback.
Retain your *nombre*	The members state Spanish names and express feelings associated with them.
Color	Each member focuses on skin color and feelings associated with their lightness or darkness (for example, guilt associated with being light-skinned).
Sonidos	Members become familiar with a Spanish musical instrument; they then pair off and try to communicate with their partners just by playing the instrument.
El grito	Members give "the yell," a spontaneous catharsis done to Mariachi music.
Chicano handclap	Members begin clapping softly in a slow, steady rhythm. Gradually, the pace increases, and spontaneous expression of feelings is encouraged.
Journey to **Aztlan**	Members close eyes and journey in their imaginations to *Aztlan*. Then, after a few minutes, members discuss their experiences.
La realidad	Therapeutic discussion for hospitalized patients about emerging life-styles including discussion of male/female relationships, parent/child interactions, responsibility to one's family and culture, ethnic pride, alternatives to drug use, and so on.
Rollo	Group members give short impromptu speeches about themselves and their opinions on various subjects. In groups not highly skilled in English, speeches are presented in English, and feedback is given in Spanish. The group is structured to teach its members more effective ways of dealing with Anglo society.
El grupo	Spontaneous expression and catharsis by employing a "hot seat." The person on the hot seat is the focus of the group's attention. The individual expresses feelings and receives feedback. Attack and confrontational therapy, which are alien to Hispanic values, are discouraged.

Sources: "Chicanoizing the Therapeutic Community," by W. S. Aron, N. Alger, and R. T. Gonzalez, *Journal of Psychedelic Drugs,* 1974, *6*, 321–327 and "Chicano Group Catalysts," by A. S. Ruiz, *Personnel and Guidance Journal,* 1975, *53*, 462–466.

effectiveness of counseling groups that incorporate Hispanic cultural concepts versus counseling groups with no cultural content has seldom been studied. One investigator compared the personal growth (as measured by academic achievement, self-concept on a semantic differential, and feelings about one's nationality) of Mexican Americans participating in traditional group counseling with that of Mexican Americans in bicultural group counseling (emphasizing pride in ethnic background). Change was not significantly different between treatment groups (Leo, 1972). With three experimental and three control groups of Puerto Rican sixth graders in an inner-city school, the addition of ethnic content (language and culture) did not enhance group interaction (Ciaramella, 1973).

The generally positive trend of research about group counseling suggests that it is a viable approach for facilitating growth among Hispanics. Much more research is needed to measure the relative effectiveness of various group-counseling modalities, especially those built on cultural premises.

Family Therapy

Family therapy offers particular promise with Hispanics because of the importance of and support inherent in kinship ties. A close family member can serve as a powerful auxiliary therapist (Ramirez, 1972) if he or she understands the goals and techniques of therapy.

If the entire family is interviewed in therapy, disturbances in the kinship support system can be identified. Once difficulties in the family system are rectified, the patient's symptoms may decrease significantly (Padilla et al., 1975). The case of Ramon (Goldstein & Palmer, 1975) illustrates that the identified patient—in this case, a 15-year-old named Ramon—may be acting out stress in the family system.

> THE CASE OF RAMON.[2] About my backaches, *señor*, I think I find it hard to tell you, though my wife here knows too. You see it is like this, I am going down the street, my two little children want a piece of candy, but I do not have ten cents, I feel sick. I decide I will go home and lie down, my back aches. My back aches very bad and yet I would like to get up. I do not feel much of a man. I know my son will come home. He will not

---

[2]From *The Experience of Anxiety: A Casebook*, Second Edition, by M. J. Goldstein and J. O. Palmer. Copyright 1975 by Michael J. Goldstein and James O. Palmer. Reprinted by permission of the authors and publisher, Oxford University Press.

respect me. He will say "you are an old man with a bad back. You do not work, you do not take care of your family, I cannot respect you." And again I will not feel much of a man. How can I get my son to respect me? He too will not be a man, he will be a bum. He will not get to school. He walks around like a proud cock all the time. He does no work. He takes drugs. He does not go to school. He will not be a man either.

The speaker, Mr. R., was a 50-year-old illiterate Mexican laborer. He had come with his wife to the psychiatric clinic on referral from a juvenile probation officer regarding their second oldest son, Ramon, age 15. It was obvious that Mr. R. was extremely concerned about Ramon and Ramon's adjustment, as well as the welfare of the rest of his family. He and his wife had to travel a long way across the city, out of the area where they lived and worked, to talk to people who did not speak Spanish. Furthermore, Mr. R. was a proud man who normally did not ask for help from anyone regarding his family.

. . . Ramon had committed no crime whatsoever; he had been referred to the courts mainly because he had stayed out all night after having had a violent quarrel with his father. Such quarrels had become increasingly frequent over the past year, and Ramon often would storm out of the house to spend the night with some friend. However, from time to time he would wander the streets late at night and would be picked up by the police. This time he was found to be in possession of a small amount of marijuana.

A quick review of Ramon's history might lead one to conclude that Ramon was an insubordinate teenager with poor but caring parents. However, the therapist gleaned information suggesting that Ramon was a victim of family problems such as poverty and sibling rivalry. Ramon was the only fair-skinned member of the family, and his distinctiveness made him an easy target for family frustration.

. . . Jesus R., who preferred to be called Jack, his wife, Marguerita, known as Rita, and their eight children lived in a two-bedroom home in a section of Los Angeles inhabited mostly by people of mainly Mexican or Latin

American descent. The adolescents voice the opinion that the crowded conditions of their home and the lack of privacy created conflicts between them and the rest of the family. The parents shared one bedroom, the four youngest children the other bedroom. The dining room was curtained off for Olivia, age 19, and her younger sister Marta, age 12. Ramon and Salvador slept on a screened-in porch that had been added to the back of the house. The living room was usually taken over by the four smaller children and Jack, who commandeered the television. Thus, there was no space for teenage activities of any kind . . .

There was a great deal of rivalry between Ramon and his brothers and sisters. Ramon felt that he was given many more chores to do around the garden and home since Salvador was excused from household chores, on the grounds that he had special jobs to do at school. It was evident that Jack was extremely proud of his oldest son and often made invidious comparisons with Ramon. Ramon often was at daggers' points with Marta, who was praised for carrying out many tasks without complaint or hesitation. Ramon hated to have to care for the yard or run errands for his mother and was always ducking out or had to be ordered three or four times before he complied. Moreover, Marta was the one member of the family who resembled her father very much, having the high forehead and peak nose of his predominantly Indian ancestry. In fact, Jack referred to Marta as "my little Indian". On the other hand, Ramon was quite fair-skinned, and resembled his mother much more so than the other children in the family. Sal and Olivia teased him and called him "pretty boy" which usually infuriated him. One of the most recent family quarrels occurred when 10-year-old George observed Ramon primping his new moustache in the mirror and yelled "pretty boy" at him; Ramon swung and knocked George into the wall bloodying his forehead, whereupon Jack grabbed Ramon by the collar, and Ramon swung at him also. Before Rita could intervene, Ramon had run out of the house . . .

Ramon was not seen in individual therapy. Rather, family discussions were initiated. Through the therapist's support and leading questions, members gained new insights about one another. This new information increased their respect for one another as exemplified in the following excerpt in which family members gain empathy for their father, Jack.

> When he (Jack) arrived in Los Angeles, he stayed with friends who were relatives of Rita's father . . . In fact, his first job was in the same factory where Rita's father worked and thus he saw quite a bit of Rita and her sisters over the following year. During this year his war wounds healed considerably. He learned to operate heavy construction earth-moving machinery, a job which paid considerably more than most unskilled labor. He now felt far more able to support a wife and family, and he married Rita . . .
>
> Despite the fact that Jack was earning more money than he could on most any other job, he realized that since he and the other Mexican workers did not belong to the union, they were paid far below union scale. With the encouragement of some of his friends Jack approached the union and asked to have some help in having him and his friends join and having a union shop where they worked. Given encouragement by the union, he and the other Mexicans gathered together and formed a local union and went on strike demanding union conditions. Backed by the union headquarters in Los Angeles the Mexican workers under Jack's leadership were able to force the employer to recognize them as union members and to give them conditions held by other union workers in Los Angeles. However, at this time the union officials no longer gave Jack any personal support, and he was fired. Jack was advised by friends that the union felt that he was acquiring far too much political power because he had led the workers in the particular company to organize. There were no Mexican officials in this union at that time, nor have there been since. Jack thereafter found it very difficult to find any job in construction because most of them were under union contract, and he found it difficult to get back into the union . . .
>
> Again his children seemed to be astounded. They were unaware that their father had ever been any kind of a community leader, that he had actively fought

prejudice and discrimination, and that he had worked
very hard against so many odds for them. Most of all,
they had not previously understood his despair. Again it
was Ramon who seemed to identify with his father and
to be most indignant over the injustices which he saw
his father having to endure.

As treatment progressed, the children learned of the sorrow in their
mother's life. They gained more understanding of Rita's repressive
attitude toward sex, and Rita began to perceive her children's interest in
sexuality as less threatening. Dilemmas between the parents were also
uncovered and resolved—with the help of feedback from the children.

. . . The family discussions continued every week
for approximately eight months. At this time, the family
was much more open with one another, and there was
much less quarreling in the house. When Jack finished
his schooling he was promptly hired by the same agency
which had trained him, to teach the use and maintenance
of large construction machinery to younger men.
Although the pay was not very high, at least it was a
full time job, and Jack felt he gained a considerable
amount of respect from these students. Sal finished high
school and was promptly drafted into the military. His
girl friend was pregnant, and he married her the week
before he went into the Army. Thus both "repeated
history," according to his father. Ramon was still at
loose ends but succeeded in completing the school year
without further incident. He took his brother's job when
his brother went into the military and thus had some
money and felt a bit more secure.

The case ends tragically, but at least communication pathways had
opened enough for family members to support one another through their
unexpected crises.

. . . However, over the following year or so the
family continued to suffer tragedies. The next fall Ramon
was again arrested for possession of marijuana and was
sent to prison for six months. The money for the agency
where the father worked gave out, and he was again
unemployed within a year. The worst tragedy was Sal's

death in Viet Nam. At this point, the mother returned to the clinic for several visits, quite grief-stricken. Jack joined her and was able to reveal his intense grief. He was quite embarrassed to be unemployed again, but in this matter, he did not feel his outlook was exceedingly grim.

There is a special model of family therapy that is designed to assist Puerto Rican patients. This model emphasizes the role of teacher or confidant that is assigned to older siblings in many Puerto Rican families. Therapy is offered in groups of eight patients. The three therapists represent an older sibling, the father, and the mother. During the first three or four weeks of therapy, a young therapist who dresses and talks like the patients (thus modeling behavior of elder siblings) meets seven patients in informal settings. Eventually two older therapists, a man and a woman, are introduced. The older male therapist behaves with dignity, in a somewhat aloof fashion, akin to how the Puerto Rican father might behave. The female therapist is friendly and nurturing, somewhat like the traditional Puerto Rican mother. The simulated family allows for interpretation of the patients' attitudes about family members and presents opportunities for patients to develop more appropriate ways of interacting with family members. In three groups of eight patients involved in such family therapy, eleven were discharged from further treatment, seven were improved, and six showed little change (Maldonado-Sierra & Trent, 1960).

Success has been reported employing a "family group constellation" approach with lower- and middle-income Hispanic families (Pollack & Menacker, 1971). In this mode of family counseling, three or four families meet jointly with three to four counselors for weekly two-hour sessions. The counselors offer feedback about family dynamics, and families attempt to help one another resolve their dilemmas. In addition to the family-constellation meetings, counselors meet separately with each adult and child in an effort to improve communication skills that members will then employ in constellation meetings and in their private lives.

Family counseling has been effective in increasing the academic performance of Hispanic children. A parent-education program conducted for two years with families increased Hispanic children's performances on two IQ tests. In the first year of the program, the counselor felt that parents needed encouragement to participate in the program. Therefore the program was conducted in the families' homes. Mothers were taught home management, preventive health, and driver education. In addition, mothers and children were observed and recommendations offered for increasing children's curiosity and improving their learning style. In the second year, fathers participated in an evening program, and mothers and children joined in a daily nursery-school program (Johnson, Leler, Ríos, Brandt, Kahn, Mazeika, Frede, & Bisett, 1974).

Although research is sparse, limited findings show family counseling and therapy to be quite promising with Hispanic clients. The family can be included in the therapy hour in a number of ways: by asking specific family members to join in the counseling process; by working directly with the whole family; or by working with a member of the family as a consultant who will, in turn, work with the client (Christensen, 1977). The therapist should consider Hispanics likely candidates for family therapy and should be particularly alert for new methods of family counseling reported in the literature.

Another aspect of family counseling that needs consideration is counseling on parenting. Child rearing among Hispanics is still a relatively unresearched area. In her extensive counseling with Hispanic families, Boulette (1977) noted many questions concerning punishment of children, insufficient or inappropriate sex education, degradation of one parent by the other or by other family members, and excessive attachment between mother and child combined with lack of attachment between father and child. As yet, no models for counseling parents have been proposed. It is our conviction, however, that, because of the emphasis placed on children in Hispanic culture, counselors must give more attention to counseling on parenting. Hispanic parenting models should take acculturation stress, intergenerational conflict, and the implications of poverty in child rearing into account.

Psychodrama

Because of the importance of *hospitalidad*—social graciousness—to many Hispanics, it might be predicted that psychodrama (psychotherapy built around the adoption of appropriate social roles) would be a particularly effective treatment modality. Systematic research on this technique has not been conducted with Hispanics, but therapists' evaluations of the technique are very promising. A therapist who works with Puerto Ricans explains that psychodrama is particularly well suited to his clientele because of their sensitivity to social roles and settings (Fink, 1967).

The therapist who conducts psychodrama with Hispanics will want to be certain that patients perceive the psychodrama setting as warm and non-threatening. Psychodrama can be conducted in an informal setting such as a community center or a patient's home. Therapists should be aware that Hispanic males may not accept sex-reversal role playing (Fink, 1967).

Assertiveness Training

Boulette (1976) has observed that the response of many Hispanic females to stress is one of **llorando** (crying), **rezando** (praying), and **aguantando** (enduring). Many Hispanic women try to hide their problems from their families and themselves. Assertiveness training may be effective in helping these clients increase appropriate behavior, protect their rights, and express feelings of anger, affection, and concern.

Pluralistic assertiveness training involves several steps. First, the person learns about the relationship of his or her nonassertive behavior to symptoms. Then the therapist and the client explore factors that inhibit assertion, and the therapist may offer advice as necessary. The client may be informed about child-care centers, women's groups, and so on. Then the therapist models assertive behavior, and, finally, behavioral rehearsal allows the individual to test out new assertive behavior (Boulette, 1976).

Research on the effectiveness of assertiveness training with Hispanics is just beginning. With low-income families, a combination of behavioral rehearsal, social modeling, and role playing were at least as successful as a variant of client-centered therapy on all outcome scales (Boulette, 1972).

The use of assertiveness training with Hispanics raises several issues. In the traditional Hispanic family, the female generally is not assertive. Would assertiveness training assist Hispanic females in adjusting to a traditional life-style? Assertiveness training could disrupt a husband/wife relationship if that relationship depended on the female assuming a passive role and the male a dominant one. Maladaptive responses to racism include withdrawal, psychosomatic disorders, and denial of ethnicity. Could assertiveness training be an effective tool in helping males as well as females cope with discrimination? It is hoped that research on assertiveness training will be conducted with various Hispanic populations and that answers to these questions will be found.

COUNSELING ADDICTS

As we have mentioned previously, drug addiction is the most frequent diagnosis among young adult Hispanic males hospitalized in mental institutions. Counseling with drug addicts is generally a difficult process and may be more so with Hispanics. The therapist working with Hispanic drug addicts, *tecatos*, will confront some issues that are common to all addicts and some problems that are associated with ethnic status. The therapist must determine whether the person is primarily an addict who steals to support his or her habit or a criminal who, among other illegal activities, uses illegal drugs. The focus of treatment will differ for these individuals. In the first case, the reason for the addiction and ways of "kicking the habit" must be emphasized. For the criminal addict, the basis of hostility and/or psychopathology must be considered.

An important key to treating the *tecato* is to raise the psychological and financial cost of the habit so high that the addict cannot maintain the habit. In an earlier chapter, we explained that addiction may be tacitly accepted by the Hispanic family. The therapist must make certain that the extended family does not provide counterproductive support (Rivera, 1975). For example, allowing the *tecato* to live at home amounts to tacit support of the habit.

Another important key in treating the *tecato* is to minimize the possibility for manipulation. New York City has established therapeutic communities called Phoenix Houses, patterned after Synanon. The addicts who reside in these centers are subject to great pressure to "kick the habit" from peers and administrators (who are usually former addicts), and excuses are not accepted. Life is highly structured and controlled by residents of the Phoenix House (Fitzpatrick, 1971).

Research conducted with Mexican-American drug addicts in a detoxification unit in California indicates that successful drug counseling requires intervention on two levels: (1) counseling to improve self-image and to encourage the expression of feelings about discrimination and (2) education and training so that rehabilitated clients can obtain employment after discharge. Hispanic drug addicts need to be counseled toward a goal, such as a career. Positive reinforcement, contracts, and group therapy were successful approaches with Hispanic addicts in the California detox unit. Rules were explained in group processes. Patients were allowed to express their views about the rules but could not veto a policy. Discipline was administered by the group of patients and staff, **la familia.** Therapy was divided into four phases. During Phase 1, of two to three months' duration, the *tecato* is involved in intensive therapy and has limited contact with individuals outside the center. In Phase 2, of another two to three months' duration, the patient lives in the center, and educational and vocational training are emphasized. In Phase 3, the patient lives in the center and works outside. Phase 3 also lasts approximately three months. In the final two months, Phase 4, the patient lives outside and works outside but continues to visit the center for counseling (Aron et al., 1974).

Casavantes (1976) interviewed 26 counselors (mostly former addicts) who had reported success working with *tecatos* and arrived at several recommendations. Treatment programs must be individualized to make optimal use of the patient's strength. For example, it may be effective to have the *tecato* help plan and administer the treatment program. Many of the skills that a drug addict needs to survive "on the street" can be put to work toward more positive goals. It is important to foster personal relationships—*el carnalismo*—with agency personnel and to take any progress as significant.

In general, successful therapy with *el tecato* requires a combination of personal, family, and vocational counseling, vocational training, and patience. If a therapist is not equipped to provide a full range of services, including occupational guidance, referral to a drug clinic is appropriate. Contact with the therapist should be continued even after the patient has "kicked the habit." Organizations of drug addicts, such as LUCHA in Los Angeles, provide long-term support for those who need it.

More programs are needed that are aimed at prevention. In New York City, the Horizon Project has attempted and successfully offered widespread information about the hazards of drugs (Fitzpatrick, 1971). But the drug problem will not be rectified until the psychosocial stresses that lead to escape into drugs are confronted squarely. As long as psychosocial stresses confront minorities and the poor, the pluralistic therapist will encounter many *tecatos*.

COUNSELING ALCOHOLICS

There is a serious need for effective treatment for Hispanic alcoholics. Many alcoholics seek help from Alcoholics Anonymous. However, Madsen (1964) argues that association with this group is almost impossible for the traditional Hispanic since the required abstinence is a threat to *machismo* and disrupts social relations. More recently, this argument has been challenged by Hispanic-oriented Alcoholics Anonymous groups throughout the country. The current feeling is that the program can be effective with Hispanic alcoholics if it is built on cultural strengths such as the importance of the family as a support system and the role of religion in helping the individual develop the strength to abstain from alcohol.

The treatment of alcoholics is generally a difficult task. The therapist can expect some of the same difficulties with Hispanic alcoholics as with those of other ethnicities, such as slow recovery or frequent relapses. Exactly how Hispanic alcoholics differ from those of the other ethnicities has not been determined, and therefore culturally specific treatment modalities have not been developed.

GERIATRIC COUNSELING

Since the 1950s social scientists have attended increasingly to the aged as a quasi minority group. Early forced retirement and other youth-oriented attitudes in our society discourage the elderly from engaging in many vital activities. Competition, aggression, and action are not sanctioned; rather, the aged are expected to be passive and cooperative. Yet research has shown that, in general, persons who remain most active and engaged have the highest morale (Haven, 1968; Reynolds & Kalish, 1974). Because of stereotyping and forced disengagement, this group has special psychological needs and may require specialized counseling.

One wonders whether the plight of the Hispanic aged is similar to that of other elderly Americans. A basic tenet of the pluralistic-counseling approach is that the counseling techniques appropriate with majority-group Americans are not necessarily directly applicable to particular ethnic groups. Do the Hispanic aged require a specialized kind of geriatric counseling? In traditional Hispanic culture, the extended family is a primary source of support. The aged may live with their families and are given much respect and attention (Maldonado, 1975; Moore, 1971). Nevertheless, in an extensive survey in Los Angeles County, Black, Mexican-American, and White residents, ages 45 to 74, were asked about their experiences with race and age discrimination in finding or staying on a job; and 60% to 88% of each ethnic subsample reported both ethnic and age discrimination. Smaller percentages of each ethnic subsample (20% to 45%) stated that their own families and acquaintances experienced age and ethnic discrimination, and 8% to 34% identified personal experiences with age and ethnic prejudice. Blacks reported the most discrimination, and Mexican Americans reported more age and ethnic discrimination than Whites (Kasschau, 1977).

Perhaps the discrepancy between the support given the aged in traditional Hispanic culture and the reported age discrimination cited in Kasschau's 1977 study can be explained if one views the Hispanic aged as a bifaceted group. In their study of the aged in San Francisco, Clark and Mendelson (1969) describe some Hispanics as "community aged." The community aged maintain close contacts with family in the United States and Mexico. They base their self-esteem "not on those values which are models for young Americans, but on a contrasting profile, including congeniality, conservation, resilience, harmoniousness, cooperation, continuity, and an orientation on the present" (p. 90).

A second group of Hispanic aged are "disengaged" not only from employment and the larger American society but also from family and friends. In a survey of the aged in Los Angeles, Reynolds and Kalish

(1974) report that Black respondents were significantly more likely to expect to live and want to live longer than Japanese Americans, Mexican Americans, and Anglo Americans. The authors speculate that those wanting to live a long life feel that life is engaging them; they are not ready to leave it. The disengaged Hispanic aged are products of the American mobile society. Their families move away from the *barrios*, out of town in search of new employment opportunities. The isolated Hispanic aged are poorer than most Mexican Americans and poorer than most Anglo aged. They have little education, and census data suggest that, in the next generation, there will be an even wider gap in education between the Mexican-American aged and the Anglo aged. Many of these Hispanic aged are immigrants and experience added stress associated with the acculturation of their children (Maldonado, 1975; Moore, 1971).

The Hispanic community aged may require a different counseling orientation than the isolated Hispanic aged. Among the community aged, it would seem appropriate to deal with themes of fear of death or incapacitation, as it is appropriate to consider these issues among the elderly of other ethnicities. It is important to foster family support and to include family members in counseling programs. For the isolated Hispanic aged, it is appropriate to deal with themes of poverty and loneliness. An important part of such counseling is helping the isolated elderly Hispanic become involved in social programs and apply for financial support (de Armas, 1975). Therapists need to reach out to this elderly population; they usually will not come to a mental-health clinic. A likely place to contact the aged is in church. Time can be set aside as part of the church service to discuss their problems. Advertising over television or radio has also been quite effective.

Therapeutic recommendations specific to the aged Hispanic can be postulated. More research is needed to ascertain the particular needs of the isolated and community aged and of Hispanic aged of other than Mexican origin. Counseling approaches for special groups of Hispanic elderly can then be more fully developed and evaluated.

BEREAVEMENT COUNSELING

Bereavement counseling is a broad field that recognizes that issues having to do with death affect people on several levels: first, how does our abstract concept of death affect our style of living? Second, how do we deal with ourselves and with significant others when they are dying? And, third, how do we mourn the loss of significant others when they die? A small but growing body of research suggests that Hispanics may differ from members of the majority culture on each of these dimensions.

Abstract Concepts of Death

Research suggests that the Mexican is much more open about considering death than the typical American. Death, as symbolized by the bullfight, is a constant and uncontrollable presence. Recognizing the arbitrary power of death helps one to be grateful for each day of life. The world is transient; life is merely a passage from one state of being to another. The dead are treated with much respect, and it is felt that their spirit is ever present. As Paz (1961) eloquently explains, to

> the resident of New York, Paris, or London, death is a word that is never spoken because it burns the lips. In contrast, the Mexican frequents death, makes fun of it, caresses it, sleeps with it, fetes it; it is one of his favorite games and his deepest love . . . Our songs, verses, fiestas and popular sayings demonstrate unequivocally that death does not frighten us because "life has cured us of fears" [p. 52].

For this reason, **el Día de los Muertos** (the Day of the Dead), November 2, is a very special day in Mexico. It has no equivalent in the United States. On this day, altars are erected in homes, and food is set out to nourish the dead who may choose to return and visit their families. The holiday carries implications of appeasement, forgiveness, and repentance. The candies, breads, and papier-mâché figures of the Day are death figures, but they all are engaged in activities of life, such as dancing, singing, and eating (Aguilar & Wood, 1976). The importance of death and of significant others who have died is emphasized.

The extent to which this traditional Mexican attitude toward death is a facet of life for Hispanics in the United States has been the subject of several recent investigations. The results suggest that Mexican Americans do emphasize death in their abstract thinking, although perhaps not to the same degree as the Mexicans. In a dream survey, Mexican-American university students reported that they experienced significantly more death-related dreams than Anglo students (Roll, Hinton, & Glazer, 1974). In a follow-up study in which similar students were asked to record their dreams over a two-week period, Mexican Americans again reported significantly more dream content (Roll & Brenneis, 1975). In an extensive survey conducted with a stratified sample of Anglos, Blacks, Mexican Americans, and Japanese Americans in Los Angeles, Mexican Americans reported more than others that they dwelled on thoughts of their own death, thinking about it at least weekly, and claimed less often that they did not think about their own death. Mexican Americans tended to report more frequent unexplainable feelings that they or others were about to die, and they were slightly more willing to admit fear of dying than were the other groups. They seemed to feel that death was arbitrary and out of their control. They were more apt to report that people cannot hasten or postpone their own death through their will to live or will to die. They opposed the notion that people should be allowed to die if they wished, and more believed that accidental deaths reflect the hand of God working among people. Although these attitudes seem very similar to those expressed by Mexicans, no celebration of the Day of the Dead was reported in Los Angeles on November 2 (Davis, 1976).

Concern about death appears to be more pervasive and more likely to enter into daily life for Mexican Americans than for Anglos or members of other American ethnic groups. Therapists should recognize that Mexican-American clients may be more likely to raise issues about death and that this concern does not include a moribund personality. The Hispanic client fears death but wants to confront those fears. It would seem most effective to fully discuss issues about death with Hispanic clients as a means of self-liberation.

> Prior to an honest facing of one's own death, we tend to have feelings of omniscience and to plan as though the results of our planning would be permanent. Facing death drives home the truly finite role of man: nothing is forever, this too shall pass. Having recognized that life shall not stretch into an infinite future, people can more effectively deal with the concerns of the day. To do so requires some acceptance of the inevitable and acceptance of one's finite being [Davis, 1976, pp. 175–176].

Dealing with the Dying

Davis' 1976 Los Angeles survey reveals some rather surprising findings about Mexican Americans' styles of responding to the dying. Although the Mexican Americans were the most preoccupied with abstract themes of death, they were the least likely to discuss dying with the terminally ill. They were also the least likely to encourage communication about a terminal condition to a dying person. Similarly, they were the least likely to wish to be told themselves, if they were dying. However, significantly more often than the other groups, the Mexican Americans said that, if they had six months to live, they would focus their concern on others and want to be with their loved ones. They would encourage their families to visit them, even if it were somewhat inconvenient for the family members, and they would want funerals with lots of friends and acquaintances present. We can conclude from this study that Mexican Americans tend to discuss dying in general terms but not in specific cases. When an individual is terminally ill, solace is provided primarily by comradery, not by direct confrontation of issues about death.

In her classic study of death and dying among Anglo patients, Kubler-Ross (1969) explains that the American style of denial of death issues fosters feelings of great isolation among the dying. She recommends gently confronting the denial by the patient and significant others in order to reduce those feelings.

Such unwillingness to confront death may be more adaptive in Hispanic culture than in Anglo culture; it does not lead to isolation of the terminally ill person. Although research has been limited, it seems appropriate that the counselor working with a terminally ill Hispanic should focus on building support systems rather than on breaking down denial mechanisms.

Mourning

Mourning among Mexican Americans differs in several critical ways from the styles that Anglos and other ethnic groups employ. In Davis' 1976 Los Angeles survey, Mexican Americans and Japanese Americans were consistently more likely to opt for long mourning periods than were Anglos and Blacks. Again Mexican Americans and Japanese Americans tended most to turn to the family for help with practical problems such as preparing meals, babysitting, shopping, and cleaning house. A second major resource, utilized more by the Mexican Americans than by the other groups, was prayer and the clergy. Importantly, Mexican Americans sanctioned the most overt emotional expression during mourning. They were the most likely to report that "they let themselves go" and would "cry themselves out" at funerals and that they would worry if they could not cry at the death of a spouse. Observation at Mexican-American and Anglo funerals revealed more spontaneous and intense expression of grief among Hispanics (Davis, 1976). Along with their intense expression of emotion, Hispanics tend not to speak ill of or joke about the dead during the period of mourning. Even after the official mourning period is over, many Hispanics may continue to feel the spiritual presence of those who have died and continue to refer to the dead with grave intensity (Aguilar & Wood, 1976).

Kubler-Ross (1969) describes the stages of mourning among majority Americans as denial and isolation, anger about one's fate, attempts to bargain in hopes of changing reality, depression, and final acceptance. Aguilar and Wood (1976) describe the stages among persons of Mexican descent as depression, the initiation of mourning (consisting of the wake and the lying in state), acceptance of reality, burial and collective acceptance of reality by family and friends, a second depression followed by collective condolence, and final acceptance. The paradigms seem to differ primarily in Kubler-Ross' greater emphasis on anger and frustration among Anglo Americans and Aguilar and Wood's greater emphasis on recurring depression and collective support among Hispanics. It would seem that Hispanics' greater abstract emphasis on death as a part of life and on *personalismo* for psychological support enables them to abridge feelings of anger about the arbitrary nature of death. The Hispanics move toward acceptance of a loved one's death by expressing their loss rather than fighting against it. The counselor may expect less anger and frustration among Hispanic mourners but more intense depression.

When counseling Mexican-American clients who are in mourning, the therapist may need to allow for an extended period of catharsis. Aguilar and Wood further suggest that, in keeping with *personalismo*, this catharsis is best achieved in supportive group sessions.

Summary

A comparative view of death attitudes of Mexican-Americans and other groups reveals a number of differences of great theoretical and practical importance. These differences affect the counseling process of the living, of the dying, and of mourners. It is very important that we continue to study this vital area and extend our investigations of attitudes, feelings, and behaviors related to death and dying with other Hispanic groups.

VOCATIONAL COUNSELING

Vocational counseling with Hispanics requires an appreciation of their attitudes about particular jobs. For example, the degree of status associated with certain jobs may differ between Hispanics and the majority culture. Responses of Anglo and Mexican-American post-high school students to one social-status scale, however, demonstrated few differences in the status ascribed to various occupations (Plata, 1975).

Hispanics have avoided government positions because of negative attitudes about the government, language difficulties with exams, low educational level, or fear of rejection and discrimination. For similar reasons, Hispanic representation in law-enforcement agencies has been low. Despite a few differences, as a whole Hispanic occupational aspirations are similar to those of other Americans. For example, Mexican-American and Anglo college students responded to a questionnaire concerning occupational plans. The attitudes of the two groups about occupations, college, vocational counseling, higher education, academic counseling, study, themselves, and their counselors were similar (Gares, 1974).

For some Hispanics, a discrepancy may exist between occupational aspirations and educational plans. In one study, the vocational aspirations of tenth-grade Chicanos matched those of Anglos. The Chicanos expressed slightly less realistic educational aspirations than the Anglos. The Chicano students expressed either very high goals that they would have trouble reaching or very low goals that underestimated their potential. Furthermore, Anglos were more vocationally-oriented; Chicanos were apt to aspire "to college" rather than to a specific career (Cole & Davenport, 1973). In another study, Blacks, Mexican Americans, and Anglos were interviewed by examiners of their own ethnicity. Educational aspiration was highest among Blacks and lowest among Mexican Americans. In contrast, vocational aspiration was highest among Mexican Americans and lowest among Blacks (Hindelang, 1970).

If Hispanics' educational and occupational aspirations are not congruent, an important facet of vocational counseling involves bridging this gap. Very often then, vocational counseling needs to be combined with educational counseling and tutoring. Considering their socioeconomic history, experiences with discrimination, frustration with the educational system, and high vocational aspirations, the following recommendations for vocational counseling with Hispanics are offered: (1) Attempt to widen students' horizons about job possibilities; (2) respect the client's views of jobs and their status; (3) suggest that students obtain special tutoring and join summer job programs when needed; (4) maintain a job pool to help students find part-time employment; (5) develop an extensive pool of financial-aid programs for Hispanics who want to go to college; and (6) encourage more than one student to attend a particular college (Pollack & Menacker, 1971).

Group counseling is often useful to people who are making educational and career decisions. In one program, university students studying for health careers chatted informally with high school Hispanics. The university students interpreted and discussed the results of career inventories with the high school students and talked about various careers with the adolescents and their parents (Burstein & Kobos, 1971). A school counselor reported success in furthering high school Hispanics' educational goals by establishing informal meetings that continued over a three-year period. For two years the students met with a counselor almost every day. The following year they met bi-weekly, and the third year they talked occasionally. Issues such as the need for education and procedures for getting accepted at a college and obtaining scholarships were discussed. This informal vocational counseling helped 30 to 35 participants enter and remain in college (Klitgaard, 1969). One researcher (Ganschow, 1970) used films and videotapes to explore vocational and educational opportunities with tenth-grade Anglos and Hispanics. Subjects who saw social models of their own ethnicity scored higher on measures of interest and occupation and engaged in slightly more information-seeking behavior. Another effective group activity for facilitating wise career choices among Hispanics involves studying about Hispanic heroes. Familiarity with the lives of well-known Hispanics may increase awareness of career options and optimism about occupational mobility. In recent years two magazines for Hispanics, *La Luz* and *Nuestro*, have appeared that contain articles about successful Hispanics. Vocational counselors would be well advised to consult these magazines for ideas concerning career choices for Hispanic youth.

Group counseling may also focus on developing skills that are needed for job interviewing. The importance of assertiveness in applying for a job should be explained. Finally, role playing may help Hispanics develop effective interviewing skills.

IMPLICATIONS FOR PLURALISTIC THERAPISTS

Our review of the therapeutic process with Hispanics reveals one major finding: *we cannot assume that any of the tools and techniques that are effective with majority-group clients will be applicable to the same degree with Hispanic clients.* Nonverbal signals may have different meanings for Hispanic clients. The amount and rate of self-disclosure may vary between Hispanic clients and those of other ethnicities. Finally, Hispanics may respond in unexpected ways to various therapeutic modalities.

We must, therefore, subject each tool and technique to a test of "cultural adaptiveness." We need to look at the way theories of personality and counseling interact with ethnicity. Are behavioral approaches more or less effective with Hispanics? Do Hispanics accept or reject humanistic counseling? Are individuals who desire advice and who are willing to assume responsibility for their own behavior similar or different in personality makeup across cultures? We need to investigate the dynamics of the counseling process across cultures. How do we establish rapport and project empathy and confidentiality across cultural groups? To what extent are empathy, positive regard, and genuineness universal traits? Research about the effectiveness of various kinds of therapeutic leads (such as silence, restatement of ideas, reflection of feelings, reassurance, and information giving) with ethnic clients would be helpful.

When we subject each tool and technique to a test of "cultural adaptiveness," we should ask "Will this therapeutic approach allow the Hispanic client to cope more effectively within his or her chosen environment?" A number of therapeutic approaches have met the test of cultural adaptiveness:

1. The therapist should ascertain whether a client's problems are due primarily to intrapsychic or to extrapsychic stress. If extrapsychic conflict is predominant, therapy aimed, for example, at social action and the alleviation of discrimination and poverty may be appropriate. If intrapsychic conflict is most basic, introspective or behavioral therapy is the treatment of choice.

2. The therapist should expect less self-disclosure from Hispanics than from clients of other ethnicities. It will be the therapist's responsibility to differentiate between personal privacy that is culturally sanctioned and psychological resistance.

3. The therapist should employ a different style of nonverbal communication with the Hispanic client. The therapist should attempt to greet the client as soon as he or she arrives, shake hands, and sometimes embrace the client. The therapist may sit closer to the Hispanic than to the Anglo or Black client. When possible, the therapist should respect the Hispanic concept of time by structuring sessions according to the time needed to resolve conflicts rather than the 50-minute hour. The therapist should look for culturally specific gestures, such as bowing the head as a sign of respect, especially among children.

4. Family counseling should be emphasized. Treatment modalities that facilitate action and interpretation of family interaction, such as psychodrama and role processing, are vital tools.

Our review of culture and therapy reveals processes that require further research. More study is needed to determine the relative effects of directive and nondirective therapies with Hispanics. Research is needed to ascertain preferred treatment for several target groups, such as alcoholics and the elderly. Future investigations are needed to explicate the effectiveness of various treatment modalities with particular groups of Hispanics. As the title of this chapter suggests, culture interacts with therapy in a continuous fashion, and most of our knowledge about pluralistic therapy with Hispanics is in "process of becoming."

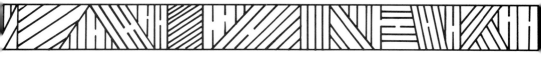

Chapter 9 Pluralistic Considerations in Therapy

CULTURE AND PERSONALITY REVIEWED

At the beginning of this book, we asked the question "How extensive are the psychological differences among cultural groups?" We suggested that the answer to this question was critical for understanding the degree and kind of special intervention needed in pluralistic therapy. Our study of the culture and personality of Hispanics provides an answer to this basic issue.

Study of Hispanic culture and comparison with Anglo values suggest that the differences are indeed large and significant. Recall our two-fold definition of culture as both the environmental context of a population and the life-style that is handed down from one generation to the next through language and imitation (Barnouw, 1963; LeVine, 1973). This definition does not imply that members of a cultural group are homogeneous. Rather, our definition of culture as environment suggests that a range of attitudes, values, and personalities will be found among members of any culture. The range can best be understood by studying the total historical, economic, and social environment of which the members are a part. Furthermore, our definition of culture as life-style suggests that some behaviors and attitudes may be similar across cultures. When we study these behaviors and attitudes more closely within the context of the whole way of life of a people, we may find that they are serving very similar or very different functions in the varied cultures. With these definitions in mind, let us review the differing parameters between Hispanic and majority American cultures.

The history of Hispanics in the United States is diversified. It is so variegated, in fact, that a Cuban and a Mexican American, for example, may have very little in common concerning their immigration, or that of their ancestors, to the United States. The historical period during which a Hispanic group settled in the United States affects its culture. Political and economic circumstances in the United States at the time of immigration also affect cultural adaptation of the immigrants. A particular socioeconomic role and set of values may be passed down from generation to generation.

The earliest Spanish and Mexican settlers claimed much untamed land and developed an economic system based on community property and ranching. Although the interface with Yankee culture enormously reduced their numbers, a few of these Hispanics in the Southwest have maintained the Spanish-American traditions of their ancestors. The legal immigrants who moved to the United States during its industrial, expansionary period adapted to a very different environment than did the early settlers. The construction of the Santa Fe railroad and the agricultural boom in California created a need for a cheap, migrant labor force. Because of extensive poverty and political upheaval in Mexico, many people willingly fled to the United States. A large number of these Mexican immigrants became poor, urban dwellers in the United States. The culture of many present-day Mexican Americans who are descendants of the early legal and illegal workers is a blend of Mexican rural culture, migrant culture, values associated with traditional Hispanic culture, and urban American attitudes and values. Current Mexican legal and illegal immigrants enter into a high-paced, highly technological work force for which they are largely untrained and unprepared. As Hispanics of longer residence move up the socioeconomic ladder, new immigrants assume the most menial jobs. The culture of the more recent Mexican immigrants will reflect more Mexican values and probably much frustration about their limited economic opportunity in both Mexico and the United States.

Early transportation between New York and Puerto Rico and the need for cheap blue-collar labor spurred the development of Puerto Rican enclaves in the eastern continental United States. Since Puerto Rico is a commonwealth of the United States, migration back and forth between the continental United States and the island is frequent. Mainland Puerto Rican culture is a combination of island culture and blue-collar urban majority-group values and attitudes.

Castro's rise to power spawned an influx of Cuban immigrants (first the educated, then the middle class, and finally the working class) to the southeastern United States. Their difficulties and successes in adjusting to American society and regaining status in a new land have created a unique Cuban-American culture. Their culture reflects aspects of working- and middle-class Cuban culture, middle-class American culture, and some special values and attitudes associated with bicultural life-styles.

One could continue to specify the particular economic and historical factors associated with the migration of members of other Hispanic groups such as Dominican Republicans, Panamanians, Peruvians, and Costa Ricans. Moreover, one can look further into each group and study how individuals of a particular age, status, and economic background adjust to particular settings in the United States. For example, the adjustment of a rural, lower-socioeconomic-class Puerto Rican to life in New York City may be different from the adjustment of a middle-class urban Puerto Rican to life in the southwestern United States. In each case, Hispanic culture will evolve differently. Of course, it is impossible to operationalize all the factors associated with cultural variance, and we must settle for the generalization that economic and historical differences among Hispanics account for many of the cultural differences among Mexican, Cuban, Puerto Rican, and Central and South American immigrants and between Hispanics and members of the majority culture and other minority groups.

Yet, despite great diversity among the Hispanic groups, we also find commonality among them. We see that in many ways the differences between the Hispanic and majority American cultures are greater than those within either group. For example, at the core of each Hispanic group is the influence of Spanish colonization. A majority of Hispanics speak Spanish, and the language transmits European and Central and South American values and attitudes that cannot be translated easily into Anglo-American terms.

In the final analysis, the question of whether differences are greater between or within the Hispanic and majority American cultures is of secondary importance. What is of primary importance is that the differences are vast enough to make Hispanics easy targets for prejudice and discrimination. Hispanics are different because of their culture, their physiognomy, and/or their language. Differences can be used to subjugate a group, relegating its members to inferior socioeconomic positions. Majority Americans attain better-paying jobs and higher education, while those who are "different" are treated as inferior and are denied upward mobility. According to the political needs of the country, the fear of the differences may be exploited and racism institutionalized in educational, housing, governmental, and legal policies. A vicious circle is established in which the "inferior" cultural differences are increasingly devalued. The Hispanic who is the subject of discrimination may experience personal discomfort or deny or criticize his or her own background. If the individual expresses hostility toward the majority group, he or she is likely to be perceived as overreactive or emotionally disturbed. Discrimination in education and employment prevents Hispanics from bettering their socioeconomic lot, and thus more negative stereotypes are added to the cultural differences between Hispanics and Anglos.

Also of primary importance is the fact that the cultural differences are so vast that the dynamics of maladjustment vary across Hispanic and majority cultures. The frequencies of some mental-health-related problems differ across the groups. Among psychiatric-hospital admissions, drug addiction and senile psychosis are more common and personality disorders less common among Hispanics than among Anglos. Some sets of symptoms are specific to Hispanics. For example, *ataque* is not found among Anglos. Symptoms differ in import across cultures. Hearing voices may be less indicative of psychosis among Hispanics than among Anglos.

Not only the system of classification but also the stressors that lead to maladjustment tend to vary in frequency and intensity across cultural groups. Obviously, the Hispanic may be more concerned with issues of prejudice than most Anglos. The counselor must be cautious about interpreting the Hispanic client's anger as due to intrapsychic, familial, or childhood factors. Much hostility may be precipitated by extrapsychic factors such as pervasive discrimination by the community, employers, and private or government agencies.

Another theme of conflict common among Hispanics and infrequent among Anglos is concern about skin color. Dark skin may retard a Hispanic's acceptance into American society, whereas light skin may retard his or her acceptance by the minority group. Moreover, definitions of "White" and "Black" differ across cultures. Many Puerto Ricans are considered White on the island and are considered Black when they move to the continent. Many Hispanics believe "Brown is beautiful," but some are in conflict about this issue.

A third theme of conflict common among Hispanics but uncommon among Anglos has to do with achieving a bicultural and bilingual life-style. Many Hispanics feel caught between the majority and minority cultures and experience guilt or fear about moving toward either one. They remain in a marginal life stance, a stance that appears to correlate with a range of personal disorders. Some Hispanics become fully and happily acculturated; yet some acculturated Hispanics experience discomfort and even guilt when interacting with members of their minority group. Still others choose to remain unacculturated; they may experience stress when forced to leave the *barrio* sanctuary.

A fourth theme of conflict—frustration about poverty—is found among both Hispanics and Anglos, but it seems to be more pressing among the former group. Most majority Americans enjoy relative economic comfort, whereas most Hispanics are poor. Ethnic discrimination compounds frustration about poverty among the poor Hispanics, and they feel powerless to change their economic situation. Therefore, in many cases the pluralistic counselor needs to be an advisor, directing ethnic-minority clients to social-service agencies.

Anglos and Hispanics may make different interpretations of the causation of maladjustment. Among Anglos, physical and social factors are viewed as the primary basis of maladjustment. Among Hispanics, family factors may be emphasized. For example, embarrassing the family may be considered worse than losing a job and may be more indicative of pathology. Those practicing *curanderismo* and *espiritismo* perceive metaphysical factors to be as important as physiological and psychosocial factors in causing maladjustment.

Of course, the cultures and personalities of Hispanics and Anglos are not exclusively variant. A number of socioeconomic factors cut across the majority and minority cultures in the United States. If individuals live in rural settings, have low socioeconomic status, receive limited education, and have immigrated recently, they are likely to ascribe to more traditional values. Similarly, the poor, uneducated and/or rural person, whether Hispanic or Anglo, is more likely to hold some fatalistic attitudes, be present-time oriented, and be oriented toward an external locus of control than are middle- and upper-class urban Americans. It is clear that Hispanics suffer maladjustment syndromes such as depression, suicidal impulses, and other neuroses with symptoms that are quite similar to those experienced by members of the majority culture. Yet the causes and frequency of such symptoms may be similar or different across cultures. It would be inappropriate to consider Anglo and Hispanic culture as completely variant from each other since they are in constant interaction.

It is imperative not to overgeneralize about differences between cultural groups, and it is important not to overgeneralize about individuals within those groups. The concept of a modal personality or national character type often leads to oversimplified and overgeneralized descriptions. Such stereotypes become the basis for institutional discrimination and unreliable research conclusions.

In contrast, it is appropriate and helpful for a therapist to focus on cultural differences as they reveal styles of positive adaptation and stresses leading to maladjustment. Simmons (1961, p. 298) writes "Mexican American culture represents the most constructive and effective means Mexican Americans have yet been able to develop for coping with their changed natural and social environments." We may add that various Hispanic cultures are very supportive to their members in times of extreme social and personal stress. Therapists can be more empathic and set more constructive goals if they understand a client's stresses within the context of the social and cultural milieu. With this sensitivity to culture and personality differences, the therapist implements pluralistic counseling, counseling that enables clients to live fulfilling lives within their own environmental context.

IMPLEMENTING PLURALISTIC THERAPY

Implementation of pluralistic therapy involves setting therapy goals, selecting environment and staff, and employing counseling techniques that facilitate the clients' adaptation to their chosen cultures. In Chapter 1 we focused on the primary issues of pluralistic implementation. Let's consider those issues again in terms of what we have discussed in this book.

In Chapter 1 we asked "How much separatism should cultural groups in the United States maintain?" Some social scientists believe full assimilation is necessary for peaceful coexistence. Others believe that total assimilation is impossible but that without it peace is also impossible. Greeley (1969) proposes that minority groups go through a process consisting of culture shock, assimilation of the elite, militancy, and, finally, emerging adjustment and acceptance of ethnic and American identity. He warns, however, that too much pluralism increases prejudice. Unfortunately, he does not tell us how much is "too much." Pettigrew (1976) sees assimilation and pluralism as part of the same social process and proposes that a balance can be reached. The current literature contains multiple answers to the question of degree of separatism. What conclusion can we draw from our study of Hispanics?

We have learned that marginality correlates highly with maladjustment. Personal and ethnic identity can be confused when there is a lack of support in the family, when parents are not valued by the majority culture, and when a child feels conflicting loyalties to two cultures. The personal consequences can include anxiety, psychosomatic illnesses, drug or alcohol addiction, neurosis, and psychosis. The majority institutions push for assimilation. Our review of Hispanic literature leads us to believe that the majority definition of deviance is often not objective but is, rather, a function of who is in power. Thus, it is clear that marginality or pressure to assimilate can be destructive to the individual.

However, when ethnic-minority people choose to assimilate or to remain unacculturated, the effects may not be adverse. Some Hispanics are happily assimilated; others enjoy living unacculturated lives in rural settings or in urban *barrios*. Other Hispanics may try desperately to assimilate but be unable to do so. These individuals probably will experience feelings of rejection and distress. Similarly, those individuals who out of fear or peer pressure remain unacculturated may also experience personal pain. The critical factor is that individuals be aware of their options and feel free to follow the life-style of their choice.

Setting therapy goals involves helping the client understand his or her life-style options and the implications of each. Research with Hispanics suggests that a therapist should attempt to lead a client out of a marginal life-style. This ambiguous position, in which the client feels inadequate to deal with the majority culture and disappointed with the minority culture, is associated with high stress for many individuals. The counselor should help other clients choose the identities they wish to forge for themselves. The option of moving toward assimilation or toward biculturalism is a reflection of the variety and freedom of the human condition. By allowing the client to set his or her own goals about life-style, the counselor shows respect for varied cultures and leaves ultimate responsibility to the individual (Perry, 1969).

We propose another far-reaching question in the introductory chapter: "What principles can we employ to design pluralistic therapy appropriate for specific cultural groups?" Part of the answer to this question lies in determining if there are aspects of good therapy that are cross-cultural. We have reviewed literature that attests to the success of both Anglo and Hispanic therapists with Hispanic clients and thus confirms that there are aspects of good therapy that can cross cultures. Torrey (1972) emphasizes three qualities that are characteristic of all good healers—from witch doctors to psychiatrists—and these qualities are confirmed by our study of the mental-health needs of Hispanics. First, good therapists exhibit *personableness*; they project warmth and empathy. In numerous case studies cited throughout this text, Hispanic clients asked for counselors who were sensitive to their feelings, who did not overgeneralize, and who were accepting and nonprejudicial. Torrey explains that good healers in various cultures seem to have charismatic personalities. Our study of Hispanic culture suggests that such charismatic qualities are not mysterious and that they can be operationalized. The effective pluralistic counselor exhibits a genuine caring for minority clients, yet genuine caring is only part of the nonprejudicial and accepting stance. An effective pluralistic therapist offers accurate empathic reflections—feedback that demonstrates understanding of the complexity and nuances of the client's feelings. Accurate empathic reflections and interpretations require practice and also a full understanding of the client's culture. It is true that the counselor never knows precisely how any individual client feels, since each person's life and subjective experience are unique. However, the more the counselor knows about a client's cultural, social, and familial environment, the more accurately he or she can picture the client's roles and attitudes and the more appropriate the counseling feedback will be.

The effective pluralistic counselor learns to offer accurate feedback in part by actively listening to the client. Pluralistic counselors solicit feedback from the client about the accuracy of their reflections and interpretations, and, in doing so, the counselors modify their views and broaden their understanding of the client's situation.

A second characteristic common to all effective therapists, according to Torrey, is *the ability to label a problem*. An effective therapist assists clients to interpret their emotional problems in terms of their world view. Naming the problem with the right language and appropriate sense of causality brings conflict and resistances to a conscious level. We have learned that many bicultural and unacculturated Hispanics prefer therapists to speak in Spanish. Therapists who do not speak Spanish are likely to interpret symptoms differently than bilingual therapists. Yet language is only one part of effective labeling. An understanding of the Hispanic world view is as important as the language used. For example, with some traditionally oriented clients, it may be good therapy to incorporate folk beliefs and/or a folk healer into the helping process.

A third characteristic of a good therapist is the ability to raise the client's *expectations for change*. Counseling mobilizes the client's hopes and trust so that he or she feels confident to lower resistances and resolve conflicts. The effective therapist recognizes which personal and social changes will create hope. Thus, hope will increase more for many poor Hispanics when counselors guide them to a social-service agency that can provide financial assistance than when counselors reflect clients' feelings about poverty. In other cases, resolving issues of how to cope with prejudice, how to appreciate one's physiognomy, and how to live successfully in two cultures increases hope.

Given that skill at providing empathy, labeling a problem, and offering hope are critical to good therapy, how can we measure a particular counselor's effectiveness? An effective pluralistic therapist can interpret the attitudes and feelings, points of stress, and system of maladjustments according to the client's cultural conceptualizations (Torrey, 1972). The effective therapist works within a dynamic and open framework. The therapist embraces varied goals that include helping the individual fit into his or her chosen environment and changing the institutions and social systems to fit clients' needs. The therapist does not overreact or assume that all minority clients are alike. Therapy goals are set in accord with the clients' value systems (Casas, 1976). Our study of Hispanic culture suggests that paraprofessionals and ombudsmen from the community are knowledgeable about many of these factors, and may therefore be vital additions to a pluralistic mental-health team.

Broad appreciation of a culture is necessary but not sufficient to ensure effective pluralistic therapy. Our review of Hispanic culture reveals that Hispanic patients have avoided conventional mental-health facilities—even though the facilities may have been planned to service them—and that Hispanics on the whole express positive attitudes toward therapy and therapists. Yet certain environmental conditions appear to be necessary before services will be utilized. Services must be offered at reasonable rates within the ethnic community. Mobile crisis units are helpful. Research findings are inconsistent about the importance of the therapist's ethnicity, but professionals need to speak the language that their client feels most comfortable using. Having the ethnic community participate in the establishment and management of mental-health facilities increases use of those facilities by members of ethnic minorities. Services should focus on crisis intervention. The traditional 50-minute hour for counseling may not be sufficient to ameliorate many crises, so time scheduling must be flexible. Therapy should be offered for special groups; among Hispanics, groups for *los tecatos* (drug addicts), alcoholics, women, the aged, and families may be particularly needed.

After the appropriate environment and therapeutic attitude are created, therapists must employ culturally relevant therapeutic techniques. Research about the most effective techniques with Hispanics is incomplete, but some specific recommendations are emerging. The therapist must be alert to different styles of nonverbal communication across cultures. For example, Hispanics are more likely to touch than Anglos. Hispanics tend to sit and stand close together, while Anglos require more personal space. Having chairs placed fairly close together may increase comfort and trust in Hispanics in counseling sessions. Each client's attitudes about physical contact, physical space, and the meaning of nonverbal gestures are considered in effective pluralistic therapy.

The impact of directive versus nondirective counseling must be evaluated in terms of the client's cultural and idiosyncratic attitudes about authoritarianism, respect, and support. Some Hispanic clients are comfortable with an older male therapist in what they feel is an authoritarian role, whereas a directive approach in a female therapist may clash with the client's view of what is appropriate sex-role behavior. A well-educated middle-class Hispanic suffering anxiety may respond well to supportive, nondirective counseling. An uneducated illegal immigrant may need directive counseling and advice concerning his or her precarious status in the United States.

The pluralistic counselor must recognize that the significance of psychological-test results differs across cultural groups. For example, results of projective tests, such as TAT or Rorschach protocols, differ in frequency and intensity of themes. Results of standardized tests demonstrate adaptation to majority-group norms and may not reflect adjustment within an ethnic-minority enclave. The pluralistic therapist employs results of standardized tests with discretion, seldom using results of a single test to diagnose clients. When possible, culture-fair tests are employed. The pluralistic therapist strives to obtain and develop criterion-referenced tests, tests that measure behavioral adjustment within areas of concern that have been identified in the counseling process.

The pluralistic therapist will stay abreast of and employ new therapeutic modalities designed for the ethnic-minority client. For example, group-counseling games have been developed that build on Chicano culture. Family therapy and psychodrama seem to be particularly effective approaches for Hispanic clients whose upbringing has involved strong family supports. Some specialized assertiveness-training techniques may be helpful for Hispanic women who have been somewhat isolated in traditional settings and are beginning to interact with the majority culture. Bereavement counseling may involve a different process and more group catharsis with Hispanics than with Anglo clients. Our review of Hispanic literature uncovered many new therapeutic techniques, but the effectiveness of these techniques is largely undocumented. Pluralistic therapists must avoid becoming overzealous about therapeutic approaches that are of little value with Hispanics. Therapists must assume responsibility for continued evaluation of their therapeutic approaches. Research must be conducted to measure the gains associated with each technique, and new programs must be undertaken energetically but with caution, until their effectiveness can be assessed. With the active participation of individual professionals, we can anticipate improved styles of pluralistic therapy.

LOOKING FORWARD

The final question of our opening chapter was "What is the future direction of pluralistic therapy?" Ideally, the future will bring improvement and expansion in research and increased application of research to practice.

Techniques are available for improving research about pluralistic therapy. Longitudinal studies of single disorders will provide reliable evidence about biological and social etiology (Kiev, 1969). Epidemiological studies should not be based on the dubious construct of the modal personality. However, investigation of the prevalence of maladjustment, particularly at the local level, provides guidelines in planning centers and programs (Opler, 1967). Researchers should exploit the anthropologist's technique of participant observation. By living and participating in a culture and by studying daily cycles of activity and inactivity, bodily and affective reactions, and literature and artifacts, researchers can learn specifically about culturally preferred methods for mitigating stress (Opler, 1967). Future research needs to focus on the complex etiology of maladjustment. Our study of Hispanic culture illustrates that maladjustment is rarely precipitated by a single event but is bound in a person's entire psychosocial and biological history.

Future research needs to focus on a number of unresolved issues in pluralistic therapy. More research is needed to determine conditions that are conducive to directive and nondirective therapy. Research about the effect of therapist ethnicity on client gain is highly inconsistent. Studies investigating this question should control a number of potential confounding variables, such as the therapist's personality, sex, and age; therapeutic modality; client's sex and age; and length of treatment. Moreover, means for measuring client gain must be sought. Another primary focus of research would be to increase the number of culturally relevant standardized and projective personality tests. The techniques for creating criterion-referenced and culture-fair tests are well established. We need to implement these procedures to develop tests of values, attitudes, and behavior appropriate to particular cultural groups. We know that many individuals in need of help do not utilize mental-health facilities. Research can help explain why, and proposals for increasing use by the target groups can be examined. Research about verbal and nonverbal communication styles in different cultures has been quite helpful in developing pluralistic-therapy procedures. Continued research in this area will open new avenues for exploration in therapy.

As results of cross-cultural research are applied in clinics and by private professionals, pluralistic therapy will become increasingly effective. Ethnic-minority clients will no longer be stigmatized or alienated by traditional majority-group methods and techniques. Misunderstanding between counselor and client will decrease as the counselor's understanding of the client's world view and preferred life-style increases. The intrusion of cultural stereotypes into the therapeutic process can be eliminated.

The future of pluralistic therapy will entail not only the alleviation of human misery but also the enhancement of human functioning. The highest priority should be given to preventive mental health. Our study of Hispanic mental health reveals how prejudice, poverty, and marginality immobilize Hispanic Americans with despair and defiance. In the future, pluralistic therapy should involve emphasis not only on one-to-one therapy but also on crisis intervention and social action. Some pluralistic therapists need to become involved in establishing local and national policies that foster the mental health of ethnic-minority groups. Policies strengthening family and neighborhood life, accurate historical education about ethnic-minority groups, public institutions recognizing the diversity of the American people, and subsidized programs to facilitate intergroup relations are all needed.

Our review of the literature on culture and personality, particularly as it relates to Hispanics, leads to the conclusion that, whenever counselors work with clients from minority groups, the crossing of cultures must be considered. Ethnic-minority clients may grapple with the interface of their own and the majority culture on one or more levels. If the client's problems are of a social nature, the points of interface are obvious. These clients need to develop skills for dealing with prejudice and discrimination so that they do not abandon their cultural heritage or identity in order to "fit." When a client's problems are more strictly personal, majority and minority cultures may cross at several other points in the counseling process. The minority clients may express their personal despair in metaphysical or philosophical terms not easily translated into majority-culture terms. The minority client may express symptoms that are unknown or less common within the majority culture. Yet some link between the minority and majority views of etiology must be made in order that the minority client not feel alienated from the larger stream of American society. Although research data are unclear about the importance of counselor's ethnicity, research findings do suggest that several facets of the counseling relationship are affected by the client's minority ethnicity.

Our basic premises about the core conditions of an effective counseling relationship must be modified somewhat when cultures cross in therapy. Whether the counselor is a majority- or minority-group member, the amount and pace of self-disclosure appear to vary with ethnicity. Similarly, the effectiveness of various counseling techniques —for example, confrontation or nondirective therapy—varies with the client's ethnicity. The results of psychological tests must be interpreted cautiously. Counselors must be particularly aware of cultural differences when interpreting test results, as the modal profiles may reflect different degrees of adaptation to minority- and majority-cultural stresses. The crossing of the majority and minority cultures is always present in counseling with ethnic-minority clients. Recognition of the points of interface is necessary so that counseling does not foster cultural anonymity or conformity but, rather, enhances personal identity within a pluralistic society.

By now you are probably considering specific techniques for counseling ethnic minorities—particularly Hispanics—that are congruent with your own style of counseling. If, as we propose in this text, the future of psychology lies in the cojoining of experimental efforts and the applied study of pluralism, the reader can play a vital role in furthering this field. As you integrate pluralistic techniques into your own treatment programs, investigate their effectiveness and share the results with other professionals. The future lies with all of us, and it begins today.

Glossary

Aguantando. Enduring.

Aguantar. To suffer or endure; to put up with.

Aspira. An organization of Hispanics, predominantly Puerto Ricans, the primary goal of which is to increase the number of Hispanics in higher education and the professions.

Ataque. A seizure, considered psychogenic in origin and usually confined to Puerto Rican women. *Ataque* occurs on occasions when a show of grief is called for (such as funerals) or when one has witnessed or received news of a shocking event, particularly an event affecting a loved one. Also referred to as the "Puerto Rican Syndrome."

Aztlán. In Mexican mythology, the land where the Aztecs are believed to have originated. Contemporary Chicanos consider the southwestern United States as Aztlán.

Barrio. A neighborhood or area of a town or city occupied by Hispanics. (See **colonía.**)

Braceros. Mexican workers admitted to the United States to do seasonal farm labor, under the U.S. Bracero program.

Brown Berets. A radical Chicano political organization of the 1960s.

Castigo de Díos. A punishment given by God.

Chicanismo. Of or pertaining to being Chicano.

Chicano (a). A sociopolitical term by which a segment of Mexican Americans identify. Indicates pride in their ethnic and cultural heritage and a commitment to maintain their cultural tradition.

Cholos. A term used mainly in South America to refer to Indian or **mestizo** groups. Sometimes used in a pejorative sense.

Colonía. A designated subdivision or neighborhood where Hispanics reside.

Comadre. Literally "co-mother"; the kin name between women, one of whom is godmother to the other's child.

Compadre. The male member of kin relationships between parents and godparents.

Curanderismo. Folk medicine practiced among individuals of Mexican descent.

Curandero (a). Folk healer knowledgeable about massage and medicinal herbs.

Deshonorar. To dishonor.

270

Día de los Muertos. In Mexico, "the Day of the Dead," when deceased friends and relatives are remembered.

Dignidad. Dignity—a personality trait generally attributed to Hispanics and highly valued by them.

Dueña. A woman chaperon of young unmarried girls.

Embrujado (a). Bewitched.

Empacho. A physical disorder believed to be caused by the formation of a hard "ball" in the stomach from eating certain foods.

Espiritismo. Spiritism; also called "the work of the white table" or "the work of the dead." It is the traditional healing practice among Puerto Ricans. Spiritists believe in the coexistence of a material or visible world and a spiritual or invisible world, both inhabited by *seres* (beings) or *espíritus* (spirits). In this belief "good" spirits are called upon to counter the forces of "bad" spirits.

Es una buena joda que le dan a uno. An expression meaning that one has been given an unjustly deserved burden.

La familia. The family.

Familismo. High regard for and dedication to the family, an important value among Hispanics.

Gringo. Hispanic term for Anglo American, sometimes derogatory.

El grito. The traditional yell that marked the beginning of Mexican independence.

El grupo. The group.

Guapo (a). Attractive; good looking.

Hembrismo. The female complement of *machismo*, characterized by passivity, submissiveness, and weakness.

Hijo de crianza. A child who is raised by adults other than his or her parents.

Hispanics. A generic term for all people of Spanish surname and/or origin in the U.S. or Puerto Rico.

Hospitalidad. Hospitality; practice of entertaining travelers and strangers.

Huelga. Strike; *"Viva La Huelga"* (long live the strike) became a popular slogan during the migrant farm workers' struggle in California and the Southwest.

Inglesado (a). Americanized or anglicized.

Llorando. Crying.

Llorar. To cry.

Machismo. A set of values and personality traits attributed to Hispanic men, including a strong sense of manliness, honor, and self respect. Stereotypically machismo also connotes sexual prowess, overindulgence in alcohol, and physical aggressiveness.

Macho. Adjective used to describe Hispanic males. Used with a sense of pride it means strong, virile, and vigorous. Used negatively, it means dominant, brutal, and promiscuous.

Mal de ojo. Literally "evil eye"; a folk belief that harm can be inflicted on others, usually children, in some magic way.

Mal puesto. A bewitchment or hex.

Mañana. Tomorrow; morning.

Mestizo. A term applied to people of mixed Spanish (White) and Indian blood.

Metas. Goals; aims.

Mijito. A term of endearment used by parents with their children.

Personalismo. The characteristic of dealing with others on a personal level; among Hispanics, the desired way of interacting with others.

La plática. Conversation.

Pochismo. Usually used to describe the spoken Spanish of *pochos*, characterized by frequent mixing of Spanish and English in speech.

Pocho. A derogatory name for the Americanized Mexican.

Promesa. Promise.

La raza. Literally "the race"; refers to people of Mexican descent or, more broadly, of Latin American descent.

La realidad. Reality.

Respeto. Respect for others (especially the elderly) and for social customs; a personality trait of great value in the Hispanic culture.

Rezando. Praying.

Rezar. To pray.

Rolla. A Chicano slang term for role; a *pochismo*.

Santería. An Afro-Cuban cult characterized by the worship of African deities and equated in part with Catholic saints. Rituals involve the offering of foods, including live animals, to the deities. Santería is African in its world view and social organization. The cult is organized in "houses" or lineages, not congregations. It is an alternative religion with some Hispanics and involves a lifelong commitment.

Señoras. Married women; also used as a name for female folk healers.

Susto. Literally, "fright"; refers to a folk belief that a severe scare can cause lasting physical or psychological damage.

Te amo; te quiero. Two ways of saying "I love you."

Tecato. A Chicano slang term for heroin addict.

Tenia su rajita. An expression referring to the fact that a person has some African or Black physical traits.

Vergüenza. Shame; disgrace.

Los veteranos. Older men who no longer participate in *barrio* gang activities; former gang members.

Wetbacks. A term, often used derogatorily, for Mexicans who enter the United States illegally. Comes from the fact that many of them swam the Río Grande.

Zoot Suit. Baggy trousers and long suit coat, a popular style of dress among young Mexican Americans in the late 1940s; the term is also associated with riots that occurred in Southern California among Mexican American youths and sailors during World War II.

References

Abad, V., Ramos, J., & Boyce, E. A model for delivery of mental health services to Spanish-speaking minorities. *American Journal of Orthopsychiatry*, 1974, *44*, 584–595.

Acosta, F. X. Etiology and treatment of homosexuality: A review. *Archives of Sexual Behavior*, 1975, *4*, 9–29. (a)

Acosta, F. X. Mexican American and Anglo American reactions to ethnically similar and dissimilar psychotherapists. In R. Alvarez (Ed.), *Delivery of services for Latino community mental health*. Los Angeles: Spanish Speaking Mental Health Research and Development Program, 1975 (Monograph 2). (b)

Acosta, F. X., & Sheehan, J. G. Psychotherapist ethnicity and expertise as determinants of self-disclosure. In M. Miranda (Ed.), *Psychotherapy for the Spanish-speaking*. Los Angeles: Spanish Speaking Mental Health Research Center, 1976 (Monograph 3).

Acuña, R. *Occupied America: The Chicano's struggle toward liberation*. New York: Canfield Press, 1972.

Aguilar, I. Initial contacts with Mexican-American families. *Social Work*, 1972, *17*(3), 66–70.

Aguilar, I., & Wood, V. N. Aspects of death, grief and mourning in the treatment of Spanish-speaking mental patients. *Journal of the National Association of Social Workers*, 1976, *21*, 49–54.

Aiello, J. R., & Jones, S. E. Field study of the proxemic behavior of young school children in three subcultural groups. *Journal of Personality and Social Psychology*, 1971, *19*, 351–356.

Albright, V. H. A comparison between the self-concept of Mexican American pupils taught in a bilingual program and those taught in a monolingual program (Doctoral dissertation, George Washington University, 1974). *Dissertation Abstracts International*, 1975, *36*, 7520A. (University Microfilms No. 75–12, 605)

Alford, H. *The proud peoples*. New York: David McKay, 1972.

American Psychiatric Association. *Diagnostic and statistical manual of mental disorders* (DSM-II) (2nd ed.). Washington, D.C.: Author, 1968.

Amin, A. Culture and the post-hospital community adjustment of long term hospitalized Puerto Rican schizophrenic male patients in New York City (Doctoral dissertation, Columbia University, 1974). *Dissertation Abstracts International*, 1975, *35*, 5964-B. (University Microfilms No. 74-26579).

Anderson, J. E. Cultural democracy in psychotherapy: Mexican-American client, Anglo-American therapist. (Doctoral dissertation, California School of Professional Psychology, 1973). (University Microfilms No. 74–7921).

Anderson, J. G., & Johnson, W. H. Stability and change among three generations of Mexican Americans: Factors affecting achievement. *American Educational Research Journal*, 1971, *8*, 285–307.

Anderson, T. Bilingual schooling: Oasis or mirage? *Hispania*, 1969, *52*, 69–74.

274

Antunes, G., Gordon, C., Gaitz, C. M., & Scott, J. Ethnicity, socioeconomic status and the etiology of psychological distress. *Sociology and Social Research*, 1974, *58*, 361–368.

Aron, W. S., Alzar, N., & Gonzales, R. T. Chicanoizing the therapeutic community. *Journal of Psychedelic Drugs*, 1974, *6*, 321–327.

Atencio, T. Mental health and the Spanish speaking. In *Mental Health Planning Conference for the Spanish Speaking*. Rockville, Md.: National Institute of Mental Health, 1972.

Bachrach, L. L. *Utilization of state and county mental hospitals by Spanish Americans in 1972*. Rockville, Md.: National Institute of Mental Health, Division of Biometry, June 1975 (Statistical Note 116).

Barberio, R. The relationship between achievement motivation and ethnicity in Anglo American and Mexican American junior high school students. *Psychological Record*, 1967, *17*, 263–266.

Barnouw, V. *Culture and personality*. Homewood, Ill.: Dorsey Press, 1963.

Baxter, J. C. Interpersonal spacing in natural settings. *Sociometry*, 1970, *33*, 444–456.

Beckner, B. L. Counseling Black students: Any place for whitey? *Journal of Higher Education*, 1970, *41*, 630–637.

Bender, P. C., & Ruiz, R. A. Race and class as differential determinants of underachievement and underaspiration among Mexican Americans. *Journal of Educational Research*, 1974, *68*, 51–56.

Benedict, R. *Patterns of culture*. New York: Penguin, 1946.

Bloombaum, M., Yamamoto, J., & James, Q. Cultural stereotyping among psychotherapists. *Journal of Counseling and Clinical Psychology*, 1968, *32*, 99.

Boulette, T. R. Problemas familiares: Television programs in Spanish for mental health education. *Hospital and Community Psychiatry*, 1974, *25*, 282.

Boulette, T. R. Assertive training with low income Mexican American women. In M. Miranda (Ed.), *Psychotherapy for the Spanish speaking*. Los Angeles: Spanish Speaking Mental Health Research Center, 1976 (Monograph 3). (a)

Boulette, T. R. Personal communication, December 10, 1976. (b)

Boulette, T. R. Parenting: Special needs of low-income Spanish-surnamed families. *Psychiatric Annals*, 1977, *6*, 95–107.

Brand, E. S. Psychological correlates of ethnic esteem among Anglo, Black, and Chicano second-grade and fifth-grade children (Doctoral dissertation, University of Missouri, 1974). *Dissertation Abstracts International*, 1974, *35*, 3861A. (University Microfilms No. 74–1742).

Brand, E. S., Ruiz, R. A., & Padilla, A. M. Ethnic identification and preference: A review. *Psychological Bulletin*, 1974, *81*, 360–390.

Bronson, L., & Meadow, A. The need achievement orientation of Catholic and Protestant Mexican Americans. *Revista Interamericana de Psicología*, 1968, *2*, 159–168.

Bryant, G. Mexican immigrants in the United States. *Survey*, 1912, *28*, 726–730.

Burger, H. Ethnicity: An anthropological approach to ecstasy and sanity. *General Systems*, 1974, *24*, 59–71.

Burma, J. *The Spanish-speaking groups in the United States*. Durham, N.C.: Duke University Press, 1954.

Burruel, G. La Frontera, a mental health clinic in the Chicano community. *Report of the Southwest States Chicano Consumer Conference on Health*, 1972, pp.

27–33.

Burstein, A. G., & Kobos, J. Psychological testing as a device to foster social mobility. *American Psychologist*, 1971, *26*, 1041–1042.

Bustamante, C. J., & Bustamante, P. L. *The Mexican-American and the United States*. Mountain View, Calif.: LAR Publications, 1969.

Bustamante, J. A. Cultural factors in hysterics with schizophrenic clinical picture. *International Journal of Social Psychiatry*, 1968, *14*, 113–118.

Butcher, J. N., & Garcia, R. E. Cross-national application of psychological tests. *Personnel and Guidance Journal*, 1978, *8*, 472–475.

Carlos, M. L., & Sellers, L. Family, kinship structure, and modernization in Latin America. *Latin American Research Review*, 1972, *7*, 95–124.

Carrier, J. M. Family attitudes and Mexican male homosexuality. *Urban Life*, 1976, *5*, 359–375. (a)

Carrier, J. M. Cultural factors affecting urban Mexican male homosexual behavior. *Archives of Sexual Behavior*, 1976, *5*, 103–124. (b)

Carrier, J. M. "Sex-role preference" as an explanatory variable in homosexual behavior. *Archives of Sexual Behavior*, 1977, *6*, 53–65.

Carter, T. P. The negative self concept of Mexican-American students. *School and Society*, 1968, *96*, 207–209.

Carter, T. P. *Mexican Americans in school: A history of educational neglect*. New York: College Entrance Examination Board, 1970.

Casas, J. M. Applicability of a behavioral model in serving the mental health needs of the Mexican American. In M. Miranda (Ed.), *Psychotherapy for the Spanish-speaking*. Los Angeles: Spanish Speaking Mental Health Research Center, 1976 (Monograph 3).

Casavantes, E. J. A new look at the attributes of the Mexican American. Albuquerque, N.M.: Southwestern Cooperative Education Laboratory, 1969. (ERIC Document Reproduction Service No. ED 028 010)

Casavantes, E. J. Pride and prejudice: A Mexican American dilemma. *Civil Rights Digest*, 1970, *3*, 22–27.

Casavantes, E. J. *El tecato: Social and cultural factors affecting drug use among Chicanos*. Washington, D.C.: National Coalition of Spanish-Speaking Mental Health Organizations, 1976.

Castañeda, A. Persisting ideological issues of assimilation in America. In G. Epps (Ed.), *Cultural pluralism*. Berkeley: McCutchan, 1974.

Chandler, C. R. Value orientations among Mexican Americans in a Southwestern city. *Sociology and Social Research*, 1974, *58*, 262–271.

Chandler, J. T., & Plankos, J. *Spanish speaking pupils classified as educable mentally retarded*. Sacramento: California State Department of Education, Division of Instruction, 1969.

Christensen, E. W. Counseling Puerto Ricans: Some cultural considerations. *Personnel and Guidance Journal*, 1975, *53*, 349–356.

Christensen, E. W. When counseling Puerto Ricans. *Personnel and Guidance Journal*, 1977, *55*, 412–415.

Ciaramella, V. A comparative study of ethnic versus dominant culture group counseling: An interaction process analysis (Doctoral dissertation, Fordham University, 1973). *Dissertation Abstracts International*, 1973, *34*, 2289A. (University Microfilms No. 73–26, 707).

Clark, M., & Mendelson, M. Mexican-American aged in San Francisco: A case description. *Gerontologist*, 1969, *9*, 90–95.

Cobbs, C. W. Community mental health services and the lower socioeconomic class: A summary of research literature on outpatient treatment (1963–1969). *American Journal of Orthopsychiatry*, 1972, *42*, 404–414.

Cole, S. G., & Davenport, K. Reported friendliness toward Mexican-Americans as a function of belief similarity and race. Paper presented at the Midwestern Psychological Association, Chicago, May 1973.

Coleman, J. S., Campbell, E. Q., Hobson, C. J., McPartland, J., Mood, A. M., Weinfeld, F. D., & York, R. L. *Equality of educational opportunity*. Washington, D.C.: U.S. Government Printing Office, 1966.

Coopersmith, S. *The antecedents of self-esteem*. San Francisco: W. H. Freeman, 1967.

Cordova, I. R. The relationship of acculturation, achievement, and alienation among Spanish American sixth-grade students. (Doctoral dissertation, University of New Mexico, 1969). *Dissertation Abstracts International*, 1970, *44*, 13371a.

Cornett, J. D., Ainsworth, L., & Askins, B. Effect of an intervention program on "high risk" Spanish American children. *Journal of Educational Research*, 1974, *67*, 342–343.

Cruz, M. Social factors and self-esteem among Puerto Rican and non-Puerto Rican students. (Doctoral dissertation, University of Illinois, 1974). (University Microfilms No. 74–14, 525).

Currier, R. L. The hot-cold syndrome and symbolic balance in Mexican and Spanish-American folk medicine. *Ethnology*, 1966, *5*, 251–263.

Dashefsky, A. (Ed.) *Ethnic identity in society*. Chicago: Rand McNally, 1976.

Davis, R. H. *Mexican Americans*. Los Angeles: University of Southern California Press, 1976.

de Armas, E. The "supersystem" and the Spanish-speaking elderly. In D. J. Curren (Ed.), *Proceedings of the Puerto Rican conferences on human services*. Washington, D.C.: National Coalition of Spanish-speaking Mental Health Organizations, 1975.

DeBlassie, R. R. *Counseling with Mexican American youth: Preconceptions and processes*. Austin, Texas: Learning Concepts, 1976.

Del Castillo, J. C. The influence of language upon symptomatology in foreign born patients. *The American Journal of Psychiatry*, 1970, *127*, 160–162.

Delgado, M. Social work and the Puerto Rican community. *Social Casework*, 1974, *55*, 117–123.

Demos, G. D. Attitudes of Mexican-American and Anglo-American groups toward education. *Journal of Social Psychology*, 1962, *57*, 249–256.

Derbyshire, R. L. Adolescent identity crisis in urban Mexican Americans in East Los Angeles. In E. B. Brody (Ed.), *Minority group adolescents in the United States*. Baltimore: Williams and Wilkins, 1968.

Diaz-Guerrero, R. The active and the passive syndromes. *Revista Interamericana de Psicología*, 1967, *1*, 263–272.

Diaz-Guerrero, R. *Psychology of the Mexican: Culture and personality*. Austin: University of Texas Press, 1975.

Diaz-Guerrero, R. A Mexican psychology. *American Psychologist*, 1977, *32*, 934–944.

Dohen, D. A new juvenile court role in an ethnically controlled community agency. *Social Work*, 1971, *16*, 25–29.

Dohrenwend, B. P. Social status and psychological disorder: An issue of substance and an issue of method. *American Sociological Review*, 1966, *31*, 14–34.

Dohrenwend, B. P., & Dohrenwend, B. S. *Social status and psychological disorder: A causal inquiry.* New York: Wiley, 1969.

Duling, J. A. The use of the Miller Analogies Test as a screening device for Mexican-American graduate students. *Journal of NAWDAC*, 1974, *37*, 133–136.

Dworkin, A. G. National origin and ghetto experience as variables in Mexican American stereotype. In N. Wagner & M. J. Haug (Eds.), *Chicanos: Social and psychological perspective.* St. Louis: C. V. Mosby, 1971, pp. 80–84.

Edgerton, R. B., & Karno, M. Mexican-American bilingualism and the perception of mental illness. *Archives of General Psychiatry*, 1971, *24*, 286–290.

Edgerton, R. B., Karno, M., & Fernandez, I. Curanderismo in the metropolis: The diminishing role of folk-psychiatry among Los Angeles Mexican-Americans. *American Journal of Psychotherapy*, 1970, *24*, 124–134.

Ellis, J. M. Spanish surname mortality differences in San Antonio Texas. *Journal of Health and Human Behavior*, 1962, *3*, 125–127.

Escarsega, Y. D., Mondaca, E. C., & Torres, U. G. *Attitudes of Chicana Lesbians towards therapy.* Unpublished master's thesis, University of Southern California, 1975.

Evans, F. B., & Anderson, J. G. The psychocultural origins of achievement and achievement motivation: The Mexican American family. *Sociology of Education*, 1973, *46*, 396–416.

Fabrega, H., Swartz, J., & Wallace, C. A. Ethnic differences in psychopathology II. Specific differences with emphasis on the Mexican American group. *Psychiatric Research*, 1968, *6*, 221–235.

Fabrega, H., Jr., & Wallace, C. Value identification and psychiatric disability: An analysis involving Americans of Mexican descent. *Behavioral Science*, 1968, *13*, 362–371.

Farb, P. *Word play: What happens when people talk.* New York: Alfred A. Knopf, 1974.

Feldman, C., & Shen, M. Some language-related cognitive advantages of bilingual five-year-olds. *Journal of Genetic Psychology*, 1971, *118*, 235–244.

Fellows, D. K. *A mosaic of America's ethnic minorities.* New York: Wiley, 1973.

Fernandez-Marina, R. The Puerto Rican syndrome: Its dynamics and cultural determinants. *Psychiatry*, 1961, *24*, 79–82.

Fernandez-Marina, R., Maldonado-Sierra, E. D., & Trent, R. D. Three basic themes in Mexican and Puerto Rican family values. *Journal of Social Psychology*, 1958, *48*, 167–181.

Fernandez-Marina, R., & Von Echardt, U. M. Cultural stresses and schizophrenogenesis in the mothering-one in Puerto Rico. *Annals of the New York Academy of Sciences*, 1960, *84*, 864–877.

Fink, A. K. Psychodrama in the Puerto Rican setting. *Group Psychotherapy*, 1967, *20*, 121–122.

Fitzgibbons, D. J., Cutler, R., & Cohen, J. Patients' self-perceived treatment needs and their relationship to background variables. *Journal of Consulting and Clinical Psychology*, 1971, *37*, 253–258.

Fitzpatrick, J. P. *Puerto Rican Americans: The meaning of migration to the mainland.* Englewood Cliffs, N.J.: Prentice-Hall, 1971.

Fogel, W. *Mexican Americans in southwest labor markets.* Advance Report

5, University of California, Los Angeles: Mexican American Study Project, 1966.

Friedman, M., & Rosenman, R. H. *Type A behavior and your heart.* Greenwich, Conn.: Fawcett, 1974.

Fuller, R. Occupations of the Mexican-born population in Texas, New Mexico, and Arizona 1900–1920. *Journal of the American Statistical Association,* 1928, *23*, 64–67.

Galarza, E., Gallegos, H., & Samora, J. *Mexican-Americans in the Southwest.* Santa Barbara: McNally & Loftin, 1970.

Galli, N. The influence of cultural heritage on the health status of Puerto Ricans. *Journal of School Health,* 1975, *45*, 10–16.

Galvin, J. A., & Ludwig, A. M. A case of witchcraft. *Journal of Nervous and Mental Diseases,* 1961, *133*, 161–168.

Gannon, T. M. Dimensions of current gang delinquency. In M. Wolfgang (Ed.), *The sociology of crime and delinquency.* New York: Wiley, 1970.

Ganschow, L. H. Stimulating educational information-seeking and changes in student attitude toward vocational education by videotape and film presentations. Final Report. Palo Alto, Calif.: American Institute of Behavioral Sciences, 1969. (ERIC Document Reproduction Service No. ED 043 778)

Garcia, A. The Chicano and social work. *Social Casework,* 1971, *52*, 274–278.

Garcia, A., & Zimmerman, B. The effect of examiner ethnicity and language on the performance of bilingual Mexican American first graders. *Journal of Social Psychology,* 1972, *87*, 3–11.

Garcia, J. Intelligence testing: Quotients, quotas, and quackery. In J. Martinez (Ed.), *Chicano psychology.* New York: Academic Press, 1977.

Gares, V. D. A comparative investigation of the occupational counseling given to Mexican-American and Anglo-American students upon entering the community college (Doctoral dissertation, United States International University, 1974). *Dissertation Abstracts International,* 1974, *35*, 187A. (University Microfilms No. 74-14, 313).

Garrison, V. The "Puerto Rican Syndrome" in psychiatry and espiritismo. In V. Crapanzano & V. Garrison (Eds.), *Case studies in spirit possession.* New York: Wiley, 1977.

Garza, R. T., & Ames, R. E., Jr. A comparison of Anglo- and Mexican-American college students on locus of control. *Journal of Consulting and Clinical Psychology,* 1974, *42*, 919.

Geismar, L., & Gerhart, U. Social class, ethnicity, and family functioning: Exploring some issues raised by the Moynihan report. *Journal of Marriage and the Family,* 1968, *30*, 480–487.

Gilbert, M. J. *Qualitative analysis of the drinking practices and alcohol-related problems of the Spanish speaking in three California locales.* Alhambra, Calif.: Technical Systems Institute, 1977.

Giordano, J. *Ethnicity and mental health: Research and recommendations.* New York: Institute of Human Relations, 1973.

Glatt, K. M. An evaluation of the French, Spanish, and German translations of the MMPI. *Acta Psychologica,* 1969, *29*, 65–84.

Glick, L. B. The right to equal opportunity. In J. Samora (Ed.), *La Raza: Forgotten Americans.* Notre Dame, Ind.: University of Notre Dame Press, 1966.

Goffman, E. *Asylums: Essays on the social situation of mental patients and other inmates.* Chicago: Aldine, 1961.

Goldman, R. D., & Richards, R. The SAT prediction of grades for Mexican-American versus Anglo-American students at the University of California, Riverside. *Journal of Educational Measurement*, 1974, *11*, 129–135.

Goldstein, M. J., & Palmer, J. O. *The experience of anxiety: A case book* (2nd ed.). New York: Oxford University Press, 1975.

Gonzales, E. The Mexican American in California. *California Education*, 1965, *3*, 19–22.

Gonzales, E. The role of Chicano folk beliefs and practices in mental health. In C. Hernandez, M. Haug, & N. Wagner (Eds.), *Chicanos: Social and psychological perspectives.* St. Louis: C. V. Mosby, 1976.

Goodenough, W. H. *Cooperation in change.* New York: Russell Sage Foundation, 1963.

Goodman, M. E., & Beman, A. Child's-eye-views on life in an urban barrio. In N. N. Wagner & M. J. Haug (Eds.), *Chicanos: Social and psychological perspectives.* St. Louis: C. V. Mosby, 1971.

Gordon, S. Are we seeing the right patients? Child guidance intake: The sacred cow. *American Journal of Orthopsychiatry*, 1965, *35*, 131–137.

Gorer, G., & Rickman, J. *The people of great Russia: A psychological study.* New York: Chanticleer, 1950.

Gough, H. G. *Manual for the California Psychological Inventory.* Palo Alto, Calif.: Consulting Psychologists Press, 1957.

Grace, W. J. Ataque. *New York Medicine*, 1959, *15*, 12–13.

Graves, T. R. Acculturation, access, and alcohol in a tri-ethnic community. *American Anthropologist*, 1967, *69*, 306–321.

Greeley, A. M. *Why can't they be like us?* New York: Institute of Human Relations Press, 1969.

Gunther, J. *Inside South America.* New York: Harper & Row, 1967.

Gutierrez, A., & Hirsch, H. The militant challenge to the American ethos: "Chicanos" and Mexican Americans. *Social Science Quarterly*, 1973, *53*, 830–845.

Guttentag, M. Group cohesiveness, ethnic origin and poverty. *Journal of Social Issues*, 1970, *26*, 105–132.

Haley, J. *Strategies of psychotherapy.* New York: Grune & Stratton, 1963.

Hall, C. S., & Lindzey, G. *Theories of personality* (2nd ed.). New York: Wiley, 1970.

Hall, D. C., Chaikin, C., & Piland, B. *A review of the problem drinking behavior literature associated with the Spanish-speaking population group: Volume III.* Menlo Park, Calif.: Stanford Research Institute, 1977.

Hall, E. *The silent language.* Garden City, N.Y.: Doubleday, 1959.

Hallowell, A. I. *Culture and experience.* Philadelphia: University of Pennsylvania, 1955.

Hallowitz, E., & Riessman, F. The role of the indigenous non-professional in a community mental health neighborhood service center. *American Journal of Orthopsychiatry*, 1967, *37*, 766–778.

Hamilton, L. S. An experimental study of the effectiveness of small group discussions in facilitating interethnic group communication and understanding (Doctoral dissertation, New Mexico State, 1969). *Dissertation Abstracts International*, 1969, *30*, 2849A. (University Microfilms No. 70–01233)

Harwood, A. *Rx: Spiritist as needed.* New York: Wiley, 1977.

Haven, B. J. An investigation of activity patterns and adjustment in an aging population. *Gerontologist,* 1968, *8,* 201–206.

Healey, G. W., & De Blassie, R. R. A comparison of Negro, Anglo and Spanish-American adolescents' self concepts. *Adolescence,* 1974, *9,* 15–24.

Heiman, E. M., Burruei, G., & Chavez, N. Factors determining effective psychiatric outpatient treatment for Mexican Americans. *Hospital and Community Psychiatry,* 1975, *26,* 515–517.

Heiman, E. M., & Kahn, M. W. Mexican-American and European American psychopathology and hospital course. *Archives of General Psychiatry,* 1977, *34,* 167–170.

Heller, C. *Mexican-American youth.* New York: Random House, 1966.

Henderson, R. W., & Merritt, C. B. Environmental background of Mexican-American children with different potentials for school success. *Journal of Social Psychology,* 1968, *75,* 101–106.

Henzlik, W. L. B. A comparison of migrant and ex-migrant Mexican-American children on locus-of-control, intelligence test performance, self-concept, and personality (Doctoral dissertation, Purdue University, 19743. *Dissertation Abstracts International,* 1974, *35,* 3298A. (University Microfilms No. 74–26, 720)

Hernandez, C. A., Haug, M. J., & Wagner, N. N., (Eds.). Mexican-Americans and the administration of justice in the southwest: Summary of a report of the United States Commission on Civil Rights, 1970. *Chicanos: Social and psychological perspectives.* St. Louis: C. V. Mosby, 1976.

Hernandez, D. *Mexican American challenge to a sacred cow.* Los Angeles: University of California, Aztlan Publications, 1970 (Monograph No. 1).

Hernandez, N. G. Variables affecting achievement of middle school Mexican-American students. *Review of Educational Research,* 1973, *43,* 1–39.

Herrera, A. E., & Sanchez, V. C. Behaviorally oriented group therapy: A successful application in the treatment of low-income Spanish-speaking clients. In M. Miranda (Ed.), *Psychotherapy for the Spanish-speaking.* Spanish-Speaking Mental Health Research Center: Los Angeles, 1976.

Hidalgo, H. A., & Christensen, E. H. The Puerto Rican lesbian and the Puerto Rican community. *Journal of Homosexuality,* 1976–77, *2,* 109–121.

Hindelang, M. J. Educational and occupational aspirations among working class Negro, Mexican American and White elementary school children. *Journal of Negro Education,* 1970, *39,* 351–353.

Holland, W. R. Mexican-American medical beliefs: Science or magic? *Arizona Medicine,* 1963, *20,* 89–101.

Holtzman, W. H., Diaz-Guerrero, R., & Swartz, J. D. *Personality development in two cultures.* Austin, Texas: University of Texas Press, 1975.

Holtzman, W. H., Diaz-Guerrero, R., Swartz, J. D., & Tapia, L. L. Crosscultural longitudinal research on child development: Studies of American and Mexican school children. In J. P. Hill (Ed.), *Minnesota symposia on child psychology* (Vol. 2). Minneapolis: University of Minnesota Press, 1968.

Honigmann, J. J. *Personality in culture.* New York: Harper & Row, 1967.

Hosford, R. E., & Bowles, S. A. Determining culturally appropriate reinforcers for Anglo and Chicano students. *Elementary School Guidance and Counseling,* 1974, *8,* 290–300.

Hountras, P. T. The use of the Miller Analogies Test in predicting graduate student achievement. *College and University*, 1956, *32*, 65–70.

Jackson, G., & Cocsa, C. The inequality of educational opportunity in the Southwest: An observational study of ethnically mixed classrooms. *American Educational Research Journal*, 1974, *11*, 219–229.

Jaco, E. G. Social factors in mental disorders in Texas. *Social Problems*, 1957, *4*, 322–328.

Jaco, E. G. Mental health of Spanish Americans in Texas. In M. F. Opler (Ed.), *Culture and mental health: Cross-cultural studies.* New York: Macmillan, 1959.

Jensen, A. R. Learning abilities in Mexican American and Anglo American children. *California Journal of Education Research*, 1961, *12*, 147–159.

Jensen, A. R. Intelligence, learning ability and socioeconomic status. *Journal of Special Education*, 1969, *3*, 23–35.

Jensen, A. R. Level I & Level II abilities in three ethnic groups. *American Education Research Journal*, 1973, *10*, 263–276.

Johnson, D. L., Leler, H., Ríos, L. Brandt, L., Kahn, A. J., Mazeika, E., Frede, M., & Bisett, B. The Houston parent-child development center: A parent education program for Mexican-American families. *American Journal of Orthopsychiatry*, 1974, *44*, 121–128.

Johnson, D. L., & Sikes, M. P. Rorschach and TAT responses of Negro, Mexican-American, and Anglo psychiatric patients. *Journal of Projective Techniques*, 1965, *29*, 183–188.

Johnson, G. B. The origin and development of the Spanish attitude toward the Anglo and the Anglo attitude toward the Spanish. *Journal of Educational Psychology*, 1950, *41*, 428–439.

Jones, S. E. A comparative proxemics analysis of dyadic interaction in selected subcultures of New York City. *Journal of Social Psychology*, 1971, *84*, 35–44.

Jourard, S. *The transparent self.* New York: Van Nostrand, 1971.

Kagan, S., & Carlson, H. Development of adaptive assertiveness in Mexican-American and United States children. *Developmental Psychology*, 1975, *11*, 71–78.

Kagan, S. M. *Adaptation mode and behavior of urban Anglo American and rural Mexican children.* Unpublished doctoral dissertation, University of California, Los Angeles, 1973. (Abstract)

Kahn, M., & Heiman, E. Factors associated with length of stay in treatment in a barrio neighborhood mental health service. Paper presented at the American Psychological Association, New Orleans, August, 1974.

Kaplan, B. Reflections of the acculturation process in the Rorschach test. *Journal of Projective Techniques*, 1955, *19*, 30–35.

Kaplan, B., Rickers-Ovsiankina, M. A., & Joseph, A. An attempt to sort Rorschach records from four cultures. *Journal of Projective Techniques*, 1956, *20*, 172–180.

Kaplan, R. M., & Goldman, R. D. Interracial perception among Black, White, and Mexican-American high school students. *Journal of Personality and Social Psychology*, 1973, *28*, 383–389.

Kardiner, A. *The individual and his society.* New York: Columbia University Press, 1939.

Karno, M. The enigma of ethnicity in a psychiatric clinic. *Archives of General Psychiatry*, 1966, *14*, 516–520.

Karno, M., & Edgerton, R. B. Perception of mental illness in a Mexican-American community. *Archives of General Psychiatry*, 1969, *20*, 233–238.

Karno, M., & Morales, A. A. A community mental health service for Mexican-Americans in a metropolis. *Comprehensive Psychiatry*, 1971, *12*, 116–121.

Kasschau, P. L. Age and race discrimination reported by middle-aged and older persons. *Social Forces*, 1977, *55*, 728–742.

Kelly, L. M. Community identification among second generation Puerto Ricans: Its relation to occupational success (Doctoral dissertation, Fordham University, 1971). *Dissertation Abstracts International*, 1971, *31*, 2223a. (University Microfilms No. 71–26, 977)

Kershner, J. Ethnic group differences in children's ability to reproduce direction and orientation. *Journal of Social Psychology*, 1972, *88*, 3–13.

Kiev, A. *Curanderismo: Mexican-American folk psychiatry*. New York: The Free Press, 1968.

Kiev, A. Transcultural psychiatry: Research problems and perspectives. In S. Plog & R. Edgerton (Eds.), *Emerging patterns of mental health*. New York: Holt, Rinehart & Winston, 1969.

Kiev, A. *Transcultural psychiatry*. New York: The Free Press, 1972.

Kitano, H.H.L. *Race relations*. Englewood Cliffs, N.J.: Prentice-Hall, 1974.

Kline, L. Y. Some factors in the psychiatric treatment of Spanish-Americans. *American Journal of Psychiatry*, 1969, *125*, 1674–1681.

Klitgaard, G. C. A gap is bridged: Successful counseling of college potential Mexican Americans. *Journal of Secondary Education*, 1969, *44*, 55–57.

Klovekorn, M. R., Madera, M., & Nardone, S. Counseling the Cuban child. *Elementary School Guidance and Counseling*, 1974, *8*, 255–260.

Kluckhohn, F., & Strodtbeck, F. *Variations in value orientations*. Evanston, Ill.: Row Peterson, 1961.

Knoll, F. R. Casework services for Mexican Americans. *Social Casework*, 1971, *52*, 279–284.

Kobrick, J. The compelling case for bilingual education. *Saturday Review of Education*, April 29, 1972, pp. 54–58.

Komaroff, A., Masuda, M., & Holmes, T. The social readjustment rating scale: A comparative study of Negro, Mexican and White Americans. *Journal of Psychosomatic Research*, 1968, *12*, 121–128.

Kramer, J. *The American minority community*. New York: Corwell, 1962.

Kreisman, J. J. The curandero's apprentice: A therapeutic integration of folk and medical healing. *American Journal of Psychiatry*, 1975, *132*, 81–83.

Kubler-Ross, E. *On death and dying*. New York: Macmillan, 1969.

Kuvlesky, W. P., & Patella, V. M. Degree of ethnicity and aspirations for upward social mobility among Mexican American youth. *Journal of Vocational Behavior*, 1971, *1*, 231–244.

Laosa, L., Swartz, J. D., & Diaz-Guerrero, R. D. Perceptual, cognitive and personality development of Mexican and Anglo-American children as measured by human figure drawings. *Developmental Psychology*, 1974, *10*, 131–139.

Lehmann, S. Selected self-help: A study of clients of a community social psychiatric service. *American Journal of Psychiatry*, 1970, *126*, 1444–1454.

Leininger, M. Witchcraft practices and psychocultural therapy with urban U.S.

families. *Human Organization*, 1973, *32*, 73–83.

Leo, P. F. The effects of two types of group counseling upon the academic achievement and self-concept of Mexican American pupils in the elementary school (Doctoral dissertation, University of the Pacific, 1972). *Dissertation Abstracts International*, 1972, *32*, 1442A. (University Microfilms No. 72–25, 740)

Leon, R. An experiment with early group counseling practicum in a Chicano counselor training program (Doctoral dissertation, University of South Carolina, 1973). *Dissertation Abstracts International*, 1973, *33*, 4840A-4841A. (University Microfilms No. 50–3817)

LeVine, R. A. *Culture, behavior and personality*. Chicago: Aldine, 1973.

Lewis, O. *La vida: A Puerto Rican family in the culture of poverty—San Juan and New York*. New York: Random House, 1966.

Leyva, R. Educational aspirations and expectations of Chicanos, non-Chicanos, and Anglo-Americans. *California Journal of Educational Research*, 1975, *26*, 27–39.

Lindholm, K. J., & Padilla, A. M. Language mixing in bilingual children. *Journal of Child Language*, 1978, *5*, 327–335.

Linton, R. *The cultural background of personality*. New York: Appleton-Century-Crofts, 1945.

Littlefield, R. P. An analysis of the self-disclosure patterns of ninth grade public school students in three selected subcultural groups (Doctoral dissertation, Florida State University, 1969). *Dissertation Abstracts International*, 1969, *30*, 588–589A. (University Microfilms No. 69–11, 309)

Locascio, R., Nesselroth, J., & Thomas, M. The career development inventory: Use and findings with inner city dropouts. *Journal of Vocational Behavior*, 1976, *8*, 285–292.

Logan, D. L. An empirical investigation of the cultural determinants of basic motivational patterns (Doctoral dissertation, University of Arizona, 1966). *Dissertation Abstracts International*, 1966, *27*, 2874A. (University Microfilms No. 67–01077)

Longres, J. F., Jr. Racism and its effects on Puerto Rican continentals. *Social Casework*, 1974, *55*, 67–75.

Lopez, R. W., & Enos, D. D. Spanish-language only television in Los Angeles County. *Aztlan: Chicano Journal of the Social Sciences and the Arts*, 1973, *4*, 283–313.

Lorion, R. P. Socioeconomic status and traditional treatment approaches reconsidered. *Psychological Bulletin*, 1973, *79*, 263–270.

Lorion, R. P. Patient and therapist variables in the treatment of low-income patients. *Psychological Bulletin*, 1974, *81*, 344–354.

Lubchansky, I., Ergi, G., & Stokes, J. Puerto Rican spiritualists view mental illness: The faith healer as a paraprofessional. *American Journal of Psychiatry*, 1970, *127*, 312–321.

Macías, R. F. U.S. Hispanics in 2000 A.D.—Projecting the number. *Agenda*, 1977, *7*, 16–19.

Mack, C. N., James, L. E., Ramirez, J., & Bailey, J. The attitudes of Mexican American "non-help seekers" regarding help for personal problems: A pilot study. Paper presented at the Southwestern Psychological Association, El Paso, Texas, May 4, 1974.

Madsen, M. C. Development and cross-cultural differences in the cooperative and competitive behavior of young children. *Psychology*, 1971, *2*, 365–371.

Madsen, W. The alcoholic agringado. *American Anthropologist*, 1964, *66*, 355–361. (a)

Madsen, W. Value conflicts and folk psychiatry in South Texas. In A. Kiev (Ed.), *Magic, faith, and healing*. New York: The Free Press, 1964. (b)

Madsen, W. Mexican-Americans and Anglo-Americans: A comparative study of mental health in Texas. In S. C. Plog & R. E. Edgerton (Eds.), *Changing perspectives in mental illness*. New York: Holt, Rinehart & Winston, 1969.

Maes, W. R., & Rinaldi, J. R. Counseling the Chicano child. *Elementary School Guidance and Counseling*, 1974, *8*, 279–284.

Maldonado, D., Jr. The Chicano aged. *Social Work*, 1975, *20*, 213–216.

Maldonado-Sierra, E. D., & Trent, R. D. The sibling relationship in group psychotherapy with Puerto Rican schizophrenics. *American Journal of Psychiatry*, 1960, *117*, 239–244.

Maldonado-Sierra, E. D., Trent, R. D., & Fernandez-Marina, R. Neurosis and traditional family beliefs. *International Journal of Social Psychiatry*, 1960, *6*, 237–246.

Malzberg, B. Mental disease among the Puerto Ricans in New York City, 1949–1951. *Journal of Nervous and Mental Disease*, 1956, *123*, 262–269.

Malzberg, B. *Mental disease among the Puerto Rican population of New York State, 1960–1961*. Albany, N.Y.: Research Foundation for Mental Hygiene, Inc., 1965.

Mansfield, C. C. Black, Mexican-American and Anglo graduates' perceptions of their secondary school counselors (Doctoral dissertation, University of Arizona, 1972). *Dissertation Abstracts International*, 1973, *33*, 159a–160a. (University Microfilms No. 49–3246)

Manuel, H. T. *Spanish-speaking children of the Southwest: Their education and the public welfare*. Austin: University of Texas Press, 1965.

Marcos, L. R. Linguistic dimensions in the bilingual patient. *American Journal of Psychoanalysis*, 1976, *36*, 347–354.

Marcos, L. R., & Alpert, M. Strategies and risks in psychotherapy with bilingual patients: The phenomenon of language independence. *American Journal of Psychiatry*, 1976, *133*, 1275–1278.

Marcos, L. R., Alpert, M., Urcuyo, L., & Kesselman, M. The effect of interview language on the evaluation of psychopathology in Spanish-American schizophrenic patients. *American Journal of Psychiatry*, 1973, *130*, 549–553.

Marcos, L. R., Urcuyo, L., Kesselman, M., & Alpert, M. The language barrier in evaluating Spanish-American patients. *Archives of General Psychology*, 1973, *29*, 655–659.

Marden, C. *Minorities in American society*. New York: American Book Company, 1952.

Martinez, C. Community mental health and the Chicano movement. *American Journal of Orthopsychiatry*, 1973, *43*, 595–601.

Martinez, C., & Martin, H. W. Folk diseases among urban Mexican-Americans. *Journal of the American Medical Association*, 1966, *196*, 161–164.

Martinez, J. L. Cross-cultural comparison of Chicanos and Anglos on the semantic differential: Some implications for psychology. In J. L. Martinez (Ed.), *Chicano psychology*. New York: Academic Press, 1977.

Martinez, T. M. Advertising and racism: The case of the Mexican-American. In

O. I. Romano-V. (Ed.), *Voices: Readings from El Grito.* Berkeley: Quinto Sol Publications, 1971.

Mason, E. P. Comparison of personality characteristics of junior high school students from American Indian, Mexican, and Caucasian ethnic backgrounds. *Journal of Social Psychology,* 1967, *73,* 145–155.

Matluck, J. H., & Mace, B. J. Language characteristics of Mexican-American children: Implications for assessment. *Journal of Social Psychology,* 1973, *11,* 365–386.

Mayeske, G. W. Educational achievement among Mexican-Americans: A special report from the educational opportunities survey. *Integrated Education,* 1968, *6,* 32–37.

McClelland, D. C. *The achieving society.* New York: The Free Press, 1961.

McCreary, C., & Padilla, E. MMPI differences among Black, Mexican American and White male offenders. *Journal of Clinical Psychology,* 1977, *33,* 171–177.

McGehearty, L., & Womble, M. Case analysis: Consultation and counseling. *Elementary School Guidance and Counseling,* 1970, *5,* 141–144, 147.

McLemore, S. D. Ethnic attitudes toward hospitalization: An illustrative comparison of Anglos and Mexican Americans. *Southwestern Social Science Quarterly,* 1963, *43,* 341–346.

McWilliams, C. *North from Mexico, the Spanish-speaking people of the United States.* New York: Greenwood Press, 1968.

Mercer, J. *Labeling the mentally retarded.* Berkeley: University of California Press, 1973.

Mercer, J. R. Identifying the gifted Chicano child. In J. L. Martinez (Ed.), *Chicano psychology.* New York: Academic Press, 1977.

Miller, M. V., & Preston, J. D. Vertical ties and the redistribution of power in Crystal City. *Social Sciences Quarterly,* 1973, *53,* 772–784.

Mingione, A. D. Need achievement in Negro, White, and Puerto Rican children. *Journal of Consulting and Clinical Psychology,* 1968, *32,* 94–95.

Miranda, M. R., Andujo, E., Caballero, I. L., Guerrero, C. C., & Ramos, R. A. Mexican American dropouts in psychotherapy as related to level of acculturation. In M. Miranda (Ed.), *Psychotherapy for the Spanish-speaking.* Los Angeles: Spanish Speaking Mental Health Research Center, 1976 (Monograph 3).

Moll, L. C., Rueda, R. S., Reza, R., Herrera, J., & Vasquez, L. P. Mental health services in East Los Angeles: An urban community case study. In M. Miranda (Ed.), *Psychotherapy for the Spanish-speaking.* Los Angeles: Spanish Speaking Mental Health Research Center, 1976 (Monograph 3).

Montalvo, B. Home-school conflict and the Puerto Rican child. *Social Casework,* 1974, *55,* 100–110.

Montijo, J. The Puerto Rican client. *Professional Psychology,* 1975, *6,* 475–477.

Moore, J. W. *Mexican Americans.* Englewood Cliffs, N.J.: Prentice-Hall, 1970.

Moore, J. W. Mexican-Americans. *Gerontologist,* 1971, *2,* 30–35.

Morales, A. Chicano police riots. In N. Wagner & M. Haug (Eds.), *Chicanos: Social and psychological perspectives.* St. Louis: C. V. Mosby, 1971. (a)

Morales, A. The collective preconscious and racism. *Social Casework,* 1971, *52,* 285–293. (b)

Morris, R. P. Self concept and ethnic group mixture among Hispanic students in elementary schools (Doctoral dissertation, Columbia University, 1974). *Dissertation Abstracts International*, 1975, *35*, 5087A. (University Microfilms No. 75–9299).

Moustafa, A. T., & Weiss, G. *Health status and practices of Mexican Americans* (Advance Report II). Los Angeles: University of California, Mexican American Study Project, 1968.

Muller, D., & Leonetti, R. Self-concepts of primary level Chicano and Anglo students. *California Journal of Educational Research*, 1974, *25*, 57–60.

Munns, J. G., Geis, G., & Bullington, B. Ex-addict streetworkers in a Mexican American community. *Crime and Delinquency*, 1970, *16*, 409–416.

Murillo, N. The Mexican American family. In N. Wagner & M. Haug (Eds.), *Chicanos: Social and psychological perspectives*. St. Louis: C. V. Mosby, 1971.

Naun, R. J. Comparison of group counseling approaches with Puerto Rican boys in an inner city high school (Doctoral dissertation, Fordham University, 1971). *Dissertation Abstracts International*, 1971, *32*, 742A. (University Microfilms No. 71–20, 200).

Nava, J. Forward. In N. Wagner & M. Haug (Eds.), *Chicanos: Social and psychological perspectives*. St. Louis: C. V. Mosby, 1971.

Negron, F. Aspira today, accountability tomorrow: An interview. *American Personnel and Guidance Journal*, 1971, *50*, 109–117.

Normand, W. C., Iglesias, J., & Payn, S. Brief group therapy to facilitate utilization of mental health services by Spanish-speaking patients. *American Journal of Orthopsychiatry*, 1974, *44*, 37–42.

Northrop, F. S. C. Cultural mentalities and medical science. In I. Galdston (Ed.), *Medicine and anthropology: New York Academy of Medicine*. Freeport, N.Y.: Books for Libraries Press, 1971.

Olmedo, E. L. Psychological testing and the Chicano: A reassessment. In J. L. Martinez (Ed.), *Chicano psychology*. New York: Academic Press, 1977.

Olmedo, E. L., & Lopez, S. (Eds.), *Hispanic mental health professionals*. Los Angeles: Spanish Speaking Mental Health Research Center, 1977 (Monograph 5).

Olmedo, E. L., Martinez, J. L., & Martinez, S. R. Measure of acculturation for Chicano adolescents. *Psychological Reports*, 1978, *42*, 159–170.

Olmedo, E. L., & Padilla, A. M. Empirical and construct validation of a measure of acculturation for Mexican Americans. *Journal of Social Psychology*, 1978, *105*, 179–187.

Opler, M. *Culture and social psychiatry*. New York: Atherton Press, 1967.

Ortega, P. D. Montezuma's children. In O. I. Romano-V. (Ed.), *Voices: Readings from El Grito*. Berkeley: Quinto Sol Publications, 1971.

Padilla, A. M., Carlos, M. L., & Keefe, S. E. Mental health service utilization by Mexican Americans. In M. Miranda (Ed.), *Psychotherapy for the Spanish-speaking*. Los Angeles: Spanish Speaking Mental Health Research Center, 1976 (Monograph 3).

Padilla, A. M., & Ruiz, R. A. *Latino mental health: A review of the literature*. Washington, D.C.: U.S. Government Printing Office, 1973.

Padilla, A. M., & Ruiz, R. A. Personality assessment and test interpretation of Mexican Americans: A critique. *Journal of Personality Assessment*, 1975, *39*, 103–109.

Padilla, A. M., Ruiz, R. A., & Alvarez, R. Community mental health services for the Spanish-speaking/surnamed population. *American Psychologist*, 1975, *30*, 892–905.

Padilla, E. R. The relationship between psychology and Chicanos: Failures and possibilities. In N. Wagner & M. Haug (Eds.), *Chicanos: Social and psychological perspectives*. St. Louis: C. V. Mosby, 1971.

Padilla, E. R., Padilla, A. M., Ramirez, R., Morales, A., & Olmedo, E. L. Inhalant, marijuana and alcohol abuse among barrio children and adolescents. *International Journal of the Addictions*, 1979.

Palomares, U. H. Puerto Rican youth speaks out. *Personnel and Guidance Journal*, 1971, *50*, 91–95. (a)

Palomares, U. H. Portrait of a counselor: A group interview. *American Personnel and Guidance Journal*, 1971, *50*, 131–136. (b)

Palomares, U. H. Nuestro sentimientos son iguales la diferencia es en la experiencia. *Personnel and Guidance Journal*, 1971, *50*, 137–144. (c)

Palomares, U. H., & Haro, J. Viva la Raza! *Personnel and Guidance Journal*, 1971, *50*, 119–130.

Paz, O. *The labyrinth of solitude*. New York: Grove Press, 1961.

Peal, E., & Lambert, W. E. The relation of bilingualism to intelligence. *Psychological Monographs*, 1962, *76*(27, Whole No. 546).

Peck, H. B., Kaplan, S. R., & Roman, M. Prevention, treatment, and social action: A strategy of intervention in a disadvantaged urban area. *American Journal of Orthopsychiatry*, 1966, *36*, 57–69.

Peñalosa, F. Mexican family roles. *Journal of Marriage and the Family*, 1968, *30*, 680–689.

Peñalosa, F., & McDonagh, E. Social mobility in a Mexican American community. *Social Forces*, 1966, *44*, 498–505.

Perls, F. *Gestalt therapy verbatim*. Des Plaines, Ill.: Bantam, 1971.

Perry, L. Moral and mental health. In S. Plog & R. Edgerton (Eds.), *Emerging perspectives in mental health*. New York: Holt, Rinehart & Winston, 1969.

Peterson, B., & Ramirez, M. Real/ideal self disparity in Negro and Mexican-American children. *Psychology*, 1971, *8*, 22–28.

Pettigrew, T. F. Ethnicity in American life: A social psychological perspective. In A. Dashefsky (Ed.), *Ethnic identity in society*. Chicago: Rand McNally, 1976.

Phillipus, M. J. Successful and unsuccessful approaches to mental health services for an urban Hispano-American population. *Journal of Public Health*, 1971, *61*, 820–830.

Plant, W. T., & Southern, M. L. The intellectual and achievement effects of preschool cognitive stimulation on poverty Mexican-American children. *Genetic Psychology Monographs*, 1972, *86*, 141–173.

Plata, M. Stability and change in the prestige ranking of occupants over 49 years. *Journal of Vocational Behavior*, 1975, *6*, 95–99.

Plemons, G. A comparison of MMPI scores of Anglo and Mexican-American psychiatric patients. *Journal of Consulting and Clinical Psychology*, 1977, *45*, 149–150.

Pollack, E., & Menacker, J. *Spanish-speaking students and guidance*. Boston: Houghton Mifflin Co., 1971.

Porkorny, A. D., & Overall, J. E. Relationships of psychopathology to age, sex, ethnicity and marital status in state hospital patients. *Journal of Psychiatric Research*, 1970, *7*, 143–152.

Preble, E. The Puerto Rican-American teenager in New York City. In E. B. Brody (Ed.), *Minority group adolescents in the United States*. Baltimore: Williams & Wilkins, 1968.

Price-Williams, D. R. *Explorations in cross-cultural psychology*. San Francisco: Chandler & Sharp, 1975.

Pruneda, M. C. Acculturation, self-concept and achievement of Mexican-American students (Doctoral dissertation, East Texas State University, 1973). *Dissertation Abstracts International*, 1974, *35*, 5491A. (University Microfilms No. 74–5772)

Ramirez, M. Identification with Mexican-American values and psychological adjustment in Mexican-American adolescents. *International Journal of Social Psychiatry*, 1969, *15*, 151–156.

Ramirez, M., III. Towards cultural democracy in mental health: The case of the Mexican American. *Interamerican Journal of Psychology*, 1972, *6*, 45–50.

Ramirez, M., Castañeda, A., & Herold, P. L. The relationship of acculturation to cognitive style among Mexican Americans. *Journal of Cross-Cultural Psychology*, 1974, *5*, 424–433.

Ramirez, M., III, & Price-Williams, D. Cognitive styles in children: Two Mexican communities. *Interamerican Journal of Psychology*, 1974, *8*, 93–101.

Ramirez, M., Taylor, C., & Petersen, B. Mexican American cultural membership and adjustment to school. *Developmental Psychology*, 1971, *4*, 141–148.

Ramos, R. A case in point: An ethnomethodological study of a poor Mexican American family. *Social Science Quarterly*, 1973, *53*, 905–919.

Recio-Andrados, J. L. Family as a unit and larger society: The adaptation of the Puerto Rican migrant family to the mainland suburban setting (Doctoral dissertation, City University of New York, 1975). *Dissertation Abstracts International*, 1977, *57*, 1117A. (University Microfilms No. 75–16, 961)

Reeves, R. A study of self-concept of Title-1 third grade Mexican-American students (Doctoral dissertation, University of Nebraska, 1974). *Dissertation Abstracts International*, 1976, *55*, 5001A. (University Microfilms No. 75–3442)

Reilley, R. R., & Knight, G. E. MMPI scores of Mexican American college students. *Journal of College Student Personnel*, 1970, *11*, 419–422.

Rendon, A. *Chicano manifesto*. New York: Macmillan, 1971.

Rendon, M. Transcultural aspects of Puerto Rican mental illness in New York. *International Journal of Social Psychiatry*, 1974, *20*, 18–24.

Report of the U.S. Commission on Civil Rights. *Puerto Ricans in the continental United States: An uncertain future*. Washington, D.C.: U. S. Government Printing Office, October, 1976.

Report to the President from the President's Commission on Mental Health. Washington, D.C.: U.S. Government Printing Office, 1978.

Reynolds, D. K., & Kalish, R. A. Anticipation of futurity as a function of ethnicity and age. *Journal of Gerontology*, 1974, *29*, 224–234.

Rice, A., Ruiz, R. A., & Padilla, A. M. Person perception, self-identity, and ethnic group preference in Anglo, Black and Chicano preschool and third-grade children. *Journal of Cross-Cultural Psychology*, 1974, *5*, 100–108.

Rippee, B. D. An investigation of Anglo-American and Spanish-American students' expectations of the counseling relationship (Doctoral dissertation, New Mexico State University, 1967). *Dissertation Abstracts International*,

1967, *28*, 2520A–2521A. (University Microfilms No. 67–16, 118)

Rivera, F. Motivation factors in treating Puerto Rican addicts. In D. J. Curren (Ed.), *Proceedings of the Puerto Rican Conferences on Human Services.* Washington, D.C.: National Coalition of Spanish-Speaking Mental Health Organizations, 1975.

Rivera, F. U. The Bender Gestalt test among Mexican American children (Doctoral dissertation, Catholic University of America, 1974). *Dissertation Abstracts International*, 1974, *35*, 1536A. (University Microfilms No. 74–19, 426)

Rivera, O. A. Vocational rehabilitation of disabled Chicanos (Doctoral dissertation, University of Utah, 1974). *Dissertation Abstracts International*, 1974, *35*, 2059A. (University Microfilms No. 74–22, 707)

Rodriguez, L. V. Social work practice in Puerto Rico. *Social Work*, 1973, *3*, 32–40.

Rodriguez, R. Going home again: The new American scholarship boy. *The American Scholar*, 1974–1975, *44*, 15–28.

Rogers, C. R. *Carl Rogers on encounter groups.* New York: Harper & Row, 1970.

Rogg, E. M. *The assimilation of Cuban exiles: The role of community and class.* New York: Aberdeen Press, 1974.

Roheim, G. *The origin and function of culture.* New York: Nervous and Mental Disease Monographs, No. 69, 1943.

Roll, S., & Brenneis, C. B. Chicano and Anglo dreams of death. *Journal of Cross-Cultural Psychology*, 1975, *6*, 377–383.

Roll, S., Hinton, R., & Glazer, M. Dreams of death: Mexican-Americans vs. Anglo-Americans. *Interamerican Journal of Psychology*, 1974, *8*, 111–115.

Romano-V., O. I. The anthropology and sociology of Mexican-Americans. In O. I. Romano-V. (Ed.), *Voices: Readings from El Grito.* Berkeley: Quinto Sol Publications, 1971.

Romero, F. Employment for the Hispanic community. Paper presented at the Conference on Hi panic Leadership, Dallas, Texas, July 20–23, 1977.

Rothenberg, A. Puerto Rico and aggression. *American Journal of Psychiatry*, 1964, *120*, 962–970.

Rotter, J. B. Generalized expectations for internal vs. external control of reinforcement. *Psychological Monographs*, 1966, *80* (Whole No. 609).

Rubel, A. J. The epidemiology of a folk illness: Susto in Hispanic America. *Ethnology*, 1964, *3*, 268–283.

Rubel, A. J. Functional analysis and negative effects of some beliefs about illness causation. Paper presented at the Society for Applied Anthropology, Mexico City, 1969.

Rudolph, J. E. Self perceived and ascribed characteristics of Mexican-American, Anglo, and bicultural college students (Doctoral dissertation, St. John's University, 1972). *Dissertation Abstracts International*, 1973, *34*, 3027A. (University Microfilms No. 49–8970)

Rueveni, U. Using sensitivity training with junior high school students. *Children*, 1971, *18*, 69–72.

Ruiz, A. S. Chicano group catalysts. *Personnel and Guidance Journal*, 1975, *53*, 462–466.

Ruiz, R. A. Relative frequency of Americans with Spanish surnames in associations of psychology, psychiatry, and sociology. *American Psychologist*, 1971, *26*, 1022–1024.

Ruiz, R. A. The delivery of mental health and social change services for Chicanos:

Analysis and recommendations. In J. Martinez (Ed.), *Chicano psychology*. New York: Academic Press, 1977.

Ruiz, R. A., Casas, J. M., & Padilla, A. M. Culturally relevant behavioristic counseling. Occasional Paper No. 5, Spanish Speaking Mental Health Research Center, Los Angeles: University of California, 1977.

Ruiz, R. A., & Padilla, A. M. Counseling Latinos. *Personnel and Guidance Journal*, 1977, *7*, 401–408.

Ruiz, R. A., Padilla, A. M., & Alvarez, R. Issues in the counseling of Spanish speaking-surnamed clients: Recommendations for therapeutic services. In L. Benjamin & G. R. Watz (Eds.), *Transcultural counseling: Needs, programs, and techniques*. New York: Human Sciences Press, 1978.

Ruiz, P. A., Vasquez, W., & Vasquez, K. The mobile unit: A new approach in mental health. *Community Mental Health Journal*, 1973, *9*, 18–24.

Sanchez, G. I. History, culture, and education. In J. Samora (Ed.), *La Raza: Forgotten Americans*. Notre Dame, Ind.: University of Notre Dame Press, 1966.

Sandoval, M. C. *La religion Afrocuban*. Madrid, Spain: Playor, 1975.

Sattler, J. Racial "experimenter effects" in experimentation, testing, interviewing, and psychotherapy. *Psychological Bulletin*, 1970, *73*, 137–160.

Scheidlinger, S., & Sarcka, A. A mental health consultation-education program with group service agencies in a disadvantaged community. *Community Mental Health Journal*, 1969, *5*, 164–171.

Scheidlinger, S., Struening, E., & Rabkin, J. Evaluation of a mental health consultation service in the ghetto area. *American Journal of Psychotherapy*, 1970, *24*, 485–492.

Schensul, S. L. Commentary: Skills needed in action anthropology: Lessons from El Centro de la Causa. *Human Organization*, 1974, *33*, 203–209.

Scholes, W. E. The migrant worker. In J. Samora (Ed.), *La Raza: Forgotten Americans*. Notre Dame, Ind.: University of Notre Dame Press, 1966.

Schwartz, A. J. A comparative study of value and achievement: Mexican-American and Anglo youth. *Sociology of Education*, 1971, *44*, 438–462.

Scott, N. R., Orzen, W., Musillo, C., & Cole, P. Methadone in the Southwest: A three-year follow-up of Chicano heroin addicts. *American Journal of Orthopsychiatry*, 1973, *43*, 355–361.

Selters, R. R. An investigation of the relationship between ethnic origin and relations to the MMPI (Doctoral dissertation, Baylor University, 1973). *Dissertation Abstracts International*, 1973, *34*, 5210–B. (University Microfilms No. 74–8485).

Serrano, A. C., & Gibson, G. Mental health services to the Mexican American community in San Antonio, Texas. *American Journal of Public Health*, 1973, *63*, 1055–1057.

Seward, G. *Cultural conflict*. New York: Ronald Press, 1958.

Sheldon, P. M. Community participation and the emerging middle class. In J. Samora (Ed.), *La Raza: Forgotten Americans*. Notre Dame, Ind.: University of Notre Dame Press, 1966.

Shofield, W. *Psychotherapy: The purchase of friendship*. Englewood Cliffs, N.J.: Prentice-Hall, 1964.

Simon , A. J. Adapting the Peabody Picture Vocabulary Test for use with Mexican children (Doctoral dissertation, Hofstra University, 1974). *Dissertation Abstracts International*, 1975, *35*, A–7135. (University Microfilms No. 75–10, 674)

Simmons, O. The mutual images and expectations of Anglo-Americans and

Mexican-Americans. *Daedalus*, 1961, *90*, 286–299.

Soares, A. T., & Soares, L. M. Self-perceptions of culturally disadvantaged children. *American Educational Research Journal*, 1969, *6*, 31–45.

Sommers, V. S. The impact of dual cultural membership on identity. *Psychiatry*, 1964, *27*, 332–344.

Spiro, M. E. Culture and personality: The natural history of a false dichotomy. *Psychiatry*, 1951, *14*, 19–46.

Stedman, J. M., & Adams, R. L. Achievement as a function of language competence, behavior adjustment, and sex in young disadvantaged Mexican-American children. *Journal of Educational Psychology*, 1972, *63*, 411–417.

Stedman, J. M. & McKenzie, R. E. Family factors related to competence in young disadvantaged Mexican-American children. *Child Development*, 1971, *42*, 1602–1607.

Steward, M. S., & Steward, D. S. Effect of social distance on teaching strategies of Anglo-American and Mexican American mothers. *Developmental Psychology*, 1974, *10*, 797–807.

Stocking, G. W., Jr. Franz Boas and the culture concept in historical perspective. *American Anthropologist*, 1966, *68*, 867–882.

Stoddard, E. R. The adjustment of Mexican American barrio families to forced housing relocation. *Social Sciences Quarterly*, 1973, *53*, 749–759.

Stoker, D. H., & Meadow, A. Cultural differences in child guidance clinic patients. *International Journal of Social Psychiatry*, 1974, *20*, 196–202.

Stonequist, E. V. *The marginal man: A study in personality and culture conflict.* New York: Russell & Russell, 1937.

Szapocznik, J., Scopetta, M. A., Kurtines, W., & de los Angeles Aranalde, M. Theory and measurement of acculturation. *Interamerican Journal of Psychology*, in press.

Thomas, C. S., & Garrison, V. A general systems view of community mental health. In L. Bellak & H. Barten (Eds.), *Progress in community mental health.* New York: Brunner/Mazel, Inc., 1975.

Toffler, A. *Future shock.* Des Plaines, Ill.: Bantam, 1974.

Torres-Matrullo, C. Acculturation and psychopathology among Puerto Rican women in mainland United States (Doctoral dissertation, Rutgers State University, 1974). *Dissertation Abstracts International*, 1974, *35*, 3041A. (University Microfilms No. 74–27, 664)

Torrey, E. F. *The mind game: Witchdoctors and psychiatrists.* New York: Emerson Hall, 1972.

Trautman, E. C. Suicide attempts of Puerto Rican immigrants. *Psychiatric Quarterly*, 1961, *35*, 544–554.

Trevino, F. M., & Bruhn, J. G. Incidence of mental illness in a Mexican-American community. *Psychiatric Annals*, 1977, *7*, 33, 35, 38–39, 42–43, 47, 51.

Tuck, R. *Not with a fist.* New York: Harcourt Brace Jovanovich, 1946.

Tylor, E. B. *Primitive culture* (4th rev. ed.). New York: John Murray, 1903.

Ulibarri, H. Social and attitudinal characteristics of Spanish-speaking migrant and ex-migrant workers in the Southwest. *Sociology and Social Research*, 1966, *50*, 361–370.

U.S. Bureau of the Census. Selected characteristics of persons and families of Mexican, Puerto Rican, and other Spanish origin (Current Population

Report, Series P-20, No. 22, 4). Washington, D.C.: U.S. Government Printing Office, 1971.

U.S. Bureau of the Census. Census of Population: 1970 Persons of Spanish Origin (Final Report PC(2)–1C). Washington, D.C.: U.S. Government Printing Office, 1973.

U.S. Bureau of the Census. Language usage in the United States: July, 1975 (Current Population Report, Series P-23, No. 60). Washington, D.C.: U.S. Government Printing Office, 1976.

U.S. Bureau of the Census. Persons of Spanish origin in the United States: March, 1976 (Current Population Report, Series P-20, No. 310). Washington, D.C.: U.S. Government Printing Office, 1977.

Valdés Fallis, G. Social interaction and code-switching patterns: A case study of Spanish/English alternation. In G. D. Keller, R. V. Teschner, & S. Vierra (Eds.), *Bilingualism in the Bicentennial and beyond.* New York: Bilingual Press, 1976.

Valdez, A. Insurrection in New Mexico: The land of enchantment. In O. I. Romano-V. (Ed.), *Voices: Readings from El Grito.* Berkeley: Quinto Sol Publications, 1971.

Van Vranken, E. W. Utilization of mental health services by Mexican Americans in a military community (Doctoral dissertation, University of Denver, 1973). *Dissertation Abstracts International,* 1974, *35,* 4419A. (University Microfilms No. 73–30, 229)

Vazquez de Rodriquez, L. Social work practice in Puerto Rico. *Social Work,* 1973, *18,* 32–40.

Vidal, M. Women: New voice of La Raza. In *Chicanas speak out.* New York: Pathfinder Press, 1971.

Vigil, J. T. A comparison of selected perceptions of Spanish-speaking students and non-Spanish-speaking students (Doctoral dissertation, Colorado State College, 1968). *Dissertation Abstracts International,* 1968, *29,* 1140A. (University Microfilms No. 68–14, 747)

Wade, T. C., & Baker, T. B. Opinions and use of psychological tests: A survey of clinical psychologists. *American Psychologist,* 1977, *32,* 874–882.

Wagner, J. A. The role of the Christian church. In J. Samora (Ed.), *La Raza: Forgotten Americans.* Notre Dame, Ind.: University of Notre Dame Press, 1966.

Walker, J. R., & Hamilton, L. S. A Chicano/Black/White encounter. *The Personnel and Guidance Journal,* 1973, *51,* 471–477.

Wallace, A.F.C. *Culture and personality* (2nd ed.). New York: Random House, 1970.

Weaver, J. L. Mexican American health care behavior: A critical review of the literature. *Social Science Quarterly,* 1973, *54,* 85–102.

Weinreich, U. *Languages in contact: Findings and problems.* The Hague: Mouton, 1963.

Welch, S., Comer, J., & Steinman, M. Some social and attitudinal correlates of health care among Mexican Americans. *Journal of Health and Social Behavior,* 1973, *14,* 205–213.

Werner, N. E., & Evans, I. M. Perception of prejudice in Mexican American preschool children. *Perceptual and Motor Skills,* 1968, *27,* 1039–1046.

Whiting, J. W., & Child, I. L. *Child training and personality: A cross-cultural*

294   *References*

study. New Haven: Yale University Press, 1953.

Wignall, C. M., & Koppin, L. L. Mexican-American usage of state mental hospital facilities. *Community Mental Health Journal*, 1967, *3*, 137–148.

Wolkon, G. H., Moriwaki, S., Mandel, D. M., Archuleta, J., Bunje, P., & Zimmerman, S. Ethnicity and social class in the delivery of services: Analysis of a child guidance clinic. *American Journal of Public Health*, 1974, *64*, 709–712.

Wrenn, G. The culturally encapsulated counselor. *Harvard Educational Review*, 1962, *32*, 444–449.

Yamamoto, J., James, Q. C., & Palley, N. Cultural problems in psychiatric therapy. *Archives of General Psychiatry*, 1968, *19*, 45–49.

Zalamea, L. The modern spirit of santería. *Nuestro Magazine*, 1978, *2* (3), 61–63.

Zimmerman, B. J., & Ghozeil, S. Feedback: Educational strategies. Unpublished manuscript, Arizona Center for Early Childhood Education, Tucson, Arizona, 1972.

Zimmerman, I. L., Steiner, V. G., & Pond, R. L. Language status of preschool Mexican-American children—Is there a case against early bilingual education? *Perceptual and Motor Skills*, 1974, *38*, 227–230.

Zirkel, P., Moses, E. G., & Gnanara, J. Self concept and ethnic group membership among public school students. *American Educational Research Journal*, 1971, *8*, 253–265.

Name Index

Subject Index